THE EDUCATION OF
AMERICAN TEACHERS

THE EDUCATION OF
AMERICAN TEACHERS

by James Bryant Conant

McGRAW-HILL BOOK COMPANY, INC.

NEW YORK   TORONTO   LONDON

PREFACE

In 1961 SOME OF THE LEADERS in the field asked me to undertake a study of the education of teachers for our elementary and secondary schools. It was their belief that a volume written on the basis of a two-year investigation might make a contribution to the public's understanding of a complex subject. Knowing that the field was highly controversial, I undertook the task with some reluctance. I received a generous grant from the Carnegie Corporation of New York, which, as in the case of my study of secondary education, was effectively administered by the Educational Testing Service of Princeton, New Jersey.

I have been most fortunate in my collaborators. For the first year's study, which involved visiting teacher-preparing institutions, I was able to secure the services of Prof. Jeremiah S. Finch of Princeton University, Prof. William H. Cartwright of Duke University, Dr. Robert F. Carbone, now professor at Emory University, and Dr. E. Alden Dunham, whose assistance had proved so valuable in previous studies. Prof. John I. Goodlad of the University of California at Los Angeles was able to give me only a portion of his time, but together with Professor Cartwright he supplied the essential knowledge of the details of teacher training. Professor Finch, as a former dean of the college at Princeton and a professor of English, was in a position to assist me in my discussions with members of the academic departments in the various institutions we included in our travels.

In the second year of the study I focused attention on the state

regulations that place limitations on the local school board's freedom to employ teachers. Since changes in these regulations have
been the subject of recent controversy in more than one state capital, I decided I needed the assistance of both a political scientist
and an historian. I was lucky enough to persuade Prof. Nicholas A.
Masters, now at Pennsylvania State University, and Dr. Merle L.
Borrowman, professor of education and history at the University of
Wisconsin, to join the inquiry. Together with Dr. Michael D. Usdan,
now a professor at Northwestern University, these gentlemen
formed a traveling team that visited the capitals of the 16 most
populous states. Dr. Elbert K. Fretwell, Jr., assistant commissioner
for higher education of the state of New York, was good enough to
give me a month of his vacation time and for this period traveled
with the others.

In the preparation of the manuscript all the members of both
years' staffs have played a major part, and all have reviewed the
final draft. While I think it fair to say there was a remarkable degree of unanimity among these advisers, none of them agrees completely with everything I have written. The responsibility for the
reporting as well as for the recommendations is mine. At the same
time I must record the fact that many of the ideas set forth in the
following pages did not originate with me; a good number of them
were initially thrown into the discussion by a member of the staff.

The list of the 77 institutions that were visited in 22 states is given
in Appendix A. They included church-connected colleges or universities, private institutions not church connected, state universities, state colleges, and municipal colleges. Some were primarily
teachers colleges in that a great majority of the students were preparing to be teachers; some were former normal schools now transformed into four-year colleges with special programs for future
businessmen, journalists, and housewives as well as teachers; some
were universities with undergraduate schools of education; others
were universities like Harvard, Yale, and Notre Dame, in which all
programs for future teachers are at the graduate level. I believe we
visited all types and categories of institution, including one example
of the two-year colleges now to be found in only a few states.

In the course of our visits, I conversed with many professors,
examined catalogs, course outlines, and textbooks, sat in some
classes, and talked to students. I also met with small groups of

teachers in different parts of the United States—perhaps three or four hundred teachers in all—and discussed with them their own education. In these endeavors I was assisted by able collaborators who hold advanced degrees from graduate schools of education, and more often than not I was accompanied by a professor of education. As in my previous studies, I have relied heavily on the opinions of classroom teachers. I found that both elementary and secondary teachers who reviewed their own educational experiences had many pertinent observations to make.

As I have indicated, the second year of the study was directed primarily to the relation of the state to teacher education and certification. In this area, I soon found that the regulations affecting the employment of teachers vary from state to state, as do the arrangements for their enforcement. To report on fifty different systems in a volume written for a broad public is out of the question. Therefore, I decided early in my study to concentrate attention almost exclusively on the 16 most populous states, in which two-thirds of the population of the United States is concentrated. This group includes states in each geographical section (except the Rocky Mountain states), and regional differences are fairly well represented in my sample. The statistics in Appendix B illustrate some of the similarities and some of the differences among the states.

Although it was necessary to limit our visits largely to institutions in the 16 most populous states, my objective, of course, was to write about the national scene. I am indebted to the staff for their conscientious review of major books on past and current issues in teacher education, and for the collection of masses of statistical information on the teacher supply and demand situation throughout the country.

I am also grateful to the many educators in all phases of the teacher education field who gave so generously of their time in helping me to put complex problems into perspective. And without the sound advice of state superintendents of education, leaders of educational associations, and officials in Washington agencies, I should have been quite at sea in coping with the subject.

Finally, I would like to express appreciation to those schoolmen and school officials with whom I have been privileged to discuss educational problems in England, France, Germany, Italy, Switzerland, and Japan during the past several years. For whatever consolation it may be to Americans, we are not alone in our concern with these problems.

The majority of elementary and secondary teachers for the public schools are educated at public expense either in state universities or in state colleges; but in terms of the number of institutions involved, the majority are not publicly supported. Forty-four per cent of the institutions are church-connected, 18 per cent private but not church-connected, and 38 per cent are public. The same situation holds for the 16 states taken together, though the proportion of public to private institutions varies from state to state to some degree (Appendix C).

Lack of time has forced me to set aside a number of important issues that might be treated. I did not examine the doctoral programs intended to prepare professors of education, although certain of my recommendations have implications for this field. I have not investigated the education of teachers for the vocations and practical courses; these include school courses in home economics, business, distributive education, trade and industry, and agriculture. Many teachers leave the classroom each year to become guidance officers, curriculum supervisors, and teachers in such highly special areas as the teaching of the deaf, the blind, or the mentally retarded. I have made no attempt to assess the certification requirements for these special tasks, nor have I examined the programs offered for the training of such specialized personnel. The same is true of the special training of school administrators, though I have publicly expressed my opinion that school boards should not be restricted by state law in the employment of superintendents, the educational statesmen of the future, who should have, of course, the widest possible cultural background.

More than one person, including several of my collaborators, have urged me to expand my study by considering in detail the whole problem of recruitment and employment of teachers. The importance of this subject is equaled by its vastness; salaries, pension rights, daily scheduling, teachers' assistants, and merit pay are some of the topics that would require exhaustive treatment if a complete set of recommendations were to be made. Again sectional, state, and local differences would arise to bedevil any reporting job. I am certainly sympathetic to the complaints I have heard from the teachers with whom I have talked in the past two years. In many communities it is almost impossible for a man to support a family on what he earns as a teacher. Far too often, I have been told, he feels forced to take on other work during the school year to supplement his income. Such "moonlighting," as it is called, poses a serious problem to a school board. How the difficulty is to be met in localities with insufficient funds is another story. And it was not one of the purposes of this study to explore the important but complicated question of how to finance our public schools and our public institutions of higher learning, in which so many teachers are educated.

Despite these self-imposed limitations on my study, I hope the volume will provide at least an introduction to an area of higher education that has an almost baffling complexity. The specific recommendations I make, if they are to be implemented, will in many cases require the support of both educators and laymen. Therefore, I have written with both groups in mind. I hope that what I have to say may seem relevant to those concerned with improving public education throughout the nation.

JAMES B. CONANT

589 Fifth Avenue, Eleventh Floor

New York 17, New York

May 7, 1963

CONTENTS

1
A QUARREL AMONG EDUCATORS

UNIVERSITIES HAVE EXISTED for nearly a thousand years. Their periods of vitality have been marked by passionate debates among professors. A clash of opinion has often been the prelude to a fruitful development of new ideas. Bitter theological disputes in the Middle Ages, as well as the violent controversy over Darwin's theory a century ago, might be cited as examples of quarrels among educators. But the quarrel I have in mind in writing this volume is of an entirely different kind. Neither factual evidence nor theoretical speculations provide the battleground. Rather, this quarrel might be described as a power struggle among professors, which has come to involve parents, alumni, legislators, and trustees. Let me illustrate the nature of the battle by recording my own involvement during the course of nearly fifty years.

Early in my career as a professor of chemistry, I became aware of the hostility of the members of my profession to schools or faculties of education. I shared the views of the majority of my colleagues on the faculty of arts and sciences that there was no excuse for the existence of people who sought to teach others how to teach. I felt confident that I was an excellent teacher and I had developed my skill by experience, without benefit of professors of education. I saw no reason why others could not do likewise, including those who graduated from college with honors in chemistry and who wished to teach in high school. As joint author, with my former chemistry teacher, of a high school chemistry textbook, I was quite certain I knew all about the way the subject should be

1

presented; I doubted that my understanding was shared by any professors of education. When any issues involving benefits to the graduate school of education came before the faculty of arts and sciences, I automatically voted with those who looked with contempt on the school of education.

Suddenly, after being a member of one faculty for fifteen years, I found myself in a new position. I became the presiding officer of *all* the faculties of Harvard University. I was responsible to the governing boards for the budgets and the welfare of all our undertakings, including that of training teachers. It soon became evident that the antithesis between the views of the professors who taught the usual college subjects and those who were instructing future teachers was not as simple as I had thought. In the circumstances, it seemed reasonable to attempt to increase mutual understanding between the two hostile groups by establishing some arrangement through which they might exchange views and, if possible, learn to cooperate in their endeavors. The idea was obvious enough, though in the mid-1930s it was so unorthodox that a leading scholar in another university wrote the dean of the Harvard School of Education that "a shotgun would be needed to carry the wedding off."

As a matter of fact it did not prove too difficult for a new president to persuade the two faculties to agree to the establishment of a joint board to administer a new joint degree, the master of arts in teaching. One faculty, that of arts and science, was to certify through its usual departments that the candidate was well prepared in the subject to be taught in school—English, for example. The other faculty, that of education, was to certify that the candidate had successfully completed the courses in education that the administrative board had agreed were necessary. Since the School of Education, like the other professional schools at Harvard, was a graduate school, the question of offering courses in education to undergraduates did not arise. The candidates for the joint degree, it was assumed, would already have received a bachelor's degree.

The scheme was accepted by the two faculties, but I can hardly say it was accepted with enthusiasm. Before more than a few years had passed, some of the members of the joint administrative board asked for a new committee to review the whole arrangement. The committee, composed of a few professors of education and a few from the faculty of arts and sciences, raised a fundamental issue. Had it not been a mistake to force a Harvard undergraduate to postpone his work with professors of education until *after* he had received the A.B. degree? Obviously he had started his preparation as a future teacher early in his college course by studying the subject matter to be taught. Why not arrange for a continuous five-year program with professors from *both* faculties involved in the undergraduate as well as the graduate work? Such a modification of the joint venture did not appeal to me as president of the University. I knew far too well the degree of hostility felt toward professors of education by the majority of the faculty of arts and sciences. It would be fatal to the whole idea to present a scheme based on the premise that a candidate for the bachelor's degree could include in his program courses in education. Furthermore, the University had decided years before that professional preparation should be wholly at the graduate level. The School of Business Administration, for example, established a generation earlier, had rigidly adhered to this decision, and functioned only as a graduate school.

The entry of the United States into World War II so disorganized American colleges and universities that all concerned at Harvard lost interest in a second reformation of the education of teachers. After the war was over, the original concept of the degree of master of arts in teaching was accepted without question. And under the leadership of Dean Keppel the new system began to prosper. As the years went by, the hostility between the two Harvard faculties gradually diminished. I feel sure that a similar change was taking place in other institutions, yet from what my collaborators and I observed in the 77 institutions we visited in 1961–63, I am equally sure that the quarrel between educators is not yet over. As one dean of education remarked to me, "The boys have at least agreed to check their hatchets with their hats at the Faculty Club coatroom when they lunch together."

While I am not prepared to say that there was, or is, actual hostility between educational and academic professors on every campus, there has always been a considerable gap between the two groups in a majority of institutions. Such a gap often exists in spite of fine word spoken by administrators about "an all-university approach" to the education of teachers, and the existence of a committee that symbolized the approach.

As long ago as 1944, I took the occasion of an invitation to speak on the 50th Anniversary of Columbia's Teachers College to call for a "Truce Among Educators." By that time, I had been thoroughly exposed to the views of the two camps, including their views about each other. After pointing out that, as is always the case in academic matters, errors had been committed by both sides, I suggested the terms for a cease-fire order. In brief, they were that the professors of education admit their failure to be sufficiently concerned with the type of youth who should go to college, and that the professors of the college subjects such as English or chemistry admit their ignorance of the nature of the high school problems of the 1940s, which were quite different from those of the 1900s. Indeed, the warfare had started primarily because of the revolution in secondary education. I reminded the audience that the expansion of the high schools of the country since the 1880s has been nothing short of astronomical. Instead of being concerned with the education of a very small proportion of the boys and girls from fourteen to eighteen years of age, the high schools now must accommodate nearly three-fourths of the entire age group. The mere physical expansion, the mere change in scale, would in itself have presented a major problem to the institutions of higher education concerned with the training of teachers, but another and still more important factor entered in.

At the turn of the century, the high schools and their equivalents —the private academies and preparatory schools—were essentially concerned with a group of young people who were studying languages and mathematics, science and history. The enrollment in these schools in the nineties usually represented either impecunious youths with high scholastic aptitude and a keen desire for book learning, or children of well-to-do families who for social reasons were bent on having their offspring acquire a college education. The combination of social motivation on the one hand and high scholastic aptitude on the other presented the teachers of that day with a relatively simple problem. What we now call an old-fashioned curriculum enabled the graduates of those schools of the last century to enter college well prepared for further work in languages, in mathematics, and in the sciences. Those who could take it found the formal instruction excellent; those who couldn't or wouldn't dropped by the wayside as a matter of course. From the point of view of those on the receiving end—the professors in the colleges—this was a highly satisfactory situation. What sort of education the rest of the fourteen-to-eighteen-year-olds received was none of their affair!

In reviewing this bit of history in 1944, I was, of course, only reminding my audience of what most of them already knew. Professors of education had been pointing out for several decades that the faculties of arts and sciences had shown little interest in school problems. In the nineteenth century they had been quite ready to leave to the normal schools the task of preparing teachers for the elementary grades. When social changes in this century transformed the nature of the high school, the typical college professor himself was viewing with disgust and dismay what was happening in the schools. (I am reporting on personal observation of fifty years.) With few exceptions, college professors turned their backs on the problem of mass secondary education and eyed with envy Great Britain and the Continent, where such problems did not exist.

My plea for a truce, made while World War II was still in progress, had little if any effect. In fact the quarrel intensified in the 1950s because laymen entered the fray in increasing numbers and with increasing vehemence. Schools have always been subject to criticism by parents, but after the close of World War II, the criticism became more general and more bitter. The Russian success with Sputnik triggered a veritable barrage of denunciation of those in charge of public education. These attacks served to embitter the professors of education, who considered that the work of their former students—classroom teachers, principals, and superintendents—was being unfairly appraised. Since practically all public school administrators have studied at one time or another in teacher-training institutions or a school or department of education, they are bound by history and sympathy to the faculties of education. The same is true of a substantial proportion of classroom teachers. Mutual loyalty between professors and former students has led to the formation of something approaching a guild of professors of education and their erstwhile students. An attack on public education is therefore automatically an attack on schools and faculties of education. As a matter of fact, the connection is not always so indirect. Many a violent critic of our public schools has specifically attacked the professors of education.

One can understand the reaction of the members of the faculties of education, yet the criticism to which they were being exposed was not without its justification. The deficiencies in our public schools, particularly in our high schools, to which a number of writers (among whom I must include myself) have called attention, were in no small part a consequence of their activities. Despite the fact (often overlooked) that public school teachers and administrators have spent many more hours in the classrooms of professors of arts and sciences than in classes taught by professors of education, their attitude toward education has been largely shaped by the latter. The writings of education professors have also influenced the outlook of many parents. The emphasis on education for citizenship, on the socially unifying effects of the comprehensive high school, and on the public schools as instruments of democracy, the recognition of individual differences, and of the need for including practical courses in high school elective programs— all these characteristics, *which I applaud,* were the fruits of the labors of professors of education. These men, most of them now no longer active, are entitled to a large measure of credit for making American schools what they are. But by the same token, the historian must charge against them some of those features of our schools that their younger successors and the general public have recently criticized so heavily. In particular, the failure to challenge the academically talented youth, to provide adequate courses in modern foreign languages, and to emphasize English composition —now widely recognized as faults of the 1930s and 1940s—are in process of being corrected.

WHAT HAPPENED AFTER SPUTNIK might be characterized as the entry of the layman in force into a battle of professors. What is now involved is more than a quarrel among educators. The academic professors[1] have consciously or unconsciously enlisted the support of

[1] The word "academic" has varying connotations; I shall use it to refer to those subjects traditionally taught in faculties of arts and sciences.

their alumni. We are therefore today dealing with two hostile camps. One camp is composed of professors of education allied with classroom teachers and public school administrators (though, like all alliances, it has its strains); the other is composed of professors of the sciences and the humanities and of influential collegiate alumni. Since the latter group includes radio and television commentators, editors, and publishers, the public school people and their mentors in some communities have faced a powerful set of forces. Along with the indignation of the professors of education frequently goes a sense of anxiety. "We who have shaped and improved our public schools are now being unfairly attacked, and there is danger that the public will be led astray!" Such thoughts are in the mind of more than one aging and honored individual who proudly carries the title of emeritus professor of education.

Why are the academic professors angry? What are they angry about? Many academic professors believe that the courses given by professors of education are worthless, and that the degrees granted students who have devoted much of their time to these courses are of little value. It is generally the case that the academic professors who advance these arguments know far too little about education courses. And unfortunately, what some professors of education have written about education can be labeled anti-intellectual. But what particularly irritates the academic professors is what professors of education say about teaching. After all, those who are engaged in college teaching usually pride themselves on their skill as teachers. And here are those who call themselves "professional educators" claiming that they and only they know what is good teaching! They imply, and sometimes openly state, that if all professors had taken their courses they would be better teachers! To make matters worse, in more than one state no one is permitted to teach in a junior college unless he has taken courses in education. If this is justified, the opponents ironically demand, why not require all teachers of freshmen and sophomores in four-year colleges to study under professors of education? To this question, professors of education often answer, "Such a requirement *ought* to be on the books."

And here we come to the issue about which emotions are most easily aroused—the issue of state requirements. Time was, not long ago, when in some states a school board could hire a teacher, and give him a permanent position, even if he had never even seen a professor of education. But those days are past. As a consequence, a graduate who has majored in an academic field must by hook or by crook meet the state requirements in education. (I shall be considering in a later chapter the various hooks and crooks now in use.) The fact that schools of education are beneficiaries of a high protective tariff wall is the single aspect of the present-day education of teachers that is most maddening to the academic professors.

In most states private schools can legally hire those they want. There is in these schools a free choice between teachers trained without benefit of courses in education and those trained as the state requires. Why shouldn't there be the same free choice in our public schools? The question is implicit in many of the attacks on schools of education. It is at the base of much of the hostility of lay critics, many of whom can cite examples of high-standing college graduates who are forced by state requirements to devote a certain number of hours to courses given by professors of education. It is hard to overestimate the bitterness of those who attack schools of education with such cases in their minds.

An inquiry into the history of certification reveals that this issue has long been a breeding ground of controversy. The struggle to control entrance to the teaching office is an old one, destined perhaps to continue indefinitely. The motives for certification were clearly recognized when modern state systems of education first emerged from the medieval systems of church schools, town or guild schools, and universities. With respect to all these schools, first clerical and later secular authorities assumed responsibility to protect the young from teachers whose influence might be morally —in those days considered inseparable from religiously—destructive. As far as the lower schools were concerned, their function was viewed primarily as one of religious indoctrination. The public interest was deemed insured when competent authority attested to the religious orthodoxy and moral reliability of potential teachers. As far as the universities were concerned, a second factor—mastery of the material to be taught—was considered necessary. This mastery was attested to by the university faculty through examinations leading to a university degree.

But the university faculty was in origin a medieval guild—indeed *universitas* was a rather general term for an organized guild—and hence the granting of a degree took on the added meaning of controlling membership in a group granted exclusive vocational rights to conduct a particular social service. Thus the combination of licensure and degree-granting power served three purposes: first, it protected the students from immoral influence; second, it insured mastery of the material to be taught; and third, it defined a group to which exclusive vocational rights to the teaching office were given.

On the university level the guild was able, in some periods, to play off secular and religious authorities against each other in such a way that the guild established exclusive control of certification for persons in higher education. On the lower levels the result varied from nation to nation and school to school. In some cases religious authority held, in others secular, and in still others a blending of the two.

In the United States local secular authorities early established control, with respect to publicly supported schools, of the total process of certification, though, of course, religious leaders sometimes acted as agents of the secular community. These authorities utilized two screening devices: character witnesses, and oral or written examinations. But since local boards were often hard pressed to find any teacher, they were sorely tempted to tailor the examinations to whatever candidate became available. Indeed in some rural areas the examiners themselves were too unschooled to develop and evaluate rigorous examinations even if they were inclined to do so. Finally, local ethnic or religious prejudices, personal favoritism on the part of some board members, and, it must be said, simple graft often entered the process.

As state systems of education developed in the middle decades of the nineteenth century, the emerging state Departments of Education began to take over the examination function. The rate of change varied from state to state, and in some cases the system of local examination persisted well into the present century. Though the legal sovereignty of the state in educational matters is clearly recognized, the state has never assumed total control of the actual certification processes from such major communities as New York City, Chicago, Philadelphia, and St. Louis.

In many states, public normal schools (later teachers colleges), controlled by the state Departments of Education, emerged simultaneously with the state system of public schools. Before 1850, state Departments of Education had begun to accept as a basis for certification completion of a course of instruction in one of the normal schools or colleges they controlled. This alternative to examinations simplified their tasks. Thus, by 1850 several states had two certification devices: first, completion of an approved course of studies in a state-regulated institution; and second, examinations.

When, at the turn of the century, American education expanded in terms of the number of students and schools, a further complicating factor entered the picture: the amount of knowledge available increased explosively; and the amount required for effective citizenship and employment rose rapidly as the social and economic system grew more complex and technologically oriented. The question raised in England by Thomas Arnold and Herbert Spencer about "what knowledge is of greatest worth" became acute in American education generally, and in teacher education explicitly.

Among the bodies of knowledge, or literature, that grew most rapidly, was that having to do with the process of education itself. The normal-school people developed an extensive literature concerning the "science and art of teaching," and as university departments of education developed, research and speculation flourished both in them and in the related social science fields. Instructional materials ostensibly tailored to the growing interests and aptitudes of school-age youngsters came to abound. By 1900 the field of "education" had so developed that doctoral degrees were being awarded, and shortly thereafter one could specialize on the doctoral level in such fields as educational psychology, school administration, curriculum and instruction, and the history or philosophy of education.

In the normal schools, material concerning curriculum and instructional problems secured a major place. In universities in which a minority of the students and professors were directly concerned with teacher education, and in which the atmosphere was traditionally hostile to vocational education of any kind, the process moved more slowly. Since the state came more and more to depend for its supply of teachers on graduates of the universities and of colleges with traditional academic orientation, those who believed in the desirability of pedagogical courses found it necessary to utilize forces outside the colleges and universities. Their solution was a series of laws establishing requirements for courses in education to be taken by all candidates for certification. These early laws tended to assume that the collegiate and university faculties would make certain that the candidate was liberally educated and had adequately studied the subjects he proposed to teach. But college and university faculties were unwilling to tailor their academic requirements to the teaching assignments their graduates were to undertake, and as a result it often happened that teachers were not properly prepared in their subjects. When this became evident, the state certification officers began to require teaching "majors" of one sort or another. By this time, a new certification device had emerged: certification based on the successful completion of a specified set of courses taken in a collegiate institution which might or might not have been subject to state inspection and regulation.

It is important to note that such certification regulations were in a sense imposed on the universities and colleges as the result of pressure from a coalition of state Department officials and public school people. Just as the professors of the academic subjects had not, in general, been willing to assume active responsibility toward the public elementary and secondary schools, they did not welcome the responsibility for the professional preparation of teachers. Moreover, the academic faculties often felt that the professors of education employed to offer this instruction would not have been hired if it had not been for the state regulations, and resented what seemed to them external coercion. The professors of education, for their part, found that their own convictions coincided with those of state Department and public school personnel, and realized, too, that their source of greatest support was outside the university faculty; as a result, they were more careful to cultivate the outside group.

In modern form the traditional patterns of certification are all at present in contention. What is essentially new is the determination of academic professors, and their allies in the larger community, to minimize the influence that professors of education, state Department personnel, and other public school forces have traditionally held over the certification process.

I have perhaps stated the issue too simply. In some instances, quarrels ostensibly about teacher education serve to mask more fundamental conflicts over economic, political, racial, or ideological issues. Furthermore, there are professors of the arts and sciences who warmly support education courses, and there are professors of education and public school people among the leaders in the movement to strengthen the teachers' academic preparation. Moreover, in some institutions and states, the university faculties—academic and professional in concert—struggle to extend the institution's autonomy against attempts by the public school people, the state Departments, and other interest groups to control its programs.

Yet it remains true that certification requirements rank high among the sources of hostility between professors of education and their colleagues in academic faculties. This should not be surprising, for the importance of these requirements on campuses throughout the country is enormous.

One would like to look at the education of future teachers in terms of a free market of ideas, and this I endeavored to do in my visits to teacher-training institutions during this study. But I came to the conclusion that such an inquiry lacks reality. The idea of state certification is so thoroughly accepted that I have found it hard to get a serious discussion of the question "What would you recommend if there were no state requirements?"

As for the attitude of the students taking state-required courses, I must report that I have heard time and time again complaints about their quality. To be sure, by no means all students I interviewed were critical; so many were, however, that I could not ignore their repeated comments that most of the educational offerings were "Mickey Mouse" courses. There can be no doubt that at least in some institutions the courses given by professors of education have a bad name among undergraduates, particularly those intending to be high school teachers. To some extent, perhaps, this is simply because the courses are required. I am well aware, from my years of experience as a teacher of a subject required for admission to a medical school, that any required course has two strikes against it in the student's mind. I am also aware that in some institutions the critical attitude of the students toward the education faculty is fed by the devastating comments they hear from certain academic professors.

The subject of teacher education is not only highly controversial, but also exceedingly complicated. The complexities are hardly ever acknowledged by those who are prone to talk in such slogans as "those terrible teachers colleges" or "those reactionary liberal-arts professors." These slogans invariably represent a point of view so oversimplified as to be fundamentally invalid. This is not to say that either academic or education professors cannot be criticized. It *is* to say that neither side can be criticized to the exclusion of the other. *In the course of my investigations, I have found much to criticize strongly on both sides of the fence that separates faculties of education from those of arts and sciences.*

EARLIER IN THIS CHAPTER I referred to the fact that the quarrel among educators had come to involve laymen. I had in mind, first of all, that teachers for our public schools are employed by local boards of education on the recommendation of the superintendent. Local boards are composed of laymen; therefore, these citizens are intimately concerned with the training of the teachers whom the boards employ. I had in mind also the fact that the freedom of the school board is limited by state requirements, which directly or indirectly are determined by laymen—the members of the legislature in each state. Indeed, the role of the state has been so important in shaping the development of teacher education that I am going to consider, in the next two chapters, first of all the way certification requirements are brought about in some of the more populous states, and then some of the policies that are actually employed today.

Unless one considers the relation of the state authorities to the school boards on the one hand, and the teacher-training institutions on the other, one is apt to miss what I consider a fundamental element in any plan for improving teacher education. The essential questions are: What role should the state play in the supervision of teacher education? And to what extent should universities and colleges be left free to experiment with new and different programs for educating teachers? My own answers to these questions will follow my report in Chapters 2 and 3 on current practices. Thereafter, I shall devote the remainder of the book to suggestions for a fresh approach to a four-year college program for teachers, and for improvements in current programs for teacher education beyond college.

I am aware that many educators resent the idea that laymen should have anything to do with education except to provide the funds. I do not agree with this point of view. What goes on in schools and colleges is far too important to be left entirely to the educators. The layman as a responsible member of a school board, a board of trustees, a legislature, or any public body, has a vital part to play. The layman as a citizen who votes and pays taxes has every reason to make his voice heard; as a parent and as an alumnus he should have concern with teacher education. What he says, however, should be based on an informed opinion. It is with the hope of developing such opinions that I have undertaken to write this book.

2

WHO GUARDS THE GATES?

IN OUR TRAVELS to 16 state capitals, my colleagues and I tried to test an often-stated and rather widely accepted charge: that there is in this country a national conspiracy on the part of certain professors and their friends to use the processes of teacher certification as a device for protecting courses in education and for maintaining a "closed shop" among teachers of the public schools who, as a result of these courses, will dependably follow the National Education Association (NEA) "party line." This conspiracy, it is argued, has been so successful that highly talented people are kept from the classrooms, and responsible laymen and distinguished scholars in the academic fields have been denied a voice in the formulation of programs of teacher education.

I confess to having had some initial skepticism about this charge: first, because I have generally found "devil" theories inadequate; and second, because my earlier studies of American education had led me to conclude that any statement about a *national* situation in education fails to account for highly significant state-by-state variations. My present study has reinforced this skepticism, although I have seen considerable evidence that one could use, with some distortion and considerable oversimplification, to support the charge.

First let us look at the national scene. There does exist a loose alliance of groups continually and very actively concerned with public school education. This educational establishment, as some have called it, is made up of organized school administrators, state Department of Education personnel, classroom teachers of various

15

kinds, professors of education, and the executive staffs of such organizations as the School Boards Association and the Parent-Teacher Association (PTA). Because professional educators are generally committed to what might be called the "politics of consensus," these groups actively seek collaboration with each other. Any powerful new group that begins to make itself heard on educational matters can expect overtures from the establishment. These groups on the national level have formal or informal ties with the National Education Association, under whose umbrella they often gather: sometimes to quarrel, more often to embrace.

The educational establishment does indeed promulgate a pervasive set of beliefs concerning teacher certification, but these beliefs are couched in such broad terms that they can mean different things to different people. For example, the groups all enunciate the belief that "teacher education is a university-wide function," a statement that begs the question of precisely where and to what extent the voice of academic professors should be heard. There is widespread agreement that the universities should collaborate with public school administrators and teachers in designing teacher-education programs; but this agreement in principle masks a power struggle currently under way between certain universities and the teacher and administrator groups over accreditation.

There is only one national organization whose direct actions have affected the question of who should be certified in a particular state. This organization, which is without legal status, is a voluntary agency known as the National Council for the Accreditation of Teacher Education (NCATE). Its appraisal of a teacher-education institution is made on the basis of a report of a team of educators who visit the institution and examine its program. If the appraisal is favorable, the institution is listed as "accredited." NCATE has acquired influence largely as the result of the access it has achieved on the state level through its contacts with two other organizations: the National Association of State Directors of Teacher Education and Certification and, more important, the state affiliates of The National Commission on Teacher Education and Professional Standards (TEPS).

The role of TEPS and NCATE is important, and its importance has been steadily increasing in recent years. On the national level,

TEPS was established in 1946 as a commission of the NEA. Its Washington, D.C., operations are under the direction of an NEA official who is directly responsible for liaison with the American Association of Colleges for Teacher Education (AACTE) and NCATE. This same official has other functions as well, concerning teacher welfare, teacher ethics, and teacher employment practices. The TEPS commission itself is appointed by NEA's executive committee and includes classroom teachers, school administrators, and professors of education. Through publications, nationwide and regional meetings, and the meetings of the TEPS affiliates in every state, TEPS endeavors to achieve widespread agreement on matters of teacher education and welfare, and professional standards.

On the state level, where the cooperation of the state Department certification personnel is actively enlisted, TEPS frequently becomes the central agency in enunciating and enlisting support for certification and employment regulations. In every state I visited, either a TEPS group or its equivalent has direct access to the state certification authorities. One of the major efforts of the national TEPS commission in recent years has been to give such groups legal status as the representatives of the organized profession in matters of concern to them. One major aspect of the "professional standards movement" has been this attempt to give legal participation to these NEA affiliates in controlling the gates to certification. In five of the states I visited (Florida, Illinois, Indiana, New Jersey, and Texas) the Legislatures have formally established advisory bodies, though in no case has the ultimate power to certify been delegated to them. In other states—for example, Wisconsin—a TEPS type of council exists and is systematically consulted by the state Department as a matter of Departmental policy, though at present it has no legal status in either legislative or state Department regulations. The influence of TEPS is further documented by the fact that the number of states moving toward the TEPS-supported *approved-program*[1] approach to teacher certification increased from 18 to 43 between 1957 and 1961.

[1] The term approved-program approach needs definition. Theoretically this approach is an alternative to that which depends on the meeting of specific course and credit requirements established by some agency of the state. Under the approved-program approach the teacher-education institution designs its own program, establishes its own requirements, and requests approval by some

Proponents of NCATE insist that it is an independent organization and has at times firmly resisted pressure from the other groups: NEA, TEPS, and AACTE. Its critics contend, with some energy, that it is part of a highly centralized NEA structure. What are the facts?

The national TEPS commission nominates six of NCATE's nineteen members; AACTE—whose liaison with the NEA, it will be remembered, is through the NEA executive secretary responsible for TEPS—appoints seven members. One member is appointed by the Council of Chief State School Officers and another by the National Association of State Directors of Teacher Education and Certification—groups with which state TEPS councils work intimately. Only four members are appointed by a group not affiliated with NEA. Furthermore, the major share of NCATE's budget comes from TEPS and AACTE. And it seems safe to say that TEPS is the political arm of the NEA in achieving state acceptance of NCATE accreditation. In every state where NCATE has had an impact on certification, the TEPS group has played a significant part in the initial and developmental phases. I realize that the term "political arm" might be regarded as objectionable, but one cannot escape the fact that NCATE would not have been able to achieve the legal recognition it has without strong and vigorous political support at the state level. Just how NCATE can be fully independent, in view of these circumstances, it is difficult to see.

In general, the arguments in favor of using NCATE accreditation are twofold: first, a national body can establish uniformly high standards; and second, the free movement of teachers from state to state can be facilitated if a respected national body attests—and if the state accepts its testimony—that graduates from out-of-state institutions have been well trained as teachers.

The intent expressed in the first of these two arguments is cer-

---

agency, either the state Department or NCATE. The approving agent then visits the institution, examines its structure and stated standards, and reviews the instructional program that prospective teachers are required to take. If the institution is judged adequate, then its graduates are automatically certified without an examination of their individual college records. In practice, as we shall see, the two systems are often blended and do not therefore constitute such clear-cut alternatives as the proponents of the approved-program approach claim.

tainly irreproachable; but whether the element of uniformity helps or hinders the raising of standards is open to question. As to the claim that NCATE facilitates interstate mobility of teachers, this would represent an important contribution if it were true. But is it true?

One cannot answer this fundamental question without a careful consideration of the certification process in the states, and in particular, of the many kinds of certificates issued by each state. Unfortunately there is no standard terminology referring to different kinds of certificates; the meaning of such labels as *permanent, standard, provisional, temporary, emergency,* and *highest standard* varies widely, and the situation is further confused by the fact that some states issue general certificates valid for all grades and subjects, while in other states the certificates are restricted to specific subjects or levels. I can, therefore, only describe the major types of certificates, and arbitrarily choose a set of labels that I will consistently use in referring to them, even though specific states may use the terms differently.

I shall refer to two broad types, *emergency* and *standard,* and shall further divide the standard type into two categories, *provisional* and *permanent.* An *emergency* certificate, usually issued on a year-by-year basis, is thought by the education authorities to be substandard, and those who hold it are considered to be in some critical way not yet fully qualified to teach. Such teachers are *ostensibly* employed only because no fully qualified teacher is available, but employing school boards occasionally use the emergency-certificate provisions to minimize their recruitment problems or to gain the services of a teacher who lacks only formal qualifications but who, in their judgment, is nevertheless effective.

The *provisional* certificate, as I shall use the term, assumes that the teacher is fully prepared for initial employment as a public school teacher. The state may, however, require that some additional conditions (further course work or experience or both) be met before the teacher receives the state's highest standard certificate, which I shall call a *permanent* certificate.

And where does NCATE approval fit into the state's certification policy? Graduation from an out-of-state NCATE-approved institution facilitates only the granting of the *provisional* certificate. Once employed, the teacher must, if he continues to teach in that state, fulfill whatever specific requirements that state has for its *permanent* certificate. Moreover, quite independently of NCATE, every state has some provisions by which an out-of-state teacher can be initially employed without meeting every detail of its regulations. In many cases the administrative discretion of the certification officer permits him to accept substitutes for some requirements; in any case the *emergency* certificate can be used until the teacher meets the standard requirements. It is true that the use of NCATE simplifies the certification process for the moving teacher, and it cuts down the amount of paper work in state Department offices as far as initial certification is concerned, but it rarely leads to the certification of a teacher who couldn't have been certified anyway. Nor does it significantly change the requirements one must ultimately meet to secure the highest standard certificate in the state.

As a matter of state law or Department of Education regulations, 7 of our 16 states rely, to one degree or another, on NCATE's program approval. The primary use of NCATE by the states thus far has been as a supplementary device, used only in the case of teachers prepared outside the state's boundaries. In some cases the individual transcript is examined to see if specific state requirements have, in fact, been met; in others, no such examination occurs with respect to initial certification. The hope of those supporting NCATE is that it will eventually be used as the major basis for certifying teachers for initial employment, whether they have been prepared within or without the state; but so far only Missouri, of our 16 states, has gone that far down the NCATE road. A few other states (including, for example, North Carolina) under TEPS influence, are adopting, for state-approved programs, guidelines almost indistinguishable from those of NCATE, though the interpretation and application of these guidelines may be quite different from state to state. New York, California, New Jersey, and recently Wisconsin, all for vastly different reasons, seem to be at this juncture the four states least inclined to expand the use of NCATE accreditation as a basis for certification.

NCATE does not specify the precise courses or credits that one must have to secure certification; it formally proclaims a commitment to variation and experimentation. It attempts to make certain that the *conditions* for an effective teacher-education program exist in each college it accredits. The criteria used concern such matters as standards for admitting and retaining students, training of staff, student-counseling arrangements, physical facilities, practice-teaching arrangements, administrative structure, and the existence of well-considered and internally consistent programs for the general and specialized education and the professional education[1] of teachers. It relies on the regional associations to evaluate the general academic achievement of the institution while it concentrates chiefly on other questions of more direct relevance to professional teacher education.

The regional associations themselves warrant notice. The North Central Association of Colleges and Secondary Schools is one of the more prominent, but the nation is blanketed by such regional groups. When it comes to accrediting colleges, a truce between NCATE and these associations has been worked out. But the regional associations also accredit high schools, and their accreditation is considered desirable; it sometimes facilitates the admission of the high school graduates to college. As a condition for such accreditation, the regional associations often insist that the teachers employed must have met certain requirements of prescribed courses similar to, but not necessarily identical with, those required by the state.

Since in one sense NCATE provides a potential alternative to state Department activities, and since both it and TEPS are at-

---

[1] The terms *general education, professional education, education in subject matter,* and *specialized education,* like many other terms used in educational circles, are variously defined and are themselves the subject of controversy. Though I will touch later on some of these controversies, these are the meanings I intend to convey by the terms I use: courses taught by professors of education and related directly to the theory and practice of public school teaching are designated as making up *professional education;* courses in a particular subject, required largely because the college student proposes to teach that subject, are designated as making up an *area of specialization* or, simply, *specialized education;* courses required primarily to insure breadth and depth of intellectual experience, without respect to the particular subject or grade the student is preparing to teach, will be spoken of as *general requirements* or *general education.* Quite obviously certain courses may fall into two of these categories for a particular student; for example, an English course may be a *general requirement* for all students but may also be considered part of the *area of specialization* for a prospective English teacher.

tempting to extend their influence over the universities and colleges, conflicts might well arise among the groups that make up the professional education establishment in many states. There is another NEA-TEPS project, that of applying sanctions against school boards whose employment policies seem undesirable to classroom teacher organizations. This project, too, is a source of strain—in this case between the school boards and administrator groups on the one hand and the classroom teachers on the other.

In certain quarters, one encounters vigorous opposition to NCATE and some opposition to the regional associations. In one state capital I was told by state Department personnel, "Our own standards for approving programs are obviously much higher than those of NCATE, many of whose approved institutions we would find completely unacceptable. In any case we cannot and would not dream of delegating our responsibility to such a group despite our belief that they are doing yeoman work in upgrading poor and mediocre institutions."

In several other states I was told that NCATE applied its standards concerning institutional structure in such a way that distinguished colleges and universities were offered only provisional NCATE accreditation while obviously poor or mediocre institutions were given approval. The structure and process of decision making within NCATE, its difficulties in assembling competent visiting teams, the ambiguity of its standards and their application, and the lack of a proper and identifiable constituency to whom it is responsible are cited as causes of major dissatisfaction.

This is not to say that NCATE is without adherents. On the contrary, the professional educators to whom we spoke in state Departments and universities were generally enthusiastic about it. They argue that NCATE provides a valuable service to teacher education when it visits institutions, makes recommendations for improvement, and classifies them in terms of the overall quality of program. However, when a body not subject to any public control whatsoever gains authority to determine, under certain conditions, who will and who will not be certified to teach, or when it seeks to impose undue uniformity on institutions of higher education, many people find it highly objectionable.

A very natural repugnance for such a state of affairs is at the root of the charge that certification policy is dominated by a national conspiracy. While I sympathize with the feeling underlying this charge, I cannot agree with the conclusion it expresses. To be sure, there is, on the national level, a cluster of groups holding broadly similar beliefs about teacher education, and seeking to persuade the various states to act in accordance with those beliefs. But the beliefs of the national group are significant *only as they are translated into policies on the state level.* The relevant decisions concerning certification are made in the state capitals, both the decision-making process and the policies adopted vary significantly from state to state, and one cannot talk intelligently about controlling entry to the teaching field except on a state-by-state basis.

IN THE STATES, the politics of teacher certification revolves around an alliance composed, much as on the national level, of representatives of organized teacher and administrator groups, professors of education and state Education Department officials. In every state some segment or segments of this alliance have exercised the predominant influence over the decisions reached. Although there are important deviations in detail, the political prowess of the establishment as a whole must be rated high: high enough to maintain marked influence and in some states substantial control. Using the widely accepted assumption that the state must control the gate to teaching in order to protect the public and its children, and propagating the idea that professional educators are best equipped to evaluate quality teaching, this establishment has persuaded almost every state to delegate to it major power over public school policy.

There have been challenges to the power of the education establishment in most states; in the majority of our 16 states, we found that bills had been introduced to rewrite the certification rules in opposition to the convictions of this group. In most cases, these attacks were defeated rather easily; in others, compromises have been made, and though the professional group has had to give in on some points, it has emerged with its power basically intact. The degree of compromise has generally varied with the strength of the establishment. In Virginia and Massachusetts, for example, for reasons peculiar to their own states' political systems, the establishments have never been as influential as those in some other states.

Interestingly enough, the bitterest conflicts have occurred in states that have traditionally had very strong teacher associations: California and Pennsylvania. Since these two states constitute exceptions to much that follows, we might take a closer look at these developments.

In Pennsylvania a potential conflict between the education establishment and other groups over the problems of financing public education has been building up for a number of years. By 1959 the state government's financial problems had become acute. Both the Legislature and the Governor reached the conclusion that the state was unable to meet the demands of the public school interests and competing groups and maintain a balanced budget. On the basis of authority granted by a resolution of the state Legislature, the issue of school support—along with other highly controversial education issues, including school reorganization and teacher education—was turned over to a committee of distinguished citizens appointed by Governor Lawrence in the spring of 1960. In the committee hearings and in the final report issued in April, 1961, the old argument of the academic versus the professional elements of teacher education played a major part, and it has been reported to us by representatives of all interests concerned that the educational establishment was bested in the power struggle. However, the committee's recommendations have yet to be fully implemented by the state, and it is impossible to determine whether the establishment's power has dwindled significantly.

In California the conflict between the academic professors and the public school interests, including the professors of education, has for many years been particularly acute but confined largely to the college campuses. There has also been widespread controversy over a number of other educational issues. By 1960, however, there was nearly unanimous agreement that the teacher certification picture had become overly complicated, and that something had to be done to simplify it. The California Teachers Association was preparing legislation, as was the California unit of the American Federation of Teachers (AFL-CIO), and a Legislature-sponsored citizen's committee had proposed action to upgrade the academic preparation of teachers and school administrators. By autumn of 1960 it was clear that the reform of teacher certification could be

made a profitable political issue; and Governor Brown, his appointed state Board of Education, and legislative leaders seized
upon it. The upshot was the Fisher Bill, which became law in 1961
and which was designed first, to raise the requirements for academic subject preparation at the expense of professional education,
and second, to prevent teachers who had no major in an academic
area from moving into administrative positions. The political lines
were clearly drawn and the professional education group suffered a
clear-cut defeat. Yet even in California, it seems probable that the
establishment still has enough power to maintain marked influence
over certification policies.

In the majority of our 16 states, the critical element in the decision-making structure has been the professional associations (that
is, teachers' associations, administrators' associations, and the like),
the state Departments of Education (nomenclature varies), or—
usually—both. It is under their auspices that the classroom teachers,
the school principals and superintendents, and the professors of
education are given a voice, and it is they who generally determine
the degree to which academic professors participate. In other words,
in most states the associations and state Departments have the
power to control professional policy decisions.

As a rule, the most powerful of these elements is the teachers' association. This is the group that has made the strongest defense of professional education as a state requirement. In fact, the
most vigorous support for the whole concept of certification comes
not from the college professors of education, who are frequently
portrayed as the villains, but from the teachers' associations, which
count few college professors of any kind among their membership.
These organizations have been able to muster the necessary political fire-power to contain attacks from those who would radically
reform certification regulations.

In few states can the teachers' association hold its power in respect to certification without substantial outside support from allies in other school matters. Yet as a rule, it has been the teacher
and administrator associations that "speak for the profession." In
every state I visited, these associations were well organized, having an established division concerned directly with legislative and
governmental policies. In every state this group was an active and

highly visible lobby, capable of exerting a grass-roots type of pressure upon governmental officials. In the majority of the states, this group was the central component of an alliance that included representatives of school boards and lay groups of various types, such as the PTA.

In most of the states, these associations place the highest priority on their legislative programs for increased state aid to the public schools. Normally, certification matters have a lower priority unless the association is threatened by some move that will destroy its cohesion and its hold on members. Such a threat, whether it comes from proposed legislation or, as in a few states, from the unionization of teachers, leads the association to rush to the support of certification rules, which it considers a unifying factor. Occasionally, if the threat seems to come from the teachers' union, the associations may meet it by more aggressive bargaining with the employing local school board, a tactic that puts some strain on the alliance among teachers, administrators, and school-board organizations.

The teachers' associations have worked persistently for the requirement of at least a bachelor's degree for certification, and in most of the states where a bachelor's degree is already required, for a fifth year or a master's degree. With regard to the amount of preparation, as opposed to the type, there seems to be relatively little political controversy. That is, many other groups accept the position that additional preparation is a reasonable requirement as long as commonsense considerations are observed. But the teacher groups and their allies (usually the state Departments) also insist that every person who enters teaching should have first completed a prescribed course of professional instruction analogous to that of doctors and lawyers. In essence, the argument is that public school teachers, in order to be regarded as professionals, must be in possession of some esoteric body of knowledge that sets them apart from those laymen whose general education is equivalent to theirs, or in some cases more extensive.

Quite obviously the only esoteric body of knowledge available to distinguish the teacher from other well-educated people is that provided in professional education courses. The teachers' associations are willing to engage, and do engage, in vigorous political battles to maintain this type of instruction either as specific courses required by the states or as components in state-approved programs. These teacher groups are not always greatly interested in the details of the professional education requirement, so long as a minimum amount is preserved. It is at this point that most of the conflict exists. Some academic professors and interested lay people contend that professional education has little to offer in the way of preparing good teachers. And on this score, officials or representatives of teachers' associations freely admit that there is considerable debate on the proper way to prepare teachers. They admit further that professional education remains a vague and inchoate field that needs flexibility for experimentation and adjustment. They acknowledge that some of the courses are repetitious and poorly taught. The question, then, is: Why have these associations, whenever they were threatened, defended state requirements of professional education courses as a necessary part of certification policy? Why do they exert considerable effort and use up large amounts of their political currency in an effort to protect these requirements?

Rational reasons can be given for their position. Let me emphasize that what I am about to say is based upon what was told to me and to my staff on numerous occasions in every state—by people intimately involved in public school matters.

First, the leaders of teacher associations do believe that there exists a specific body of principles that can be taught, and that such teaching does, in fact, make an individual a better teacher. Classroom teachers and administrators have convinced the association executives that new teachers who have not had such instruction perform inadequately and require close supervision and assistance. Given the disagreements among experts, however, few of those in leadership posts would attempt to specify precisely what instruction should be required, *except for practice teaching*[1] on which there is general agreement.

Second, by requiring a special type of training for all public school teachers, it is possible to control the gate to the profession and thus create conditions that will attract people of high ability.

[1] Practice teaching involves the future teacher's participating in the activities of an elementary or secondary school classroom under the guidance of the regular teacher and with the supervision of a professor of education.

The group leaders with whom we talked often argued that if certification requirements in professional education were removed, the results would be disastrous. They felt that as a matter of convenience, economy, or simple patronage, school boards would hire anybody with a college degree. Neither teaching aptitude, knowledge of the art of teaching, nor teaching experience would be required. Under such conditions the market would be flooded and it would become possible to deflate already inadequate teachers' salaries, with the result that teaching would become less attractive to talented college graduates. Control of the gate to teaching restricts the supply of teachers and makes it possible for their leaders to negotiate with political officials for better salaries and working conditions. This, they maintain, is in the public interest because it enhances the profession's appeal to the kind of people they believe should be employed as teachers. The professional courses have particular value in that they permit and encourage a screening process by which inept and otherwise undesirable candidates are eliminated.

Third, training in professional education serves as a "badge of unity" for members of the professional education association. A special type of training shared by all who enter the field provides a common experience for both administrators and classroom teachers, which keeps the two segments together. Moreover, and perhaps more important, such instruction *symbolizes* the distinctive quality of the profession in that not just anyone is eligible to join the public school enterprise. The practical importance of this symbol hinges upon the fact that much of the effort to secure favorable public and governmental support for the aims of teacher and administrator associations has been made to hinge directly upon a recognition of such associations as *professional groups*.

Finally, a specialized type of training, I was told, can serve as a protective shield for the teacher in his dealings with parents whose training may be comparable in the general education field. More concretely, the teacher, often confronted by anxious and deeply concerned parents, feels the necessity of producing in defense of his decisions convincing information that goes beyond general public knowledge. In this way, both the parent and the teacher are reassured.

These arguments obviously relate both to substantive and to political considerations. Although I do not wish at this point to pass any personal judgment on their merit, I will say that it would be unwise to discount the soundness of at least some of this reasoning.

The striking feature of certification politics in all but 3 of the 16 states is the absence of any serious attempt at lay participation. There is no organized and continuing group of nonprofessional people concerned substantially with the certification rules and offering an alternative to the proposals of the public school people. This is not to say that there are no critics or that the educational establishment is free to do as it pleases. Certification decisions are occasionally influenced by the exertions of temporary critics, but there is no noneducational group that displays continuous concern. Thus certification politics in the majority of states might be characterized as issueless politics; that is, seldom do the temporary critics present real alternatives. The professional groups who remain in control have developed the strategy of minimizing or redirecting any potential differences as to what the certification rules should be. With a few notable exceptions, public concern over teacher certification, to the extent that it exists at all, finds expression through the grooves of influence that have been carefully channeled by the educational establishment.

In THREE RESPECTS, then, the situation in the 16 states we visited is similar as far as the politics of teacher education is concerned. First, all are subject to propaganda emanating from NCATE, TEPS, and other national organizations. Second, the state educational establishment, usually led and controlled by the teachers' association, is well organized, politically effective, and exerts the major influence on certification policies. Third, this establishment is committed in every state to some form of certification that will insure, for the reasons given above, at least a minimal amount of professional education. As we shall see, however, in spite of these similarities, state regulations concerning teacher education show important variations from state to state. The question is: What produces these variations?

Here any number of factors must be taken into consideration; some of them are subtle. A state in whose communities are concentrated highly educated scientists and advanced technologists demands a kind of education different from that demanded in a state dependent on mass-labor industry. A state whose intellectual and economic leaders send their own children to private schools differs in its behavior from one in which many such people rely on the public schools. A state with a well-developed system of state universities does not pass the same kind of legislation as one largely dependent on private universities and public teachers colleges. Where there is a strong tradition of local school autonomy, the state Department of Education officials assume roles entirely different from those of their counterparts in states with a tradition of centralized leadership.

Moreover, the capacity of the schools within a state to recruit teachers will affect the extent to which certification policy can practically be enforced. The states are not alike in this respect. To understand the divergent results from state to state, one must examine such factors as these, as well as formal legal arrangements. The kind of state-by-state analysis one should make before entering the arena of state educational politics would be much more extended than I can provide here, but a few examples should serve to illustrate the complexities.

First, let us consider the states' response to the growing demand for state-supported higher education. The institutions most directly affected usually are the state universities and the state colleges; the latter originated in most cases as two-year institutions called normal schools, whose sole function was teacher preparation. The size and strength of the state university differs enormously from one state to another, as does the role of the state colleges: for instance neither Massachusetts nor New Jersey has yet developed a state university comparable to the large tax-supported universities of the states west of the Alleghenies. The state colleges in these two states are still almost exclusively teacher-training institutions; a movement to develop local two-year public colleges is in its infancy. In contrast stands California with fifteen state colleges and a state university comprising eight campuses; all the state colleges offer undergraduate vocational or professional programs in addition to training teachers. Thus, in California the state institutions that were once primarily supported for training teachers have been transformed. At the same time local two-year colleges have increased in number and have prospered, but they are not involved in educating teachers.

New York is in process of expanding its relatively new state university, which involves converting the state colleges into branches of the university. The graduate work will be concentrated on a few campuses. The proposed transformation, therefore, is unlike what has occurred in California. It is also unlike what is being talked about in Pennsylvania. In that state the fourteen former state teachers colleges will not become part of a university, but appear to be ready for a metamorphosis into colleges with many programs. Clearly, this transformation of state institutions is bound to affect one way or another the state's commitment to training teachers. Questions of curriculum control, personnel policy, and institutional finance raise complicated political problems at the state capital. Time and again as we investigated certification issues, we uncovered an argument about the proportion of state money to be received by different types of institutions. Hence state requirements for certification become intimately involved with general policies of state finance for higher education. Though the relationship of certification to these other issues may differ state by state, there is almost invariably some connection.

A practical consideration more obviously related to the politics and enforcement of teacher certification regulations is the supply and demand of teachers within the state. With reference to certification decisions, one observer told me, "People have to have their symbols," by which he meant that certain decisions, such as increasing the course requirements, had been designed simply to reassure certain groups that higher standards were being invoked. But people have to have their teachers, too; and both the formal rules and the extent to which they are enforced are shaped by the necessity to have at least a live, mature person in every classroom.

Three factors enter into judgments about the adequacy of teacher supply. One is the actual number of persons available and prepared to teach; the second is the number of pupils to be taught; and the third is the ideal size of each class. Here is another situation that must be examined state by state, and here, too, the national statistics are not very helpful to one who would understand the problems in his particular state. Even the state-by-state figures are misleading unless one notes differences in the teacher-pupil ratio that is held to be the ideal. Moreover, even within a state, the supply-demand picture for elementary school teachers is unlike that for secondary school teachers, and that for one secondary-school teaching field is unlike that for another. I have provided in Appendix D some statistical data and some discussion of the implications of these data for those who make teacher certification policy.

Such practical problems must be studied carefully by interested laymen in each state. Clearly, in any state, all efforts to upgrade teacher education, or indeed any aspect of the public school program, must take into account the funds, facilities, and personnel available within that state.

IF WE TURN from these practical considerations to the composition and political behavior of groups involved in decision making, we find again marked differences from one state to another. These differences must assuredly be included in any attempt to explain variations in state policies, and again an awareness of the situation in each state is indispensable to the layman who would affect his state's policies.

The formal structure through which policies are arrived at is often indicative of, and sometimes determines, the extent to which certain groups have an opportunity to influence certification policies; it also controls the manner in which they must make their influence felt. But I am convinced that the formal structure, as such, does not determine either the policy decided upon or its application: that is, the importance of structural considerations is more tactical than substantive. (Appendix E indicates structural differences in the 16 most populous states.)

A few of the considerations I have in mind are: Is the state Board of Education (its title may vary, and in a few states, it does not even exist) elected or appointed? Of what kind of people is it composed? And does it have extensive administrative discretion, or is its power closely restricted by the Governor or Legislature? Is the chief state school officer (usually superintendent, but again titles vary) appointed or elected? What are his formal relationships to the board? And how much legal autonomy does he have? Are there standing advisory committees that must be consulted by the chief state school officer, or does the state have a tradition of using specially appointed "blue ribbon" committees of distinguished citizens? For an example of the role of these factors in decision making, let us examine the formal structure in two states.

In New York the Board of Regents and the state Department of Education are the agencies responsible for the establishment of certification criteria. The Board of Regents, whose members are selected by the State Legislature, is steeped in tradition (one of the first regents was Alexander Hamilton), is widely regarded as a powerful body, and enjoys high prestige. It is entirely a lay board; its members are prominent and distinguished citizens of the State of New York. The title "regent" is considered evidence of one's publicly recognized acclaim and distinction. In this state, therefore, powerful lay opinion comes in at the moment of final decision-making.

The state Department of Education in New York, created by and responsible to this Board, is frequently referred to as outstanding in the United States. The Department has a large staff, it is composed of many divisions, and its functions encompass a wide range of subjects. It has considerable funds for research and administration, it recruits its professional staff members from various parts of the country, and their salaries are, by comparative standards, high. Decisions made within this structure, whether they pertain to certification or some other educational problem, are far less likely to generate widespread protest or to encounter bitter and heated opposition than might be the case in a structure that did not have these advantages. Given such a structure, outside groups feel assured that before final decisions are made their interests will have been considered—as, indeed, is the case. The formal and legal structure in New York, coupled with tradition, custom, and method of appointment, helps to insure in *any* decisions a relatively high level of acceptance and confidence on the part of both professional educators and interested laymen.

In terms of formal structure, Indiana stands in marked contrast to New York. The state has no exclusively lay board comparable to the Regents in New York. Quite the contrary, it has in reality what amounts to three separate and independent boards, which are but theoretically integrated. One board or division deals exclusively with textbooks, another concentrates on matters pertaining to finance, and the third, the one with which I am concerned, deals primarily with teacher certification and the approval of teacher-preparation programs. Each of these boards has six members who are appointed by the Governor, but the Governor must appoint, on each, at least four people who are actively engaged in some phase of public education. In further contrast to New York, the Indiana Commission on Teacher Training and Licensing has extensive administrative powers that are exercised independently of the Indiana state Department of Education. For example, it has its own staff to visit colleges and universities in carrying out its own function of approving particular teacher-preparation programs.

The Indiana state Department, which has a voice in the formation of certification policies and is charged with the responsibility of administering them, is, by its own admission, a relatively weak department. The state superintendent is elected every two years on a partisan ballot, and this fact alone makes his job an almost impossible one. Aside from the fact that a superintendent is constantly running for office, we were told that neither party has displayed any sustained interest in this office. In fact, both parties have been accused of using the nomination for state superintendent as a device to kill off a potential candidate who is considered undesirable but whose political strength cannot be safely disregarded. The Department has little in the way of funds for research purposes; the salaries of appointees to the Department are comparatively low, and those who hold staff positions on the professional level do not have civil service status; service in the agency is seldom considered to offer prestige or to provide a stepping stone to some other position; and the clerical staff is considerably overburdened. Obviously, all these factors make it very difficult for the state Department in Indiana to recruit highly trained professional people. Though informed observers told my staff that the Department was beginning to gain some stature and had in recent years enjoyed greater prestige, the same observers feel that the office must be removed from the partisan elective process and made an appointive one before it can achieve the desired level of educational leadership. In Indiana this would require a constitutional amendment—which, of course, is a lengthy and complicated process. This type of legal structure, as contrasted to that of New York, is likely to give rise to certification policies that reflect narrow thinking and allow little room for outside groups to exercise any influence.

There is another significant element that affects certification decisions and helps to explain the variations among the states, and that is the simple fact of variations in personality. Though this seems obvious, its importance is sometimes overlooked. For example, the chief state school officer in one state has been quoted as saying that a "shift toward a very high degree of centralized determination of curriculum or of school policies represents in the long run a threat to the basic function of public education." This same official has also been publicly quoted as saying that he is highly skeptical about the use of standardized tests. Given the structure of this state Department and the crucial role this man plays, his opinions have a profound effect on the policies that are formulated. It is very unlikely, as long as this individual remains the chief state school officer, that this state will adopt examinations as a major procedure for certification. I do not wish, of course, to pass judgment on his position; whether I agree with it is not the relevant point. I merely cite the instance as an illustration of the fact that personal preferences affect the decisions. It can safely be said that the personal judgments of influential leaders in every state are just as vital.

One critical question remains to be considered, and that is the degree to which the establishment is responsive to outside criticisms and the extent to which it has encouraged outside groups to work cooperatively with it. In North Carolina, for example, the teachers' association, the administrators' organization, and the school boards' association—which have long worked well with each other—made a major and successful effort to involve the academic professors in the development of a new approved-program approach to teacher certification. The state authorities were then confronted with a proposal on which the usually antagonistic groups had already reached consensus, and no major legislative row occurred. In California, on the other hand, the teachers' association sponsored a number of meetings to discuss teacher certification, but invited only people active in public school work. They were unwilling or unable to construct a consensus with the academic professors, and the latter attacked them head on by carrying the fight directly to the public and the Legislature. It must be said that in California neither the teacher and administrator associations nor the academic professors are known for their restraint.

New York is like California in that it has a large number of people interested in having their schools emphasize a high quality of academic performance, and willing to press to achieve this objective. But in New York, the Board of Regents and the Department of Education (neither of which has traditionally been dominated by the teachers' association, though all three groups work comfortably together) quickly respond to public pressures. As a matter of fact, the professional associations themselves share many of the values of those demanding reform. The public pressure that may, in a state like California, result in a Fisher Bill controversy, is absorbed by the more flexible and responsive New York system. In fact, the decision-making institutions in New York are so well fortified by public esteem that political leaders are fearful of seizing upon any educational issue to further their ambitions, and disagreements over educational policy are not as likely to become political issues as they are in some other states.

The only states in which the educational establishment did not show a marked trend toward bringing the academic professors and their allies into the decision-making structure were California, Pennsylvania, New Jersey, and Illinois. Of the first two situations I have already spoken. California and Pennsylvania are similar in two respects. In both states, for different reasons, the political leaders seized upon teacher education and made it a highly visible political issue. In doing so, they sought the total exclusion of the public school people from their deliberations.

New Jersey is atypical in many ways. Its chief state school officer is very powerful in certain policy areas and strongly supports a tradition of local autonomy in other areas. He is backed by a highly cooperative teachers' association. New Jersey's education-conscious citizens often rely on private schools; the state is only beginning to create a public university system; and its single-purpose state teachers colleges are firmly in the hands of the chief state school officer. There has as yet been very little heated controversy about teacher education.

Illinois is also quite atypical. Here the School Problems Commission, composed of key legislators and school people, constitutes a consensus system on most educational matters. Though it has not recently been deeply involved in teacher-certification issues, concerning which there *is* controversy, it stands ready to move in before the controversy reaches critical proportions. Moreover, its manner of handling other issues has prevented far-reaching educational conflicts on such matters as school support. Thus, in Illinois, battles over teacher education do not get too much attention because they are not tied up in other issues, and because the power of the teachers' association seems relatively inoffensive to people who view the School Problems Commission as a watchdog.

In the rest of the states I surveyed, the public school forces are at least attempting to bring the academic professors into their decision-making processes. In 8 of our 16 states, advisory councils on teacher education have been enlarged to include representatives from academic faculties. In another the state Department, with the support and cooperation of the teachers' association, has solicited the opinions of academic groups. In two more, elaborate claims are made that academic people have been systematically consulted, and that their views have been seriously considered whenever changes in certification requirements were being made.

Though the participation of academic people in the certification process has demonstrably increased in the past years, particularly in the post-Sputnik era, one does have to ask how effective that participation has been. More than once I was told that academic representatives had been "brought into line." This, I suppose, means that either they have adopted much of the thinking of professional educators or they have been allowed to blow off steam, so to speak, and are content to play a less vigorous role. I cannot resist at this point reporting an ironical and somewhat amusing event that occurred in one state. I heard from members of the liberal arts and science faculty of a major university in that state that they had successfully penetrated the "interlocking professional education directorate." They had secured the appointment of one of their men to a crucial post in the certification decision-making process, a man they expected to expound their point of view. The next day representatives of the professional education side of the argument described the same individual as a man who supported their general point of view and as a man who certainly wasn't a "liberal arts type."

Still, virtually no recent cases of certification reform have increased the number of education courses required in four-year collegiate programs; most have, instead, required increases in academic courses. This fact, I believe, reflects the response of the educational establishment to the public's increasing concern. Even on the national level, the TEPS group has given some support to these changes and has actively sought to involve academic professors.[1]

In those cases in which the academic professors and their allies have sought to reform teacher education, they have adopted the tactics of the educational establishment. That is, they have sought to have the state write out specific requirements for courses in general education or in the field of specialization. To implement their proposals, they have sometimes urged legislative action, with what I regard as unfortunate consequences. *When disagreement concerning teacher education is forced into the Legislature, unrelated conflicts may override the issue.* In state after state, legislators use arguments concerning academic or professional instruction to mask their concern with racial, economic, ideological, or partisan political factors. The teacher-education issue becomes a mere symbol to conceal more fundamental conflicts; both professional and academic professors become pawns in disputes that in reality have little to do with the effective preparation of teachers. Moreover, by pressing for legislation to enforce their views, ironically enough, the academic professors restrict their freedom to control the curricula on their own campuses.

Much as I deplore both the coercive method and its effects, in all fairness I must emphasize one point: those most concerned with

---

[1] The TEPS commission in conjunction with several national learned societies and professional associations has sponsored and published reports of three conferences related to teacher education. These conferences were held at Bowling Green University (1958), the University of Kansas (1959), and at San Diego State College (1960).

the certification processes act in good faith with the public. They are sincerely convinced that their desires are consistent with the public interest. This is true even though it is also true that they seek to enhance the status of themselves and others who share their beliefs. The irony of it is that in my judgment the attempt to provide *legal* support for their position actually serves to undercut the public confidence in them. The professors of education, through their dependence on legal support, have already reaped a bitter harvest. On campus after campus it is now widely believed by students and professors alike that the *only* justification for pedagogical courses is that the state requires them. Such courses are rarely judged on their own merits; in some cases they could not survive such judgment, in others they might come out very well. The academic professors on many campuses now seem determined to follow their professional colleagues down this primrose path. The consequences of the state's requiring courses, I think, are analogous to those Thomas Jefferson feared would result from the state's legal support of religion. Such legal support, he argued, would evoke the resentment of people forced to comply with things to which they were not rationally committed; and it would withdraw from those who would be leaders the incentives and rewards that came to one who, by his own effort and merit, secured uncoerced public support and respect.

Now that I have unburdened myself of this conviction, let me summarize our findings and my own views on the politics of teacher education state by state. There is in every state capital a well-organized education lobby, usually centering on the teachers' association and the state Department of Education. To some extent the state educational establishments share the beliefs of their national organizations, though when they translate these beliefs into state action, highly significant differences—both in the ways of operating and the policies they adopt—emerge among them. These differences stem from the degree of responsiveness of the establishment to other groups in the state, the legal structure within each state, and the effect of personality variables, among other things. In most of the states I am convinced that the establishment is flexible and responsive enough so that anyone actively concerned with teacher education can make his influence felt.

As we have seen, in most states the public school forces hold the greatest power as far as teacher certification is concerned. Is this situation unwholesome? The answer, of course, depends on whether or not these forces are serving the public interest and can be held in the final analysis accountable to the public.

As a general policy, I believe the public interest is well served when there exists a clearly identifiable group of people who assume continued responsibility for the operation of the public school system. The existence of an educational "establishment" is, in my judgment, as it should be. Without it no one could be called to account. And if we are to hold the establishment responsible for the management of the schools, we can only in justice yield to it the right to make fundamental decisions concerning these schools. The key word here is *responsible,* which implies *responsiveness* as well. If, as is sometimes charged, the establishment is so rigid in its responses, so closed-minded in its convictions, that the concerns of the public are not met, then indeed a most serious danger exists.

I think it must be said that in almost every state the establishment is overly defensive; it views any proposal for change as a threat and assumes that any critic intends to enlarge its difficulties and responsibilities while simultaneously undermining its ability to bear them. In short, there is too much resentment of outside criticism and too little effort toward vigorous internal criticism. In some instances I found the establishment's rigidity frightening.

I can understand, of course, that hit-and-run attacks by critics who always seem to disappear when constructive and continuous action is required, or who do not give any serious study to school problems before launching an attack, provoke legitimate anxieties. Such critics appear to public school people as connivers anxious only to gain a public forum in order to enhance their personal prestige or fatten their pocketbooks. As for criticism from the members of academic faculties, the most common rejoinder is "You can't get them to spend even a day trying to handle public school classrooms or going over the problems an administrator faces." This charge is in too many cases just.

The anxiety is understandable; the excessive rigidity is still too often a fact. Yet my overall judgment is that the educational establishment in most of the states I visited *has* responded to public con-

cern about teacher education and *has* actively sought the cooperation of other responsible groups. In most states the professional
educators have not only supported the upgrading of the academic
preparation of teachers, but have also sought to involve representatives of academic faculties in their planning. On the national level,
the TEPS commission, which I have described as the strongest
national political group actively concerned with teacher education,
has consistently turned over its speaker's platform to its most vocal
critics.

The question of who determines certification policies is at present,
as we have seen, a complicated one; it is also undeniably important. But we must also consider another even more important question: How well do our policies work? That is, do they provide well-
trained and competent teachers for the public schools? For an
answer to this question, let us turn to an examination of certification practices now in use by the states.

3

PATTERNS OF CERTIFICATION

TEMPTING AS IT MIGHT BE to discuss certification policy in national terms, any such discussion soon gets into difficulties. The magnitude of the problem alone makes it impossible to speak in wide generalizations. The total number of institutions offering teacher-training programs is large; in the whole country, there are over a thousand of them. (For the 16 states on which I am focusing attention, the number is no less than 665.) Every year in the nation as a whole, some 150,000 individuals trained in these institutions are certified as teachers by the states to take their places among the 1.5 million classroom teachers who, day after day, instruct some 39 million pupils in no fewer than 84,000 separate elementary schools and 24,000 secondary schools.[1]

The institutions in which these teachers are educated, the schools in which they are eventually employed, and the state regulations to which both are subject are profoundly affected by a number of factors, which vary widely from state to state and from region to region. For example, the state's financial resources and the supply and demand of teachers are among the most obviously relevant considerations.

In all 50 states, public money is spent on the education of teachers; in all 50 states, the state sets limits to the freedom of the local

[1] Every year, approximately one-third of all the recipients of the baccalaureate degree in the country are graduates of teacher-training programs. These facts make a consideration of the education of teachers quite unlike a similar inquiry into the education of lawyers or doctors or even engineers (about 30,000 engineers are graduated annually as compared with 150,000 classroom teachers).

42

school board to hire teachers by setting up certification requirements. Beyond these two generalizations it is hard to find many of
significance.

Indeed, among the 16 most populous states, no two states *have
adopted exactly the same requirements for entry into the profession*
on either the elementary or the secondary level. Moreover, in most
states the situation is far from stable. In some states the certification
requirements are in process of revision; in others changes have just
been made, to become effective in a few years. Thus, what I might
have reported three years ago would not be true today; what is
reported in the present volume may not be accurate three years
hence. Furthermore, in almost any state, what appears to be a stable
situation may become a rapidly changing one in a short time.[1]

In essence, certification requirements involve three things in each
state. One is the total amount of preparation, the second is the
amount of instruction in professional education, and the third is
the amount of general education and subject-matter specialization.
Let us consider these three items, in that order.

After years of agitation, 14 of the 16 states we surveyed now require a bachelor's degree as the minimal base for *standard* certification. Only two still issue standard certificates to persons with less
than four years of preparation: Wisconsin, which currently operates
several two-year teacher-training institutions whose graduates are
provisionally certifiable; and Ohio, which, in order to meet a teacher
shortage some years ago, created a two-year program for elementary
school teachers. Even these two states are only a step away from
eliminating the two-year certificates. The Ohio State Board of
Education voted in 1962 to eliminate its two-year certificate by
1968.

The major debate today is what to do about a fifth year. California has a formal certification rule requiring that a person must have

---

[1] The source of much information relating to certification is *A Manual on
Certification Requirements for School Personnel in the United States* by
W. Earl Armstrong and T. M. Stinnett. The National Commission on Teacher
Education and Professional Standards of the National Education Association,
Washington, D.C., 1961 edition. TEPS has published certification manuals
every second year since 1951. Another useful document is published by the
University of Chicago Press, which for almost thirty years has released annu-
ally a summary of the most recent requirements for certification.

had *five continuous* years of preparation to receive a standard certificate for secondary teaching, and that elementary teachers must take a fifth year's work before receiving the permanent certificate. Indiana requires a bachelor's degree for standard certification and a master's degree—based on a full year's work, to be acquired within seven years—for permanent certification. New York, too, has moved in the direction of four-plus-one. In order to be permanently certified in New York, a teacher must, within five years after obtaining the bachelor's degree, have acquired an additional 30 semester hours or its equivalent of graduate credit. Georgia issues a special certificate to a person who has six years of preparation. However, in that state, teachers may be permanently certified with less preparation. In all states there are varying laws and regulations, state and local, that encourage some teachers to take afternoon and evening courses by tying the salary schedule to courses taken.

The reader would be deceived, however, if he concluded that most teachers in many states will soon have had five years of post-high-school preparation. Even if requirements were rigorously enforced, this would still not be the case. These are relatively recent provisions and they are *not* retroactive. Moreover, most of the states will still allow persons with less than this amount of preparation to teach on an emergency basis. In all the states we surveyed, a number of teachers with less than four years of preparation are in the classrooms.

The amount of time that must be devoted to education courses also varies from state to state. Moreover, the amount required for an elementary teacher is often substantially greater than that required for secondary teachers. On the elementary level no state requires fewer than 18 semester hours, and on a secondary level no state requires fewer than 12 hours, though Virginia and Massachusetts have arrangements by which actual teaching experience may be substituted for all but 9 and 10 hours respectively. In Virginia, in fact, in certain special cases the entire requirement of course work in education may be waived, and the teacher may acquire a standard certificate without having done any such work.

Table I in Appendix F sets forth the details of the professional education requirements, including practice teaching, for both elementary and secondary teachers in the 16 states we surveyed. It should be noted that several states and numerous teacher-training institutions also require that elementary teachers complete professionalized-content courses.[1] For example, Texas and Pennsylvania require 12 and 18 semester hours[2] respectively in elementary-content subjects.

The requirements shown in the Appendix are, it must be recalled, state minimal requirements. There are no state regulations *limiting* the number of credits that might be required by a given college, and individual colleges in many states do require more than the state minimum. There are widespread misconceptions concerning the actual professional education requirements in every state. I have encountered many people who stated as fact that their particular state required at least half the collegiate credit to be in education courses. Even when I informed them of the facts, many seemed inclined not to believe me.

However one views the contribution of education courses to sound teacher preparation, there has been, in so far as credit hours are concerned, a marked trend in all 16 states we surveyed toward holding the line on these requirements. In fact, they have been de-

[1] *Professionalized-content* courses are to be distinguished from regular *education* courses. The former include such courses as children's literature, elementary school art, mathematics for the elementary school, elementary school science, etc. Though the requirements in professionalized-content courses may be listed separately from those for education courses, the two kinds of courses are combined in many programs.

[2] A few words are in order at this point regarding the use of the term "semester hours." A unit of 3 semester hours has become the standard measure of a college course meeting three times a week. It is common practice for a full-time college student to study five subjects a semester, each course meeting three times each week. If the student passes the courses, he is said to have completed 15 semester hours or "credits" of academic work. In most colleges (but not all) 120 semester hours' credit is specified for a degree. Some courses may be evaluated as 4 or even 9 semester hours if, for example, laboratory work is required. Some courses that are continuous through two semesters have a price tag of 6 or 8. Some courses that in the wisdom of the faculty take less of the student's time may be priced at only 2 or even as little as 1 semester hour's credit. Institutions on the quarter system have their own system of academic bookkeeping, but formulas for converting one account into another are available. Throughout this volume I shall write in terms of semester hours, though I dislike the implication that accomplishment in higher education can be expressed in a numerical system that is so reminiscent of a cash account.

creased more often than increased in recent years, except when a fifth year has been added, and most of the new fifth-year programs have emphasized academic preparation.

It is chiefly in the areas of general education and subject-matter specialization that the states are now moving toward increasing certification requirements. Since the wave of protest that followed the launching of the first Soviet Sputnik, the trend is clearly toward higher "intellectual" standards. This pattern was evident in all 16 of our states. In each state the tendency to tighten and increase the general education and subject-matter requirements paralleled the stabilizing of requirements in education courses. It would be possible to discuss the variations among the states almost indefinitely, but a lengthy discussion would not, I think, prove very useful. Table II in Appendix F describes the present situation well enough to indicate the different patterns followed among the 16 most populous states. For our purposes only a few highlights need be examined.

Requirements recently adopted in New York, to take effect in September, 1963, for secondary teachers, are most formidable, at least in formal specifications. To receive permanent certification to teach chemistry in New York, a secondary-school teacher must be a graduate of an accredited institution; have 30 hours beyond the bachelor's degree completed within five years; have 57 semester hours in mathematics and science, which includes the equivalent of three full year courses in chemistry and mathematics; and 60 semester hours on the undergraduate level in general education. In addition to these requirements, the candidate must also have 18 semester hours in education courses and 80 supervised periods of practice teaching in the field of chemistry.

The requirements in New York contrast rather sharply with those in Georgia. A Georgia chemistry teacher needs only 30 semester hours of science, of which 12 must be in the field of chemistry itself.[1] The general education requirement in Georgia is also lower, only 36 semester hours. Both states, however, require approximately the same amount of professional education, and both require practice teaching as a prerequisite for certification.

As long as I am using Georgia as an example, I might point out that

---

[1] Georgia's certification requirements, which are listed as quarter hours, have been converted into semester hours.

its teacher specialist certificate, which ranks higher in prestige than the permanent standard certificate, is unique. The winner of such a certificate is given a thousand-dollar raise in salary. Presumably the holders of this certificate constitute a sort of elite group among Georgia teachers. To join this group one must complete six years of formal schooling and make a high score on the National Teacher Examinations.[1]

Three other states use some kind of examination in connection with the certification process. Florida requires that all teachers take the National Teacher Examinations and attain a prescribed score or higher in order to qualify for a continuing contract and to be eligible for the benefits under the state's minimum salary law. Individuals who have failed to attain the prescribed score may still be certified, but they are ineligible for tenure and their maximum salary cannot exceed $2,500 a year. North Carolina requires that every teacher take the National Teacher Examinations, but the results are used exclusively for advisory and research purposes and are not yet conditions of certification, tenure, or salary.[2] Pennsylvania does not use the National Teacher Examinations but does require examinations for all teachers of foreign languages. The authorities in Pennsylvania have given no indication of a desire to extend the examination requirements to other fields.

In this connection, the "special requirements" imposed by a few states deserve mention. In California, under regulations in force at this writing, renewal of a standard certificate requires a course in audio-visual education. In Wisconsin, teachers of social studies, economics, and agriculture are required to take special courses en-

---

[1] The National Teacher Examinations program, administered by Educational Testing Service, consists of objective-type examinations for assessing academic preparation in both professional and general education. In addition, the tests include certain measures for appraising mental ability. The examinations do not purport to measure directly such factors as personal and social characteristics, interests, attitudes, and ability to motivate learning.

[2] One can hardly doubt that the decision by Southern states to use the National Teacher Examinations is related to the fact that Negro teachers and white teachers are prepared in separate institutions in these states, and are organized in completely separate teachers' organizations. Questions of teacher education and certification related to such separation, however, are far too important and too complex to be dealt with briefly. I have therefore decided not to discuss them in this volume.

titled "cooperatives," while social studies and biology teachers must also take a course in "conservation." Texas requires of every teacher courses that include state and Federal constitutional history or development. Pennsylvania requires of all teachers courses in both visual aids and state history, and similar requirements exist in other states. I report, happily, that the trend is against the continuation or addition of such requirements. But, again, each state must contend with political forces within its own boundaries.

BOTH FRIENDS AND FOES of state requirements agree that this whole process, regardless of how one feels about the specifics, is a nuisance and a headache and ought to be simplified. Since the credit and hour rules have created administrative problems and have failed to perform entirely satisfactorily the function assigned to them, a number of states are planning or have executed plans to certify teachers, at least provisionally, upon the basis of the approved-program approach mentioned earlier, though in these cases the state rather than NCATE does the approving.

At the time of my survey, 14 of our 16 states were at some stage in the process of switching to an approved-program approach, and the other two states were considering such a move. In a few of these—Texas, for example—the approval of the total teacher-education institution is combined with a detailed prescription of required courses in education and in the teaching field. That is to say, the inclusion of the older course-credit requirement is an explicit condition of approval. In others—New York is a case in point—the state Departments examine the colleges' requirements in detail but have no definitive statement of the courses that must be included in each institutional program they approve. The state Department may refuse approval if it considers a program lacking in the necessary elements or excessive in certain credit requirements. It does not, however, require all institutions to have the same courses and credits. The policy in such states as New York and Pennsylvania is to attempt to define certain standards and guidelines of quality within which the teacher-education institutions are allowed some freedom and flexibility for experimentation.

I must say at this point that there are hidden traps in the approved-program approach. Even in those states most liberal in granting freedom to the institutions they approve, there are differences of opinion between the state Departments and the institutions over the courses future teachers should take and the amount of credit each course should carry. Such differences are almost invariably resolved in favor of the state Department. Inevitably the result is hostility on the part of the universities and colleges affected. Despite the state's admittedly worthwhile intent, its efforts become infuriating when state officials impose detailed prescriptions in areas in which they are untrained or thought to be less competent than the college specialists who must act on their prescriptions. The problem is inherent in the structure and composition of state Departments of Education. Even the best of these Departments include few persons with significant amounts of experience in college teaching or administration. Most of the Departmental staff is made up of experts in public school administration, curriculum design, or the teaching of some subject—music, mathematics, foreign language, physical education, etc.—on the elementary or secondary school level. Rarely is an experienced college teacher of educational psychology, educational history, or philosophy of education included; and it is even more unusual to find a college teacher of English, history, mathematics, or science. Of course the state Departments can and do seek the assistance of outside experts when they visit and appraise the work on a given campus, but even in these cases an expert is rarely familiar with the particular traditions and resources of a specific college, and even he may be less informed and experienced than the professors of the college to be appraised. Moreover, the outside expert can be brought in only for a brief period; most of the work has to be done by the state Department people, and it is they who make the final recommendations.

Consider, then, the situation of a college that has worked for many years to establish a structure for administering teacher education, that has organized its curriculum so as to take maximum advantage of the talents of its faculty, and that has recruited professors in terms of its considered judgment of how teachers should be educated. In order for its graduates to be certified, it submits elaborate material to the state Department and requests approval. Someone in the state Department—perhaps an expert on the teaching of music in the elementary school, or the ex-superintendent of a small city school system—goes over the material. He also assembles a visiting committee made up of people with backgrounds similar to his own and of professors from some other college in the state who are willing to give a day's time to visit on a neighboring campus. After a brief visit, the committee makes its report and recommendations. The recommendations may include instructions to modify what the college considers a carefully developed and well-tested pattern of administrating its program, to change the courses required in general education, to add some courses it does not consider desirable, and to delete others it considers to be of great value; or, if it refuses to accept the judgment of the state Department, to give up its teacher-education program. Ironically enough, the reasons given for withholding approval are never those I would consider most important. A college is never told that a careful evaluation of the actual standards of teaching and grading on the college campus proved them to be of very low quality; that careful testing of the college's graduates showed them to be still too ignorant to teach; or that in observing its candidates actually teach, the state Department found them incompetent. Questions that would allow such statements are never asked, not only for political reasons but also because of the difficulty of measurement.

The colleges that are denied approval or forced to make modifications inevitably feel that their own judgments are superior to those of the approving group. They also feel that the design of instructional programs is their own prerogative, and that the only question the outside public can legitimately raise is the question of whether or not their graduates are effective teachers: the very question the approved-program approach does not in fact answer. On this point I believe the colleges are correct.

THE ATTITUDES of both the ardent friends and the implacable foes of certification show strikingly how much confusion abounds in this field. One side feels the requirements are reasonable, just, and necessary conditions for employment. The other side argues that they are unreasonable and unnecessary. Both sides talk as if the requirements were being regularly enforced.

My findings indicate that certification requirements are not *rigidly* enforced in any state; in all of the 16 most populous states, it is relatively simple for a local school district to circumvent them. The exact nature of the escape clauses, or "end runs," varies, but the result is the same in every state: large numbers of people are teaching in American classrooms who do not meet the state's current minimum requirements for provisional, much less permanent, certification. To anyone who takes state requirements seriously, this is surely a national scandal. A few examples should serve to illustrate this point.

Most states use a legal procedure to allow persons to teach with emergency credentials. In New Jersey, for example, the Commissioner has the authority to designate areas in which there is a shortage of qualified personnel, which in turn permits a superintendent or principal to employ persons who do not meet state requirements. Georgia follows a similar process. In Florida the state Board of Education can waive requirements county by county when in its judgment such action is needed. New York allows uncertified teachers to enter the classroom through a procedure known as "excuse of default." A school superintendent may notify the state Department that no qualified teacher is available and that efforts have been made to find one, and his application to hire an uncertified teacher may then be approved. In the school year 1960–61, 8,000, or almost 10 per cent of the teachers in New York State, exclusive of Buffalo and New York City, were actually teaching without being certifiable under the provisions in effect at the time.

New York State regulations also embody a second end run in the form of a provision under which any teacher may, without state Department permission, be assigned to teach one period a day in a subject for which he is not certified. Similar provisions exist in most other states. One state, not among our 16, specifically wrote into its legislation a provision that, although the new certificates will specify the areas one is prepared to teach, such specification can*not* be used to prevent a school administrator from assigning teaching responsibilities outside the designated field. Provisions that permit the assignment of teachers to fields for which they are not prepared are among the most common, and I think the most objectionable, evasions of the intent of certification. The New York rules, for example, make it possible for a school principal to assign a history teacher one course a day in science, mathematics, or any other subject for which a teacher is needed. It would be possible, under these arrangements, to have all the courses in a particular subject taught by persons untrained in that subject. That is, if a school has no science teacher, it might assign a general science course to an English teacher, a physics course to a history teacher, a chemistry course to the home economics teacher, and a biology course to the coach.

One cannot determine the extent to which these provisions are used, for in many cases the statistics provided by state Departments of Education or the U.S. Office of Education are ambiguous. They tell us only how many teachers are teaching outside their specified fields as the states legally define "outside." North Carolina provides an excellent example of how misleading such statistics may be. According to its state Department figures, there are only 484 teachers in the state who are currently teaching out of field; this is about 1.15 per cent of the total number of teachers in the state. The figure seems impressive; in fact, too impressive. Investigation reveals that, as one might suspect, the statistics are deceptive, for they apply only to those persons who are doing more than half their teaching outside their certified fields of instruction. In other words, a teacher who spends as much as 50 per cent of his time teaching in his own field is uncounted in the statistics, even though the rest of the time he may teach a subject for which he is not prepared.

As for the effects of these end runs that are so prevalent, a 1961 survey[1] on science and mathematics teachers provides shocking evidence. A few of the results follow:

Table I shows that on the basis of the sample drawn it would appear that, the country over, nearly half the classes in biology are taught by teachers who have devoted less than a quarter of four years (30 semester hours) to a study of that subject. The situation is somewhat worse in regard to mathematics in grades 9–12 and very much worse in chemistry, mathematics in grades 7–8, and general science and physics. In physics 23 per cent and in 7–8 grade

---

[1] From *Secondary School Science and Mathematics Teachers: Characteristics and Service Loads*, by the National Association of State Directors of Teacher Education and Certification and the American Association for the Advancement of Science for the National Science Foundation. U.S. Government Printing Office, Washington, D.C., 1961. (NSF 63-10).

TABLE I

Estimated percentage of classes taught by teachers whose hours of credit in subject total

	Less than 9	9–17	18–29	30 or more
Biology	8	13	22	57
Mathematics 9–12	11	12	32	45
Chemistry	14	20	32	34
Mathematics 7–8	34	19	26	21
General Science (Biology credits)	31	21	20	28
Physics	23	43	20	14

mathematics 34 per cent of the classes are taught by teachers who have studied the subject in college for less than 9 semester hours or about 7 per cent of the time in four years. Usually, such an exposure would be provided by a full year's course in the freshman year and a half year's course in the sophomore year.

Three points are worth emphasizing as one contemplates with horror Table I. The first is that an examination of the entire 1961 survey report (which I strongly recommend) shows that there are some regional differences. The second is that the sampling includes many (32 per cent) who are teaching in schools with a total enrollment of less than 500, and it is difficult for a small high school to provide a full schedule for a teacher properly prepared to teach in only one field (or even two such closely related fields as physics and chemistry). Third, a vast majority of the teachers in the sample received their degrees before 1957 and, therefore, probably now hold permanent appointments. The significance of this last point is that any changes in certification requirements in the direction of more study of a subject matter can only affect the teaching staff slowly over a long period of years (even if the requirements are enforced). When one studies the facts set forth in the document to which I have referred, one conclusion seems inescapable. A greater knowledge of the subject matter is a need of many teachers today, and the need will continue for many years. In the conclusion to the study, the authors divide those teachers who have had inadequate preparation into two groups: those who have had a bare introduction to the subject (less than 9 hours) and those who have had at least 9 hours but not enough. "It seems probable," the authors say, "that the teachers in the first group would welcome reassignment to the subjects that they are prepared to teach and that the amelioration of their condition and that of their students must depend upon improved planning within the school systems where they are employed."

As to the second group, the authors feel, "If a teacher has had (to use another arbitrary measure) 9–17 semester hours of college work in a subject, has some experience of teaching it to high school classes, and has some educational background in other science subjects as well, it would appear that he has potentialities that should be further developed." And the writers conclude that since the persons in question may have insufficient formal education to qualify for graduate work, "new kinds of programs need to be made readily available."

An interesting sidelight of this report is that 20 per cent of the teachers in this sample have completed at least one National Science Foundation (NSF) Summer Institute program. Other effective programs for in-service and summer-school education exist without National Science Foundation support, and I should hope that more will be developed. It does seem clear, however, that the NSF Institutes are currently filling a crucial gap and that their continuation is most important.

IN MY VIEW, any discussion of state certification policy in terms of actual course and credit specifications or of the approved-program approach must ultimately come to rest on this single, all-important question: *Do these policies effectively serve the purposes of those concerned with quality teaching?* My conclusion is that they do not.

In none of the states do the rules have a clearly demonstrable practical bearing on the quality of the teacher, the quality of his preparation, or the extent to which the public is informed about the personnel in the classrooms. In every state literal adherence to the rules is impractical and evasion is common. (See Appendix G.)

The policy of certification based on the completion of state-specified course requirements is bankrupt; of this I am convinced. Unfortunately, the newer approved-program approach, which is intended to afford increased flexibility and freedom, involves the state Department to such a degree that the dominant public school forces can use it to impose their own orthodoxy as easily as they used the older system. The specific course requirements and the approved-program approach as it is now developing have critical defects in common; they cannot be enforced in such a manner that the public can be assured of competent teachers, and they involve the states in acrimonious and continuous political struggles, which may not serve the public interest.

Moreover, in either case the layman cannot know, without special inquiry, that pupils are being taught by a teacher specifically prepared and certified to teach on that grade level or in that subject. Should he discover that a teacher is working on less than a standard certificate, he has no way of knowing whether the requirements not yet met are in fact crucial ones. If the teacher has secured the permanent certificate, he may well have done so by picking up an odd lot of late-afternoon and Saturday courses not well related to his previous education and experience or his current teaching assignment. Even if the teacher has met full state certification requirements, the public knows only that someone has looked at a formal description of courses, and may have examined the formal credentials of the instructor. There is no conclusive evidence that any specific course improves teaching ability. If the student has been trained in a first-rate institution, it *may* be that competent people observed him teach in a well-conceived practice-teaching situation, but then again it may not be. Some of our generally best institutions do a very poor job of supervising practice teaching.

In most cases all that the public can know is that the teacher somehow rang up the required number of credits in courses whose catalog descriptions appear to some state education officer to meet state specifications for courses in professional education, general education, and a field of specialization.

Since none of the present methods of teacher certification assure the public of competent and adequately prepared teachers, the reader may well ask: What should be the basis for the state's certification of teachers? The answer to this question is the subject of the next chapter.

4

THE REDIRECTION
OF PUBLIC AUTHORITY

THE EMPLOYMENT OF TEACHERS in our public schools is a legal responsibility of a local school board, which should act on the advice of a professional school administrator in whom the board has confidence. The responsibility to make wise appointments is inescapable and may not safely be neglected. The assumption that prescribed programs of teacher education, or certification procedures, can insure public protection from individual incompetence is largely illusory. The final door to the classroom is guarded, it is hoped responsibly, by the local board.

It is, however, a matter of historic record that certain boards— because of corruption, incompetence, lack of sufficient information, or an inadequate supply of candidates—have at times been unable to discharge their responsibilities well. These conditions led state governments, which are constitutionally responsible for public education, to develop screening processes by which they could create a pool of certified candidates. From such a pool local officials could select teachers with some assurance against gross incompetence. But regardless of state certification efforts, the public must ultimately rely on the local school board. To warrant this reliance it would seem important that *local school districts be so organized that the school board constituency is too broad to be easily dominated by a single interest group, and that teaching conditions be attractive enough to give the local authorities an opportunity to recruit effectively.*

56

The importance of such organization may be demonstrated by a few examples. In one community that has been brought to my attention, two families dominated—in fact, virtually constituted—the school board for a century. In such a community, the school personnel will inevitably be selected and directed according to the personal prejudices of the board. There would be little objection to this arrangement if one could be certain that the dominant interest would be responsible and intelligent. But the possibility of abuse is too obvious to require elaboration.

In a school district that is organized to provide schooling for only a very small number of students, the school must use the same teacher to cover many grade levels in the elementary school and several subjects at the high school level. The teachers are isolated from stimulating professional colleagues, the district is unable to provide the needed professional libraries and instructional materials, and able, well-prepared teachers cannot be recruited and held. Fortunately, in some of the states the proportion of adequate-sized school districts, or of smaller districts working together for teachers' employment, is reasonably high. (See Appendix H.) Moreover, the reorganization of school districts is already proceeding at a rapid pace.

Given a school system that is attractive to teachers and a board that is answerable to many interest groups, the ultimate responsibility for the appointment of teachers should be clearly laid on the shoulders of the local school board. The existing pattern of excessive dependence on state regulations as well as the not infrequent use of end runs that permit boards to evade this responsibility, whether by reason of indifference or of favoritism, should cease. At the same time the state should not, through certification, make requirements so specific that the local school authorities are denied the opportunity to try teachers with varied patterns of preparation.

What, then, should be the role of the state education authorities? The state as a whole has a legitimate interest in insuring reasonable equality of educational opportunity and in protecting its educational system from local corruption and inadequacy. It is, after all, constitutionally charged with the maintenance and supervision of the public schools. In discharging this responsibility, states have utilized teacher examinations, specific course requirements, and approval of institutional programs.

Certification by examination, whether on subject matter or on professional knowledge, has been attacked on several grounds. It is alleged that if a state were to set up such examinations, the wrong kind of information would be tested; that the ability to write test answers would not insure the ability to function effectively in the classroom; that the testing instruments would lend themselves to preparation by cramming or to corrupt administration; and that the tests would have an unwholesome effect of imposing a strait jacket on the teaching function. It is claimed that tests may discriminate against certain persons who do not perform well when taking a test, or that the tests themselves are culturally biased. Finally, since in many fields there is no way to measure the degree of mastery except in terms of relative scores within a standardized population, the issue of what score should be used as a "passing" grade raises difficult problems. For example, if one designates the average score as "passing," then half the people fail despite the possibility that all may in fact know much or little about the matter being tested.

Because of these objections, I do not favor the use by the states of standardized tests as the basis of certification. I agree with the contention that it is too difficult on a statewide basis to determine the proper cut-off score. And furthermore, I believe that the ultimate test should be *how the teacher actually performs in a classroom,* as judged by experienced teachers. I am convinced that a single test cannot be relied upon for a state judgment that has the force of law.

As I have indicated, I am also opposed to certification based on specific required courses. In my judgment, no state has been able to insure a high quality of teacher preparation by simply listing course titles and credit-hour requirements. But there is in this system an even more fundamental fault, which remains to be examined. For better or worse, the college professor actually determines what goes on in his own classroom. He may bow to state authorities concerning the title and syllabus of his course. But ultimately, he will teach what he knows and considers to be important. In brief, both the content and the quality of instruction are in fact determined on the individual campus no matter what the state may do. State regulations consistent with the beliefs of the college are unnecessary. Those inconsistent with the college's beliefs receive at best only lip service; at worst, they hamstring the able professors and faculties who, with greater understanding of their own strengths and the characteristics of their own student body, can design a superior program if given greater freedom.

The approved-program approach goes awry, as we have seen, because too often those who do the approving end by dictating the total teacher-preparation program and the total institutional structure. In these cases it often becomes even more inflexible than the process of certification by courses and credits. For example, even in what I consider to be one of the more enlightened states, I was told by one faculty member that the approval of his program depended on his bowing to a state Department official on the issue of whether to give two or three credits for a particular course in physical education. In another state, an institution's authority to prepare teachers of one language was being challenged because it did not offer enough courses in a second and unrelated language. Yet another institution had asked NCATE rather than a state Department for approval, and I was told that NCATE demanded as a condition of full accreditation that the institution abandon its present policies of offering two different programs of general education and of subject matter specialization in the sciences and social sciences.

Thus, no one of the three devices—the use of objective examinations, the requirement of specific courses, the approved-program approach—seems to offer a satisfactory basis for state certification. What, then, should the states require of candidates for teaching jobs? It seems to me that we need to find one or two critical points by which to test the quality of teacher preparation, and then focus attention on these points *so far as certification is concerned.* In other words, we need a *restricted* approved-program basis for certification.

Interestingly enough, amid all the conflict over teacher education, I have found only two points on which all are agreed: first, before being entrusted with complete control of a public school classroom, a teacher should have had opportunities under close guidance and supervision actually to teach—whether such opportunities are labeled "practice teaching," "student teaching," "apprenticeship," "internship," or something else; and second, the ultimate question the state should ask is "Can this person teach adequately?" There is also near consensus, with which I am in agreement, that public school teachers cannot be adequately educated in less than the time required to obtain a baccalaureate degree. On the basis of these agreements, I come to my first recommendation concerning state certification:

1. *For certification purposes the state should require only (a) that a candidate hold a baccalaureate degree from a legitimate[1] college or university, (b) that he submit evidence of having successfully performed as a student teacher under the direction of college and public school personnel in whom the state Department has confidence, and in a practice-teaching situation of which the state Department approves, and (c) that he hold a specially endorsed teaching certificate from a college or university which, in issuing the official document, attests that the institution as a whole considers the person adequately prepared to teach in a designated field and grade level.*

This is, I recognize, a radical suggestion. While it does more sharply hold the colleges and universities responsible for attesting that the person is prepared *to teach* as well as being a "well-educated person," it removes all state requirements for specific courses except practice teaching and closely related special methods courses, and asks the state to rely on the good judgment and integrity of these institutions in determining what instruction is required prior to, or in addition to, practice teaching.

The adoption of such a policy by a state would, I believe, invigorate the institutions. To be sure, a competition between teacher-training colleges and universities would result; but as a consequence faculties would develop more pride in the quality of their graduates; there would be gradual recognition by superintendents and school boards that alumni of certain institutions tended to be better prepared than those of rival institutions. Such a change in the climate of opinion would affect the attitude of the professors. We

[1] I do not propose in this book to discuss the ways different states police the institutions the state charters; some crack down on diploma mills, some do not!

tend to forget that faculties are made up of individuals whose personal reputations are affected by the quality of the instruction just as their own efforts determine that quality. When the state or an accrediting agency unduly restricts the program of teacher preparation (or any other program), the degree of freedom of each faculty member is thereby diminished, and individual professors do not or cannot put their creative energies into the building of a curriculum; teacher-education programs become increasingly sterile. Recommendation 1 would free the colleges without opening the doors to the appointment of incompetent teachers by the local boards.

Let me now face an objection that I am sure will spring up in many readers' minds. Those who have observed the slipshod conditions under which practice teaching is often done will be appalled at the suggestion that the state content itself with this device for certification. And unless the state authorities, the colleges, and the local school districts give very serious attention to these conditions, I, too, would find the prospects truly appalling. However, my subsequent comments will, I trust, make clear that I do not propose to perpetuate the present sometimes-chaotic system. Though the details of a practice-teaching program will have to be worked out by each state Department and each college and public school system with which it works, I would like to suggest some things that I believe must be assured if practice teaching is to serve adequately, either as a step in teacher preparation or as a basis for certification.

There must be enough time allotted to enable the student teacher to have the following experience: to participate in the overall planning of the semester's work; to observe critically for a week or so, with the guidance of someone who can tell him what to look for; to begin with simple instructional tasks involving individuals and small groups of children (note that I say "instructional tasks" —not filling out forms or pulling on rubbers); and, ultimately, to assume full responsibility for an extended period of instruction which he plans, executes, and evaluates. (See Chapters 8 and 9 for estimates of the time to be devoted to practice teaching.)

The regular teacher in whose classroom the future teacher works should be one known to his own school officials, the collegiate faculty, and the state Department as a highly competent teacher both of classroom pupils and of student teachers. Such persons, often called "cooperating teachers," should have time freed to aid the student teachers; they should also have increased compensation in recognition of added responsibility and special talent.

The college personnel directly involved should be of the type I shall call "clinical professors" (not to be confused with the cooperating teachers). The clinical professors must be master teachers who themselves periodically teach at the level of those being supervised, and who are given by the college full recognition in salary and rank of their essential function. They must not be treated as second-class citizens of the university. *The clinical professor will be the person responsible for teaching the "methods" course. Such courses, designed to guide student teachers to the best instructional material in the field as well as to assist them in the planning and conduct of instruction, should be part of the practice teaching experience.* The clinical professor must be a master of teaching methods and materials; he must also be up to date on advances in the educational sciences and know how to apply this knowledge to the concrete work in which his student teacher is involved.

The cooperating teacher, the clinical professor, and any others brought in to evaluate the practice teaching must be qualified to judge the candidate's mastery of the subject he teaches, his utilization of educational knowledge, his mastery of techniques of teaching, and his possession of the intellectual and personality traits relevant to effective teaching. It goes without saying that they must have opportunity to observe often enough and over a long-enough period so that the candidate has a chance for guided improvement, and, ultimately, a fair test. Ideally, I would hope that other professors in such fields as mathematics, science, social science, humanities, and education would observe student teachers and use their observations as a basis for revising the college curriculum as well as for judging the candidate's competence.

When I recommend, then, that practice teaching become the basis of certification, I assume that state certifying authorities will not approve practice-teaching programs that are inadequate either for certification purposes or for teacher-education purposes.

Recommendations 2 to 5 below attempt to spell out more fully—from the perspective of the colleges, the public school districts, and the state—the implications of this basic shift in certification policies.

2. *Each college or university should be permitted to develop in detail whatever program of teacher education it considers most desirable, subject only to two conditions: first, the president of the institution in behalf of the entire faculty involved—academic as well as professional—certifies that the candidate is adequately prepared to teach on a specific level or in specific fields, and second, the institution establishes in conjunction with a public school system a state-approved practice-teaching arrangement.*

This proposal calls for a contract between each college and one or more public school systems in the practice-teaching arrangements. Such a contract already exists in most cases. However, I believe that local school districts have not yet assumed the responsibility they ought to assume either for the initial training of teachers or for the introduction of teachers into service during a probationary period. To effect a full partnership among the state Departments, the universities or colleges, and the public schools, two further recommendations would have to be accepted.

3. *Public school systems that enter contracts with a college or university for practice teaching should designate, as classroom teachers working with practice teaching, only those persons in whose competence as teachers, leaders, and evaluators they have the highest confidence, and should give such persons encouragement by reducing their work loads and raising their salaries.*

To implement this recommendation, it would be necessary for the school board to formalize its relation with the institutions that send student teachers into its school. If no contract now exists, one should be prepared and signed. More important, the school board should adopt a policy that would show recognition of the continuing value of its responsibility. The board should direct the superintendent to have his principals see that the best teachers become cooperating teachers. The board should also require the superintendent to report from time to time on the way the arrangements for practice teaching are functioning.

The acceptance of Recommendation 3 and its full implementation would mean an increase in the budget. What I have in mind is a considerable raise in salary for the cooperating teacher. The board would be committed by its policy to recruiting some of its best teachers to participate in the education of future teachers. Since there is no assurance that those being thus educated will be employed by the board, it hardly seems fair to charge the extra expense to the local budget. In such an arrangement, the local board functions as an agency of the state, and plays an important part in discharging a state responsibility: the education of future teachers. If the citizens of the state want those enrolled in the teacher-preparation programs within the state (in private or public institutions) to be well educated, the role of the local board cannot be overlooked. If the job is to be well done, the state must provide the money out of state funds on a per-student basis, the money to be used for increasing the salary of the cooperating teachers. (One state at least has already made a modest step in this direction.) These considerations may be summed up in the following recommendation:

4. *The state should provide financial assistance to local boards to insure high-quality practice teaching as part of the preparation of teachers enrolled in either private or public institutions.*

So far I have left the colleges and universities free to define and control the paths to practice teaching. I assume—and in an increasing number of institutions the assumption is already fact—that professors of education and academic professors will share in designing programs leading to the teacher's diploma.

At the practice-teaching stage, I have urged that public school people become involved. And both public schools and colleges would be represented through the clinical professors. But since the state has an inescapable responsibility ultimately to certify, it, too, must act directly. I recommend that:

5. *The state should approve programs of practice teaching. It should, working cooperatively with the college and public school authorities, regulate the conditions under which practice teaching is done and the nature of the methods instruction that accompanies it. The state should require that the colleges and public school systems involved submit evidence concerning the*

competence of those appointed as cooperating teachers and clinical professors.

In referring to "evidence" in Recommendation 5, I do not have in mind the offering of special courses and credits accumulated, a practice to be found in certain states, of which I heartily disapprove.

In making these recommendations, I have hoped to encourage flexibility in teacher-education programs, and to minimize conflict by restricting the focus of state control. I have left under state scrutiny that part of the program by which the entire program can be evaluated. If a potential teacher is seriously lacking in knowledge of his field, in information concerning the conduct of schooling, or in teaching skill, such inadequacies should show up when he actually teaches under the scrutiny of two experienced teachers, namely the clinical professor and the cooperating teacher. These teachers, both acting with the sanction of the state, must be prepared to reject those who are inadequate. This obligation is of special importance with respect to the candidate's mastery of the subject he teaches.

Though I trust that the colleges will already have screened out most of those candidates whose personality traits provide obvious handicaps to teaching, those missed should also show up at this time. I repeat, however, that those who evaluate practice teaching must include persons capable of judging *every* critical aspect of the candidate's preparation. I believe that if the state provides for a careful examination of the student teacher in the actual act of teaching, it will have the most effective device by which to insure itself of competent teachers.

Since the purpose of these proposals is to provide greater flexibility, their intent would be defeated if, through the influence of such groups as TEPS, all institutions preparing teachers for a given state prescribed the same path to practice teaching. The state should not remove the tariff barrier and then permit it to be reestablished as a private cartel. Should such a cartel develop, the state may have to set up special practice-teaching centers to insure reasonable flexibility.

By these proposals responsibility is sharply focused at three gates: first, the individual colleges, whose programs may vary widely, control entrance to practice teaching; second, the state, using state Department, collegiate (or university), and public school personnel, certifies on the basis of effectiveness in actual teaching during the practice-teaching operation, and third, the local board, choosing from persons who, without exception, are certified by the state but who may have been prepared under widely varying programs, is responsible for the final choice.

These, I believe, should be the limits of *legal restraints* within which experimentation, research, and persuasion should be free to operate. No *single* program of teacher education should be granted a legal monopoly, nor should it be necessary for those wishing to experiment or reform to secure legislative action or seek escape clauses in state regulations.

On the other hand, all programs of teacher education and all local school board employment policies should be subjected to more informed public scrutiny than has often in the past been possible. The state educational authorities have unique opportunity and responsibility for this scrutiny. I recommend, then, that:

6. *State Departments of Education should develop and make available to local school boards and colleges and universities data relevant to the preparation and employment of teachers. Such data may include information about the types of teacher-education programs of colleges or universities throughout the state and information concerning supply and demand of teachers at various grade levels and in various fields.*

This recommendation reflects my conviction that the public stake in education demands the active, continuous, and informed interest of laymen on the local level. Whatever system of certification is used, there are, and will continue to be, variations in teacher-education programs. And the school board can, through carelessness or ignorance, hire easily accessible but possibly incompetent teachers. Even given the best intent, local boards and superintendents find it difficult at times to judge among candidates from a variety of colleges. The public at large might wisely explore with its local school authorities the kinds of information they use in selecting new teachers, and—in the absence of information provided by the state—might well urge the local district to make its own evaluation of the teacher-education programs in the colleges from which it recruits teachers. Most state Departments, however, are in a much better position to do the research and provide the information needed both by the local school boards and by their constituencies. In the long run, I am convinced that the improvement of teacher education will depend on an informed and articulate lay opinion.

Information placed by the state into the hands of local school boards can be useful, but it is not enough. No matter how well prepared a teacher is in one subject or for one grade level, he is likely to be incompetent when misassigned. Our survey of state laws and such evidence as that provided by the National Science Foundation study make it clear that local school boards are not only legally free to assign teachers in areas for which they are unprepared but actually do so in far too many cases. On this matter both tighter regulations and more rigorous enforcement are needed. I therefore recommend that:

7. *The state education authorities should give top priority to the development of regulations insuring that a teacher will be assigned only to those teaching duties for which he is specifically prepared, and should enforce these regulations rigorously.*

If my Recommendations 1 and 2 have been adopted, the state will have in its hands documents in which the college or university president attests that the teacher has, in the college's judgment, been prepared to teach specific subjects or at a specific grade level. It should then be possible for the state Department to check actual teaching assignments to make certain that they correspond to the attested preparation.

We have already noted how widespread are present provisions that facilitate the misuse of teachers, and I have called these the most objectionable of end runs. Moreover, even the present inadequate controls are rarely enforced, though theoretically the state has the power to enforce them. If this recommendation is to be adopted, it will require the active support of all groups interested in education.

As we have seen, in every state capital there are organized groups representing teachers, school administrators, school board members, and others interested in education. These groups are, appropriately, active in endeavoring to influence state educational policy on such matters as school finance, school district organization, teacher certification, and teacher welfare. In many states they supply valuable information and advice to state education officials, and in certain states they have been given quasi-legal status as members of an advisory board on teacher education and professional standards. Their power might well be used on the matter of teaching assignment. The best interest of the public as well as the teachers is involved.

If, as I have recommended, the states certify solely on the basis of the bachelor's degree and successful practice teaching, these interest groups can abandon their preoccupation with detailed certification regulations and can concentrate on other matters. They will, however, have a continued interest in informing and persuading the teacher-educating institutions and local school boards of their opinions concerning how teachers should be educated and what sort of teachers should be employed. Though my recommendations would deny them the power of using the state to give their recommendations on teacher education the force of law, what I propose would also deny their critics the use of the state in opposition to their beliefs.

It must by now be clear that my recommendations so far are designed first, to insure that no teacher enters a classroom without having been tested and found competent in the actual act of teaching; second, to provide both teacher-educating institutions and local school boards with as free a market as is consistent with assurance that inept teachers are kept out of our schools; and third, to increase the range of information and opinion available to those who educate or hire teachers. The "free market" provides state Department personnel, teachers' organizations, and other interested groups with a greater, rather than a lesser, stake in educational leadership, but it calls them to bring this leadership to bear in the local communities and in the colleges and universities rather than in the state capitals. Those who are bested in the struggle in one community or campus can hope to prevail in another.

We have noted that an increasing number of states has given a quasi-legal status to NCATE, and that since 1957 the NEA and its affiliates, working largely through TEPS, have conducted a widespread campaign on both the state and national levels to persuade states automatically to certify graduates of an NCATE-approved institution outside their own states. At present about half the states have given *some* weight to NCATE-accreditation in their approved-program approach to certification; in at least one state persons graduating from out-of-state NCATE-approved institutions receive automatic certification. Thus has NCATE become a quasi-legal body with tremendous national power.

We have also seen that the regional accrediting bodies, such as the North Central Association of Colleges and Secondary Schools, by selective accreditation of schools, use their power to insist that teachers be educated as these organizations believe they should be. They, too, tend to require a specific number of courses in specific fields.

Both NCATE and secondary school branches of regional accreditation agencies are controlled by people whose wide professional experience well qualifies them to *advise* colleges on how to prepare teachers and to *advise* local school boards on what kinds of teacher to hire. However, both are widely, and I believe somewhat justly, accused of representing only a narrow sector of those actively engaged in American public and higher education; in neither are the well-informed conscientious lay citizens—who, I believe, have an important role in determining educational policy—adequately represented. I, therefore, recommend that:

8. *The governing boards of NCATE and the regional associations should be significantly broadened to give greater power to (a) representatives of scholarly disciplines in addition to professional education, and to (b) informed representatives of the lay public.*

The governing council of NCATE, for example, should include distinguished citizens, scholars, and laymen.

But even given such enlarged representation, no strictly private group should have delegated to it, either directly or indirectly, the power to determine which institutions may or may not legally prepare candidates for state certification through the process I have described above. For this reason, I recommend that:

9. *NCATE and the regional associations should serve only as advisory bodies to teacher-preparing institutions and local school boards. They should, on the request of institutions, send in teams to study and make recommendations concerning the whole or any portion of a teacher-education program. They should on the request of local boards, evaluate employment policies. They should provide a forum in which issues concerning teacher education and employment are debated.*

NCATE has been most widely used as a basis of reciprocity to facilitate the migration of teachers from state to state; this function has been one of the major reasons for its development. I strongly doubt that such an institution as NCATE is really needed to achieve this purpose. Should my recommendations be followed, the certification requirements will be limited, but will also be more sharply defined. It should not be too difficult for state certification authorities to achieve comparable standards by negotiation. I do, however, recommend that:

10. *Whenever a teacher has been certified by one state under the provisions of Recommendations 1 and 2, his certificate should be accepted as valid in any other state.*

The above recommendations refer to the initial certification process. This process should insure a safe level of preparation for the initial assumption of full responsibility for a public school classroom. I believe this level of preparation can be achieved in a four-year program. However, no such program—in my judgment, no kind of preservice program—can prepare first-year teachers to operate effectively in the "sink-or-swim" situation in which they too often find themselves. Many local school boards have, I believe, been scandalously remiss in failing to give adequate assistance to new teachers. I recommend, therefore that:

11. *During the initial probationary period, local school boards should take specific steps to provide the new teacher with every possible help in the form of: (a) limited teaching responsibility;*

(*b*) *aid in gathering instructional materials;* (*c*) *advice of experienced teachers whose own load is reduced so that they can work with the new teacher in his own classroom;* (*d*) *shifting to more experienced teachers those pupils who create problems beyond the ability of the novice to handle effectively; and* (*e*) *specialized instruction concerning the characteristics of the community, the neighborhood, and the students he is likely to encounter.*

The last point merits further comment. The reader of my previous book, *Slums and Suburbs,* will recall that teachers in certain communities confront a concentration of particular kinds of student. In some schools an unusually large number of students have severe problems of adjustment to a harsh social environment and face acute vocational difficulties. In others high parental aspirations that children achieve success in college and find employment in the higher social-economic positions imposes a marked strain on pupils whose own abilities and hopes are inconsistent with parental aspirations. Though some students with these special problems are encountered in every school, special instruction in the characteristics of the community and the student population is needed. Such instruction should, I believe, be provided by the employing agency and should be directly related to the teaching assignment of the new teacher. I do not think it feasible for the colleges—which train teachers for service anywhere in the state, and are often geographically isolated from the neighborhood to be served—to provide this special instruction as part of its general teacher-education program.

One way and possibly the most promising way of implementing Recommendation 11 would be to have the new teacher become part of a teaching team. The idea of team teaching has been widely discussed in recent years, but the phrase lacks clear-cut definition. As applied to the induction of a new teacher, I would define a teaching team as an arrangement by which one or more older and experienced teachers shared a teaching responsibility with the new teacher. There might be two junior members of the team. The most junior would be the brand-new teacher; the other would be a teacher in his second or third year of a probationary period. One can only suggest such arrangements, for the details would obviously differ from grade to grade and from subject to subject. The objectives to be achieved are summed up in the recommendation.

I have made one recommendation (11) that is essentially in the hands of local school boards, and two additional ones (3, 4) will affect them. Two of my recommendations (8, 9) affect NCATE and other accrediting bodies. I have no doubt that the TEPS groups and other professional organizations will be concerned with all the recommendations.

It is surely not my prerogative to tell the reader how to bring these changes to pass if he is persuaded that my recommendations should be followed. It should be clear that both the structure and the process of decision making vary too widely from state to state to admit of a uniform strategy of reform. However, I have expressed my conviction that each structure, though possessing unique qualities, is flexible enough so that responsible men willing to study and work within their own state's system can make their influence felt.

In the later chapters of this book I will set forth my own views concerning the way colleges and universities should prepare teachers and, by implication, the sort of preparation I think local school boards should prefer in selecting their teachers. Obviously, however, if accrediting agencies and state educational authorities tighten, by detailed prescription, the certification rules, then neither my suggestions, nor those of anyone else (except him who writes the rules) can possibly be tried.

5

THE ACADEMIC PREPARATION
OF TEACHERS

WHEN AMONG LAYMEN the subject of public school teachers is mentioned, one is likely to hear a comment something like this: "The trouble is that our teachers come out of the teachers colleges, where they spend all their time telling the students *how* to teach. We ought to be getting our teachers from the liberal arts colleges, where they get a broad general education and have good solid work in a major, so that they come out knowing something!" I have heard this view expressed by a great many intelligent people in many walks of life, including college and university professors.

In my considerations of the academic preparation of teachers, I shall examine this comment in several connections, for whether the dichotomy it implies is valid or not, it is so widely held as to constitute a basic part of the debate on teacher education.

Another and even more fundamental issue is the one contention that seems to be universally endorsed: that the breadth and depth of academic achievement of future school teachers could and should be greater than they are at present. In an effort to cast some light on this issue, let us see what is involved in the academic education of future teachers. In any educational process, there are three elements: those who instruct, those who are instructed, and the program followed. In each of these, wide diversity is found throughout our system of higher education.

Instruction provided in different types of institutions

For our purposes, it is neither desirable nor possible to assess the quality and performance of individual college and university instructors. They are as varied as the autumn leaves, and such wide differences in personnel are found within institutions, and even in very small departments, that one simply cannot make generalizations about them. It is, however, very much to the point to direct our attention to the institutions in which our teachers are educated. In so doing, we encounter at once several false assumptions held among the critics of the present situation.

The first, that teachers colleges supply most of our classroom teachers, is simply not the case. Only 20 per cent of our teachers come from colleges that can clearly be designated "teachers" colleges.[1] Indeed, the greatest number of teachers come from universities that fit neither the "teachers college" nor the "liberal arts" college stereotype. Three-quarters of the four-year colleges and universities in the nation, including nearly every type of institution, are in the business of preparing teachers. The universities involved can be divided into those that offer teacher training only on the graduate level, of which there are very few, and those that maintain both graduate and undergraduate teacher-training courses. Of the four-year colleges, there are four subcategories: private "liberal arts" colleges that have no vocational programs other than teacher training; private colleges that now offer several vocational programs, including teacher training; state colleges offering a variety of vocational programs; and state colleges in which 80 per cent or more of the students plan to teach.

Of all these types of institutions, only the last can be considered primarily "teachers colleges." Moreover, the increasing demand of recent years for public higher education has given rise to the expansion of many former teachers colleges into multipurpose insti-

[1] As a case in point, the reader may recall the shocking revelations contained in the 1961 NSF survey on mathematics and science teachers that were quoted on page 52–53. Of the 3,000 teachers covered in that survey, 29 per cent received their bachelor's degrees from "teachers colleges" (presumably this includes state colleges primarily or exclusively concerned with teacher training), 39 per cent from "liberal arts" colleges, 20 per cent from university schools of education, 12 per cent from "other" institutions. (The distribution varied somewhat from region to region.)

tutions. The number of essentially teacher-training institutions now is less than 100, and is steadily dwindling. By contrast, over 900 multipurpose institutions also prepare teachers.

There is a variety of arrangements for training teachers in multi-purpose institutions. The professors of education may be organized as a department of a college faculty of arts and letters, or they may be members of a separate college of education with a considerable degree of autonomy. Extreme differences in organization give rise to noticeable distinctions in programs.

A traditional "liberal arts" college, in which only a small number of students are interested in becoming public school teachers, is obviously quite different from a school of education in a university with many students at both the undergraduate and graduate levels. And both are different from a state college almost exclusively concerned with the undergraduate education of elementary teachers or one primarily interested in secondary school teachers. But I would urge the layman to beware of labels! One large private university has an undergraduate school of education that is as much a self-contained single-purpose teacher-training institution as any state college I have visited.

Two institutions with the same label may provide very different programs of teacher education; highly similar programs may be provided by two institutions carrying different labels; and sometimes the same institution may give different credentials to two students who have completed essentially the same program. For example, I have visited two universities (one private and one public) in which the school of education is separately organized from the school or faculty in which all the courses in the academic fields are offered. Now, those who seek to graduate from either of these universities with a preparation that will enable them to teach an academic subject in a public school must complete a program that includes a study in some depth of one field, such as mathematics, and that also includes certain courses given in the school of education. But the student may be enrolled in either the college or the school of education, jumping the fence, so to speak, in order to take the courses in the other school or college. The requirements for general education are the same in the two faculties in these particular universities. The chief difference in the point of enrollment is that if the student wishes a degree from the academic faculty, some exposure to instruction in a foreign language is required; as a reward for this exposure, the degree of A.B. (or B.A.) is awarded. The student in the school of education, whose program may be identical except for the foreign language course, receives a B.S. degree, which some feel has less prestige than an A.B. Prestige aside, it is impossible to assert that the B.S. holder is less adequately equipped to teach mathematics than the B.A. holder.

However, the organizational structure of the institution and the percentage of the student body preparing for teaching careers are actually the least relevant points of contrast among types of institutions. More to the point, perhaps, is the composition of the faculty. But here again, no generalization can be made with any confidence.

Apart from comparable salary figures, names in *Who's Who,* and similar limited grounds for comparison, there is too little to go on. To be sure, the faculty of a great university would in general be superior to that of a small, struggling college; and it might be argued that an historian or a chemist would be more willing to take a position in a college with a liberal arts tradition than in a state college primarily concerned with training teachers. Statistically speaking, these considerations may be valid in broad comparisons. If one compared the academic professors in 100 institutions of one type or another, the professors in the universities and private prestige colleges might be better scholars more thoroughly acquainted with their fields than those in the teachers colleges. But by the same token, the better teachers colleges might in turn have more distinguished scholars than the poorer universities and private colleges. Moreover, excellence in scholarship is not necessarily identical with excellence in teaching. And it is also obviously true that many a strong faculty has some weak members, and many modestly staffed colleges can boast some gifted and dedicated professors. Thus, anyone who asserted that a student would be "better taught" in a particular *type* of institution would be very bold indeed!

Another variable that complicates comparisons between types of institutions, is the wide divergence in academic standards among institutions of every type. This factor is evident whenever scores on standardized examinations are made public. As an example, I quote from the reports of the Graduate Record Examinations— and specifically, from data on the natural science part—taken in a variety of colleges and universities by seniors who are candidates for graduate schools. In the institution with the highest mean score, something like 98 per cent made a score better than that made by only 25 per cent in the lowest-ranking institution. If this score had been taken as a passing score, only 2 per cent of the seniors in one institution would have failed, whereas 75 per cent would have failed in the other college—and, needless to say, in the second institution no such mortality rate was recorded.

Another example is afforded by the results on the National Teacher Examinations. Information I have seen pertaining to this examination shows that in one state, only 1 per cent of the seniors in the state university made a score of less than 500. In a private institution in the same state, 40 per cent made a score of less than 500, and in two other institutions 75 per cent made less than 500. Yet certainly all or almost all the seniors in all the institutions were graduated. If 500 had been the passing score, in the state university 1 per cent would have failed, in the private college 40 per cent would have failed, and in the two other institutions 75 per cent.

Nothing revealed by a close study of institutions designated as "teachers colleges," as compared to those designated as "liberal arts" colleges, justifies a sweeping assertion that one *type* of institution consistently gives the student a better education than the other. The belief that "liberal arts" colleges provide more "breadth and depth" than teachers colleges rests essentially on the notion that courses in education in teachers colleges displace general requirements, subject specialization, or both. My investigations have convinced me that this is simply not the case. The time devoted to education courses in teachers colleges, and in teacher-preparation programs in multipurpose institutions, is not taken away from academic requirements; rather, the courses that are displaced are electives, and such elective courses also give way in a "liberal arts" college that prepares students for certification. Thus one would be quite mistaken to believe that a student necessarily gets a better academic education in one or another type of institution.

There are certain basic procedures and policies in all types of institution that could be improved; and it is in this area that colleges and universities should be attempting to raise their standards. For example, I should like to register my dissatisfaction with the way I have seen subjects studied in both colleges that train few teachers and those exclusively concerned with teacher training. The use of a textbook may be a necessary evil; but I hope that the dreary discussions I have heard in classes of thirty are the exception and not the rule. One would expect that a stimulating lecture could from time to time set the tone; the use of closed-circuit TV makes it possible to direct such lectures to an unlimited audience. Individual reading assignments resulting in short essays and conferences in *small* groups should, but rarely do, characterize the collegiate methods of instruction as contrasted with the high school methods, and would correspond to the increased maturity of the student.

I found other unfortunate practices in many colleges: the use of graduate students as teaching assistants placed in charge of "sections" of freshman courses; heavy dependence on anthologies and textbooks; pretentious reading lists, which only a few students take seriously; and lectures poorly delivered by uninspired teachers.

I am also far from pleased with the reliance of most colleges and universities on conventional patterns of courses. Just as the notion that education can only be measured out in units of semester hours has become a sacred cow, so has the concept of the "course." Higher education in America is course-ridden. I do not propose to drive these sacred cows from the pasture. The semester-hour system seems to be a necessary medium of exchange, and the "course" is a natural and logical way to organize a large part of collegiate education. My protest is against the supine acceptance of it as the *only* way and the exclusion of other ways. One need not cite the example of Abraham Lincoln by the fireside, or the practice of "reading law," to argue that independent study has always been, and should be, a legitimate road to the mastery of a subject. It is striking that with the exception of honors programs, of provisions for independent work in some institutions, and of scattered instances of the use of examinations in place of course work, American colleges and universities of all types seem to be almost totally committed to the shibboleth of the "course" involving a certain amount of time in a certain room. One might expect widespread use of examinations both to determine whether a student is prepared for a beginning college course and as a basis for bypassing required courses when he has by independent study already achieved mastery of the subject.

This is no new idea. "Examining out" has long been the practice in certain subjects, notably in foreign languages and mathematics. But there is surprisingly *little* general use of this procedure in American colleges and universities today. Such examinations must, of course, be carefully set and rigorously evaluated. Moreover, there are some subjects in which the process of instruction—i.e., the lecture, the discussion, the demonstration, the laboratory—is such a valuable part of the educational experience that even if a student passes an examination based on independent reading, he may not have been adequately exposed to the substance of the subject. To expect a young person to gain much from the study of philosophy or economics by reading only, without benefit of discussion or interpretation, is asking a great deal; in such fields, reading would offer only a fragment of the understanding to be gained; too much would be missed.

But it is high time to challenge the assumption that education takes place only when the student is physically present in a classroom. *Opportunities for examining out should be offered much more widely than they are,* especially in the area of general education. The use of examinations in place of course work would create greater flexibility for the student in arranging his course of study, especially in the first two years, and would encourage the fruitful use of free time in the summer or during recess. It would also serve to encourage initiative, and free the student, to some degree, from the role of schoolboy. Finally, the option of meeting requirements by examination, rather than by course-taking, places the emphasis where it should be: on the subject itself rather than on the arbitrarily defined segment of it.

Opportunities for "examining out" would, obviously, be most useful for the bright students, or those whose high school preparation has been more than adequate in certain subjects. Other special provisions should be made for those whose high school work has been less than adequate. This matter is of the greatest importance in relation to those subjects whose mastery is an indispensable tool if college work is to be done satisfactorily: notably reading, writing, and the basic mathematical skills. Of these three areas, reading and writing deficiencies are the more fundamental problems; those whose mathematical skills are inadequate can often either avoid courses in which these skills are necessary, or muddle through the few that are required. But poor writing and limited reading ability are severe handicaps; as every college and university professor can testify, they are also commonplace phenomena.

The College Entrance Examination Board has long been at work on the problem of developing standards and examinations to test the writing competence of incoming freshmen. It is best, of course, if the school preparation is such that the student is ready for writing at the collegiate level when he enters college. But when remedial work is necessary, it should be outside the regular curriculum and should be regarded as the student's responsibility rather than the institution's. At least one public university has taken the stand that the taxpayers should not be expected to support for a second time training that should have been completed in high school. Nevertheless, thousands of students enter college each year seriously deficient in the ability to write clear, correct English prose; that there is some improvement on the horizon as high schools reduce the size of English classes and give more emphasis to writing I do not doubt, but the millennium is a long way off. My suggestion is simply that a standard of performance in English composition be set; if the student cannot achieve this standard, either he should be denied admission to a teacher-training course or he should be expected to remedy his deficiency through extra work for which he should pay a fee. The cost of maintaining large staffs to conduct classes in basic composition can hardly be justified. Many an institutional budget would be helped by eliminating this generous service, or at least making a moderate charge for it. This is true as well of the remedial reading clinics that some universities find it necessary to supply.

The quality of the student body

And this consideration brings us to the second element in the educational process, the students instructed. This is essentially the question of standards: who are admitted, allowed to continue, and given degrees.

I have heard a great deal of talk during the course of my study about upgrading the teaching profession. I have heard little discussion of the minimum level of scholastic aptitude to be required of candidates for teaching positions. I suggest that it is time this subject was examined and vigorously discussed state by state. The state boards of education, the state school boards' associations, and the highly influential state teachers' associations might well devote some time and energy to such an inquiry. At the outset this question would be faced: Is there a minimum level of intellectual ability we should set in this state for future teachers? I believe the answer should be yes.

I know it is often argued that there is no close correlation between teaching ability and intellectual ability (as measured by grades in courses or scholastic aptitude tests), and I am not unsympathetic to this argument. I realize that there are certainly many outstanding college students who for one reason or another would make poor schoolteachers and should be weeded out during the college course, and that there are also other college students, relatively slow in their academic work, who would yet make good teachers. This I grant, but I still maintain that *we should endeavor to recruit our teachers from the upper third of the graduating high school class on a national basis.* Why? Because the courses in the academic subjects that I believe important as part of a general education must not be pitched at too low a level or too slow a pace. The program I suggest in the following pages, which includes such subjects as college mathematics, science, and philosophy, would be too difficult for students whose intellectual ability placed them much below the top 30 per cent, in terms of the high school graduating class on a national basis.[1] In this chapter and hereafter, when

---

[1] Techniques for measuring academic aptitude abound, and all of them are subject to some criticism. A 30 per cent pool selected by one set of criteria will leave out people who belong according to a second set. Different researchers use different criteria, and the experts in the field are constantly seeking to improve their tools for prediction. I do not propose to judge which are the best tools. Those who must in practice make the selections have to decide for themselves what criteria to use. My 30 per cent figure suggests a general category, and the overwhelming number of students who fall in that category by

I suggest the kind of educational programs that should be provided in a four-year course for teachers, I shall assume that all the students fall in the upper 30 per cent category. For those with much less aptitude for academic work, what I am recommending is too stiff a program both in high school and in college.

An examination of Appendix D will make it clear that we cannot at present hope to obtain all our teachers from the upper 30 per cent, although we may be able to do so in the future. For the time being, it is plain that there will be some colleges and universities that could not follow my suggestions in this and the following chapters if they would; the students would not be up to it. Those who are interested in my specific suggestions about curricula must first examine the cutoff point in terms of academic ability for those enrolled in the teacher-training programs.

With this in mind, I suggest that if a state wishes to raise the intellectual level of those being trained within the state as teachers, it should establish for future teachers a loan policy *limited to students who can meet a certain level of scholastic aptitude*. A number of states have taken the matter in hand; some of the provisions of the NDEA are directed at helping future teachers to finance their education. But there has not been the emphasis on helping the more able that I should like. To establish any national standards of scholastic aptitude would be extremely difficult and totally unrealistic; therefore, my recommendation is for state-by-state action.

12. *Each state should develop a loan policy for future teachers aimed at recruiting into the profession the most able students; the requirements for admission to the teacher-training institutions within the state should be left to the institution, but the state should set a standard for the recipients in terms of scholastic aptitude; the amount of the loan should be sufficient to cover expenses, and the loan should be canceled after four or five years of teaching in the public schools of the state.*

Many will question such a recommendation; some will do so on the grounds that it is impossible to set up suitable standards; others

---

one criterion will also fall in it by most others. Obviously in using tools that are only statistically valid, one must use common sense in their application to particular cases.

will say that if this is done, there will not be teachers enough to meet the needs. Obviously, much depends on the pupil-teacher ratio, and much depends on the extent to which new developments can spread the effectiveness of the best teachers. These include team teaching, programmed instruction, television, and various ways of providing teachers with clerical and other assistance. It is beyond the scope of this book to examine the degree to which these new and highly important developments would enable a school system to change the teacher-student ratio. What I suggest is simply this: *If a state is faced with a shortage of teachers, it would be far better to push the new developments with the hope of decreasing the demand than to continue to recruit teachers with very low intellectual ability, as some states do at the present moment.*

Over and above the talent of the would-be teachers, there is a second factor that teacher-training institutions should consider, and that is high school preparation. Today many young people with the requisite academic talent are graduating from high school without having studied as wide an academic program as I would recommend. Therefore, in my view, the improvement of the education of future teachers in many regions of the country must start with first, more rigorous selection of those who enter the collegiate programs; and second, the improvement of the high school programs.

Judging from what I have found, I believe that far too many students intending to become teachers enter college without sufficient academic preparation.

For future teachers, I believe that the content of general education in school and college should include certain essential ingredients. Let me start with a summary of what may be accomplished in school. For those planning to be teachers I would suggest the following high school program:[1]

[1] Readers of my earlier book, *The American High School Today,* will recall my recommendation that all students in the upper 15 to 20 per cent of an age group should be urged to take a similar program including four years of mathematics. A careful reader will also note that I did not suggest that such programs be *restricted* to the upper 15 per cent. I am quite convinced that what I recommend is possible for a substantial number of students in the upper 30 per cent of the high school graduating glass (already a more select group than 30 per cent of the total age group), particularly if the fourth year of mathematics is dropped.

English (including frequent practice in writing)   4 years
Foreign language (one language studied consecutively)   4 years
Mathematics (four years preferred)   3 years
Natural science   3 years
History and social studies   3 years
Art and music   2 years

Remember, I am assuming that we are considering students whose scholastic aptitude places them in the category of the top 30 per cent of the high school graduating class on a national basis. Such students can, I believe, study with profit and without an excessive demand on time and energy the program I have suggested in high school. I would refer any who question this assumption to the academic inventories I have published in *Slums and Suburbs*, particularly that of the Newton High School in Newton, Massachusetts. The evidence there presented shows that over half the boys and girls in the I.Q. range 105–114 were taking and passing 18 academic courses in four years, including four years of mathematics. (The range I.Q. 111 and higher corresponds roughly to the upper 30 per cent of the high school graduating class on a national basis.)

I should be disposed to go even a step further, and urge that, for the most talented students, opportunities for advanced placement be extended. If these were widely enough offered, a great many students could do a good deal of general college work in high school.

In examining the high school program, the reader will note that four years of a foreign language are specified, and here I would make one reservation. Unless the student has the ability to carry the study of a language this far, and unless four years of instruction are offered in the high school, it might better be eliminated entirely. This is not a minor matter. The student who enters college with only two years of language training in high school, if he is to gain a proficiency, must devote at least two years of college study to it. This time can ill be spared from the future teacher's program. The college years are too late for this job to be done. Therefore, *I suggest that until the secondary schools are regularly offering four consecutive years of language instruction, there is little point in giving language a fixed place in the requirements for "breadth" in the combined high school and college program.*

Current programs in general education

Let me now turn to the third element of the educational process, the programs of study offered and followed in our colleges and universities. A subsequent chapter will be concerned with the question of professional—i.e., education—courses, but here I would like to discuss the breadth and depth of the collegiate studies undertaken by future teachers along with other students. In other words, I am asking this question: Apart from professional courses, what goes into the education of teachers in our colleges and universities?

I must say at the outset that I do not believe that today, in this country, a consideration of general education can be divorced from the special education that may accompany it or is soon to follow. Again, there will be those who disagree, and I can only acknowledge my awareness of their point of view. It seems to me, however, that a prescription of general education is impossible unless one knows, at least approximately, the vocational aspirations of the group in question.

In discussing general requirements for future teachers, two questions must be considered. The first is: Are the requirements adequate? And the second is: How nearly uniform are these requirements the country over? For an answer, let us look at the general requirements for the bachelor's degree in a number of American institutions representing a variety of types.

I shall include, for the sake of those readers who may harbor lingering doubts about the relative adequacy of programs in teachers colleges as compared to those in "liberal arts" colleges, examples of general academic requirements demanded of all students for the bachelor's degree in both types of schools. In this connection, there will be many who might protest; "It is only to be expected that in a wide survey of many sorts of institution one would find great diversity in general requirements. But if you look at the best colleges, the old-line institutions, you'll find some pretty stiff requirements generally held to." Just to satisfy myself on this point, I established a list of 20 institutions of the prestige category. The list could have been extended well beyond that, but it was not difficult to list 20 whose reputations could hardly be questioned. In what follows I shall compare these institutions with 10 institutions usually considered primarily teachers colleges.

There are, in the main, three patterns of general requirements: first, the actual designation of specific courses in such subjects as English, history, or natural science that all students must take, usually in their first two years; second (and the most frequent pattern), the designation of certain areas, or lists of courses in each of which the student must complete a certain number; and third, a set of integrated or interdepartmental courses,[1] all or some of which the student must take, the latter sometimes being offered by a separate division or college of the institution, with its own independent faculty.

In small or medium-size colleges, and in universities having "basic" or "general education" programs, the requirements are likely to apply to all students in their first year or first two years; but in institutions with many degree programs the requirements may vary according to the curriculum or school in which the student is enrolled.

Do the general requirements insure a common intellectual experience in varying institutions? One might suppose that there would be something approaching a uniform requirement in English, or at least in English composition. But here, I find, is an area of disagreement that would surprise the most ardent advocate of diversity.

In the 20 prestige institutions, the requirements in English composition were extremely varied, with no requirement, other than a form of screening entering students, in 4 of the 20. By contrast, all 10 of our teachers colleges require a year or a year and a half of English. Moreover, each of the teachers colleges insists on some work in speech as part of or as an accompaniment to the English requirement. Now, it would probably be wrong to conclude that

---

[1] The first two patterns involve courses that correspond to the disciplines into which a college faculty is usually divided, i.e., history, physics, sociology, English, etc. The third cuts across departmental lines and offers such courses as "Man and Society," "Contemporary Trends," "Man and His Natural Environment," in which knowledge from several disciplines is reorganized, refocused, and "integrated."

the students enrolled in the teachers colleges become more proficient in their use of the English language than those in the prestige institutions. There are too many other factors involved: the ability of the students, secondary school preparation, and so on. The presumption might be that even with less consistent attention to English composition, the quality of writing in the prestige colleges might be generally better than in other colleges. (I am bound to repeat here the almost universal complaint of faculty members in the arts and sciences that student writing is poorer than it should be!) Nevertheless, it is quite clear that somewhat more attention, in terms of formal instruction, is given to this basic need at the 10 teachers colleges than at the 20 prestige institutions.

A committee of the National Council of the Teachers of English[1] warns that when one takes a close look, there are many things wrong with the freshman course in English. Differences in aims, differences in the handling of remedial work, differences in provisions for the superior student ("It is hard to see what, other than someone's personal whim, has led to some of the patterns," reports the committee), and the wide array of anthologies and textbooks in use—all these go to make up the variegated thing called freshman English. My own investigations, while not carried out as thoroughly as the Committee's, tended to support the same conclusion. To summarize it very briefly, a requirement of a half-year or more of English composition, variously defined, was found in a majority of institutions, *but not in all*. Along with English composition—or quite separate from it—there may be a requirement of from half a year to two years of literature, or humanities, even more variously defined. It should be pointed out that many college and university teachers of English are keenly aware of the difficulties and are making strenuous efforts to improve this confusing situation. Nevertheless, it seems likely that widely different courses of instruction in English will be a familiar pattern in our colleges and universities for some time to come. One can hardly look to the field of

---

[1] "But What Are We Articulating With? Freshman English in Ninety-five Colleges and Universities," by the N.C.T.E. Committee on High School College Articulation, *The English Journal,* March, 1962, pp. 167–179. Floyd Rinker, "Priorities in the English Curriculum, *The English Journal,* May, 1962, pp. 309–312. See also *The National Interest and the Teaching of English,* prepared by the National Council of Teachers of English, 1961.

English, therefore, for a binding thread in American collegiate education.

The same diversity is found in mathematics requirements. It is surprising in this post-Sputnik era that mathematics is not often a specific requirement for the bachelor's degree, even among the prestige colleges.

Of our 20 institutions in the prestige category, only 3 specifically required any college study of mathematics. By contrast, all but 3 of the 10 teachers colleges require a semester or more of mathematics. To be sure, the mathematics required of freshmen is usually of the introductory sort; that is, it is not, strictly speaking, college-level mathematics. And yet the requirement is there; an effort is being made; there is some exposure at least—which is more than can be said of 17 of the prestige group.

When we turn to the three areas usually thought of as representing "breadth"—social science, science, and the humanities—we find among all types of institutions an even more confusing disparity of offerings and requirements. Rarely does the required college science course presuppose more than a modest acquaintance with mathematics (i.e., first or second year of high school). Rarely are both biological and physical science specifically required. In some institutions the student can meet a "science" requirement by mathematics alone, or by geography or psychology.

Among our 20 "prestige" colleges, the situation seems somewhat better. Twelve of them require the equivalent of two years of science; usually this requirement specifies both physical and biological science. Six require only one year, and two accept psychology as meeting the natural science requirement. In this area, the teachers colleges seem to be somewhat less demanding than the prestige group. Only 3 of our 10 teachers colleges require two years, though 6 of the remaining 7 require at least a year.

Social science is defined so variously that it is hard even to summarize it: all sorts of history, all sorts of general courses such as world civilization or American society, various sorts of political science, economics, anthropology, psychology, even religion and humanities may be found under the heading "social science."

Just as varied a coat of many colors are the requirements that can be said to fall under the heading of humanities. On the one hand are interdisciplinary courses in "humanities" or "Western culture," and at the other, options among many courses in many literatures, in music, and in art. Philosophy, which might be regarded as an essential element in any collegiate program pretending to breadth or coherence, is rare indeed as a specific requirement for a bachelor's degree.[1]

In our 20 prestige institutions, the social sciences displayed the same range of options found in the institutions of various types, with only 6 actually specifying the study of history. Humanities again proved to be a wide net, with many subjects acceptable, including history, mathematics, and psychology!

In both the humanities and the social sciences, the requirements of the teachers colleges are roughly the same as those of the prestige colleges. None specifies less than a year's work in each, and two years' work in either the humanities or the social sciences or both is required by a majority of the institutions in both groups. All but one of the teachers colleges require two years or more of work in the social sciences; roughly two-thirds of the prestige institutions require as much.

What about foreign language? Proficiency in this area was once held to be indispensable to the educated man. But these days, a bachelor's degree is of itself no guarantee whatever of mastery of a foreign language, or even exposure to one. In our 20 prestige institutions, the only important difference I could detect was that most require a degree of proficiency in a foreign language *for the A.B. degree,* but not for the B.S. degree. By contrast, only one of the teachers colleges has such a requirement.

Summing it all up, about all one can say is that most institutions

[1] I should make clear at this point that some church-related colleges have patterns of general requirements that are far more specific and coherent, particularly in religion and philosophy, than those usually found elsewhere. At one institution, for example, besides 16 hours of theology, the student must take 15 hours in philosophy and logic, as well as 12 hours of English, 6 hours of speech, 6 hours of mathematics, 12 hours of natural science, and 6 hours of foreign language. At another institution, far removed geographically—as well as doctrinally—from the first, the student must complete 18 hours of required courses in religion, this in addition to 6 hours of natural science, 12 hours of social science, 12 hours of a foreign language, and 6 hours, as well as a proficiency examination, in English. Having visited both church-related colleges, I may say that they contrast sharply, not only with the many looser patterns of general education I have observed, but with each other!

require the student to be involved in the study of something called the humanities, something called social science, some sort of science variously defined, frequently English composition, less frequently foreign language, and occasionally mathematics and philosophy; *no broader generalizations can be made.* The conclusion one is forced to is that a *common intellectual experience is unlikely to be an actuality in higher education in this country* in any given year, in any given state, and with some exceptions on any given campus.

I would not want to argue that diversity is a bad thing, or to suggest that American colleges and universities should march in lockstep in framing the general requirements for their degrees. I have had too many years of experience in dealing with faculty curriculum committees to indulge in hopes for even a small measure of consistency in curricular matters. But I have taken time to discuss the diversity in general requirements among our colleges simply to show the folly in assuming that because a young man or woman holds a bachelor's degree from a so-called liberal arts college or a university he will necessarily have greater "breadth" in his educational background than a graduate of a teachers college.[1]

Without intending to suggest that the *diversity* in offerings and requirements from one institution to another is necessarily undesirable, I am bound to state quite bluntly that in most institutions whose programs I have examined the level of general education requirements seems to me to fall below what should be demanded of prospective teachers at the collegiate level.

More discouragingly, one sees the weakness of the entire fabric of this part of collegiate education in the confusion among the college administrators and faculties themselves. One does not need to travel far to discover that this indictment of the general requirements found in collegiate education, whether in a "liberal arts" college or any other type, is neither overstated nor undeserved.

In this context let me caution the reader against the terms "liberal arts college" and "liberal education." Their meaning has be-

---

[1] The reader's attention is called to the survey of 18 representative colleges and universities in Russell B. Thomas's *The Search for a Common Learning: General Education, 1800–1960.* McGraw-Hill Book Company, Inc., New York, 1962. See also a summary of a survey of general requirements listed in the catalogs of 140 colleges, as reported by Prof. E. O. Leverett in the April 8, 1961, issue of *School and Society.*

come so varied as to render them almost useless in a study of this kind. A good many so-called liberal arts colleges actually devote only a part of their efforts to instruction in strictly academic fields. One finds that they may offer a variety of programs, such as business administration, journalism, social work, or pre-engineering; that their students concentrating in the sciences really think of themselves as preprofessional (and quite properly so!); and that on some campuses thu B.S. candidates will outnumber the B.A.s. Thus it is absurd to assume that all holders of a bachelor's degree have received an education that can be described by any set of words. Those who proclaim that "a teacher must be first of all a liberally educated person" are making a far from precise statement.

In writing this sentence, I am aware of the anguish with which it will be read by many professors with whose views I am generally in accord. I am aware of the ancient and honorable distinction between a liberal and a vocational education. And I shudder, as do many others, when I hear it argued that "any subject properly taught can be considered as part of a liberal education." But my negative reactions arise not so much from a horror at seeing courses in physical education counted towards a bachelor's degree in one of our oldest colleges as from the utter confusion that is a consequence of such a declaration. In terms of the knowledge and skills acquired and the attitudes developed, the distinction made in ancient Greece has held throughout the entire development of Western civilization.

The writers of the Harvard Report of 1945 on "General Education in a Free Society" pointed out that the concept of liberal education, which first appeared in the slave-owning society of ancient Greece, was concerned with education for leisure as contrasted to vocational education. They then went on to say that "modern democratic society is more likely to regard leisure with suspicion than to consider labor as odious."

As long as the distinction made by the ancient Greeks was valid, the phrases "liberal education" and "a liberally educated man" had clear meanings. In our own society, however, the education of a leisure class is no longer an issue; and now the use of the adjective "liberal" to denote the content of an educational program can only add to confusion. One of my friends, whose advice has been most helpful in my present study, has pointed up the issue as follows: "Embedded in the concept of a liberal education, as it has been held in varying ways over the centuries, there is something we may recognize and value. But it does not inhere in a program or pattern. We are close to the mark if we conceive of it as a process and as an aspiration. A liberal education, one might say, is a process begun in childhood, carried on through a varying number of years of schooling, and best tested by the momentum it sustains in adult life. It is characterized by what it aspires to, rather than by what it embraces; it aims to enlarge the understanding, to develop respect for data, and to strengthen the ability to think and to act rationally. Accordingly, the process of educating liberally is not confined to the classroom and is not circumscribed by the subjects of study or the experiences which may contribute to it. It seeks to produce an informed, inquiring, and judicious habit of mind rather than particular abilities."

In accordance with this view, I should like to urge that "liberal education," if the term is to be used at all, should be used in reference to a process rather than a program of study. As it is often used at present—that is, with the idea that it describes a consistent and generally accepted pattern of studies—"liberal education" in this country is a myth. I defy anyone to discover in the stated aims and practices of our colleges and universities anything consistent enough to justify the term "liberal education" as it is commonly employed.

What constitutes general education?

Assuming sufficient aptitude and an adequate secondary school preparation, what should be the general requirements for the bachelor's degree in a program of teacher education, and on what assumptions would such requirements rest? If I were advising a teacher-education institution, I should argue that the assumptions are neither new nor far to seek. They are: first, that there are certain areas of knowledge with which all future teachers should be acquainted; second, that in these areas of knowledge there are characteristic ways of grasping the subject; third, that in both the knowledge and the ways of understanding them there are basic principles; finally, that properly studied and taught, these subjects and the principles discoverable in them can further the *process* of a liberal education.

There is, moreover, an important practical reason for certain studies: almost any teacher inevitably faces the necessity of dealing with subjects outside his area of specialization, not only in his classroom but also in conversations with students. If he is largely ignorant or uninformed, he can do much harm. Moreover, if the teachers in a school system are to be a group of learned persons cooperating together, they should have as much intellectual experience in common as possible, and any teacher who has not studied in a variety of fields in college will always feel far out of his depth when talking with a colleague who is the high school teacher in a field other than his own.

And too, if teachers are to be considered as learned persons in their communities (as they are in certain European countries), and if they are to command the respect of the professional men and women they meet, they must be prepared to discuss difficult topics. This requires a certain level of sophistication. For example, to participate in any but the most superficial conversations about the impact of science on our culture, one must have at some time wrestled with the problems of the theory of knowledge. The same is true when it comes to the discussion of current issues.

What I am about to suggest in the way of a general education program would occupy half the student's time for four years, even assuming a good high school preparation. If one accepts my argument in the preceding paragraphs, this amount of time is not too much. Whether more time could be used profitably is a question that leads into the controversial issue of breadth versus depth, and I must postpone for a few pages weighing the particular pros and cons in this area. Here I am arguing for two years in college aimed at developing such a degree of competence in the usual academic areas that the teacher has some confidence in talking with a colleague who is a specialist in one of these areas. Such confidence is important for the elementary teacher as well as for the secondary. Even though the elementary teacher is directly concerned with arithmetic or relatively simple science or social science, he ought to know what kind of road eventually lies ahead.

General education for future teachers, then, should be a broad *academic* education. The limitation implied by the word academic is, I believe, a necessary restriction. Without it one can argue for all sorts of broadening educational experiences whose values I might or might not question. But with the time limits imposed upon formal education, I am ready to defend the restrictions implied in the word "academic."

What subjects should be included as academic? Of the fields usually studied in secondary schools, college programs should continue literature, history, government, mathematics, the natural sciences, geography, art, and music. How much further should these be pursued in college as part of a general education of teachers? One might say that ideally each subject should be studied until the student has attained enough competence to teach the subject to a 12th grade average class. But to demand any such degree of concentration in each field would be to extend the general education alone to far more than four years.

Foreign languages and mathematics, at least as they have been taught, have been the traditional stumbling blocks to many able students. I believe in the importance of having educated Americans at least bilingual by the time they graduate from high school. But I would not now push the claim that all future teachers should have something approaching a mastery of a foreign language. Such a goal is for the future.

Given time enough, good teaching, and a sufficient degree of interest, many more people could probably study mathematics in college than now do. Moreover, an understanding of much of modern science is heavily dependent on mathematics. Therefore, mathematics must be included in a college program. Further study in college is certainly a necessity in English, in literature, and in history, and probably in the natural sciences. The high school courses in art and music are so varied and the time devoted to them so uncertain that I hesitate to say what the exposure should be in college. It is enough to say that teachers should have a common background of knowledge and appreciation of our cultural heritage. Thus some time in college should be spent on increasing the understanding of literature, art, and music that was acquired in school.

In each of these fields, collegiate faculties should define the levels of knowledge and understanding or skill that should be required as the product of the total *general* education of the future teacher. *I should hope each institution that has serious concern with educating teachers would, through appropriate committees, define such levels, bearing in mind that the entire general education course should not require more than half the student's time during four years* (though the program need not be completed in the first two years, and, as I have indicated, the possibility of examining out should be available). For an illustration, I venture statements about several fields.

I am strongly of the view that a general education hardly deserves the name unless it ensures a reasonable familiarity with the nature of the language we use. A year's work devoted to an understanding of its structure, its history, its relations to other languages, and its use seems little enough. I am aware that varying emphasis will be given to such things as structural linguistics and traditional grammar, and that the kind and amount of work in composition that would accompany such language instruction would vary also. However, the serious study of the English language should be an essential component of any collegiate program and particularly of a teacher's education. I am bound to report, on the basis of my own visits, that it is rarely found as a specific requirement.

Being a sequential subject, mathematics should be the easiest in which to state the level of competence. This would be true except for the revolutions in teaching mathematics that are now in progress. As I have talked to professors during the last two years, I find some uncertainty as to what is the most fruitful use of four high school years devoted to mathematics. If I were talking in old-fashioned terms, I would define the level of competence as that of just reaching the elements of calculus and probability. For a student who has studied mathematics in high school for four years, I would hope that a minimum of one full year's course or two semesters of college work might be profitably spent. For those with only three years of high school work (or four years poorly done), more college time might be required. Conversely, for those who have taken the advanced placement examination in mathematics, a single semester course should be sufficient. In this field above all others, it should be possible to do away with semester hours and set the requirements in terms of success on a competence examination. How the student acquires the competence is of secondary importance.

I am of the opinion that the physical sciences for general education purposes should be regarded as a whole. There is often much duplication as courses have been given. For a long time I have been convinced that the teachers of freshman physics and chemistry should get together and present a single course. Ideally a general examination in physical science should be set for those not concentrating in this area, and the topics to be covered should include astronomy and geology. For those who have had good instruction in chemistry and physics in high school and who would study portions of astronomy and geology outside the classroom, a single combined full-year course in physics and chemistry should suffice. At least this statement will serve to define the level I have in mind. Physical chemistry, for example, should be studied up to but not including the use of calculus, and organic chemistry would involve only the methods of determining the structural formulas of the simplest classes of compounds.

Modern biology is based on a considerable knowledge of chemistry and physics. Therefore, I would define the level of competence in biology in terms of a full year's college course, the prerequisite for admission to which would be the mastery of physics and chemistry and mathematics at the levels I have prescribed. This means that a competence examination in this field is very unlikely to be passed by a high school student or even a freshman. For this reason, and because there is so little agreement among biologists as to which of the many topics should be included in an introductory course, I should not press for a general examination here as I have done in the case of mathematics and the physical sciences.

Anything less than the requirements I have just proposed in mathematics and science can hardly be justified in the present world. To ask the future teacher to devote two semesters to mathematics at the college level beyond three years in high school is a modest requirement. It is seeking no more than a kind of literacy in a field that touches all mankind daily, for twentieth-century science is basically mathematical. If a teacher is to be regarded as an example of an educated person, his acquaintance with mathematics and science should be at least as much as I have outlined. Yet in both those fields, as I have already said, some students whose high school work has been sufficiently advanced might be able to pass the examination and reduce the time devoted to mathematics, chemistry, and physics. A similar situation might easily obtain in regard to either art or music or both. In short, *competence examinations in all these fields are to be recommended.*

We have seen that English, mathematics, and science are studied in high school, but except in rare instances not in sufficient depth to provide the degree of understanding I think is essential; the same is true of history and literature. Since these are not sequential subjects, however, it is by no means easy to specify what should be the minimum aim of the college in these areas. *As in the field of English, I should hope a committee of the faculty would undertake to spell out what, in their opinion, were the books that must be read and the periods of history that should be studied.* Even if the coverage of American history in the high school years has been extensive and the instruction excellent, the college work must be focused upon the more mature consideration of historical evidence and interpretation. Many high schools teach world history, and the survey thus provided may serve as the basis on which to build in the college years. In history as well as in English, extensive reading, essay writing, and small group conferences are essential. The nature of the lecture courses provided will depend on the prescription of the committee on the one hand and the student's achievement in high school on the other.

There are five areas of knowledge that I believe can only be studied on the college level, namely, philosophy, sociology and anthropology, economics, political science, and psychology. I have in mind the introductory college course. In the time available only an introduction can be accomplished, but such an introduction I feel to be of the utmost importance. Properly taught, such introductory courses would lay the basis for further self-education based on reading. I shall not attempt to outline the nature of the introduction, for the essential matter is the person or persons who give the course and the way the study is conducted.

I consider it essential that a person of the maturity of a college student explore these areas of knowledge under the guidance of a person who has been trained as a scholar in these fields. All future teachers are not now required to study philosophy under a philosopher or psychology under a psychologist or sociology under a sociologist; in many cases students are first introduced to these subjects by members of a faculty of education who are by no means philosophers or psychologists or sociologists but who are experts in the application of principles from these fields to the educational process. As I shall make evident in later chapters, there is an important function to be performed by such people. But philosophy taught by a philosopher of education is definitely *not* what I have in mind in referring to philosophy as part of the general education of a teacher. This point I believe to be of some importance.

While I recognize that differences in faculties, in students, and in habits of thought and outlook in the 1,150 institutions that prepare teachers result in differences in actual practice, nevertheless I am bold enough to translate what I have just said into the following pattern of general education for future teachers. It is *not* a prescription but an illustration of my contention that, given a good high school preparation, an able student can receive a general education of some breadth in two years.

	No. of Courses	Equivalent Sem. Hours
Subjects already studied in high school		
The English language and composition	2	6
The Western world's literary tradition	2	6
History (at least one-half other than American)	3	9
Art appreciation and music appreciation	2	6
Mathematics	2	6
Science (physical and biological, each studied consecutively)	4	12
Subjects not studied in school		
Introduction to general psychology	1	3
Introduction to sociology and anthropology	1	3
Introduction to the problems of philosophy	1	3
Introduction to economics	1	3
Introduction to political science	1	3
	20	60

This general education program for future teachers should occupy about one-half of the four years, or 60 out of 120 semester hours. Such an amount is considerably larger than the amount I found in most institutions, where something on the order of 30 to 45 semester hours, i.e., a year to a year and a half, is the usual prescription. Since, as we shall see, the amount of time given to major concentration and professional courses is not enough to fill the remaining two years, the question inevitably arises: Where does the rest go? The answer is, to a fetish of American higher education —elective courses.

When I refer to the concept of providing elective courses as a fetish, I am guilty of using a negative word to cover an area of collegiate study that may be deserving of more respect. Therefore, I should make clear that I am not denying the educational value of courses chosen solely on the basis of the student's interest. This would be ignoring the universal experience that we tend to devote our best efforts to the things that interest us. A student's field of concentration represents a relatively free choice, as does the curriculum or program he pursues, the institution he attends, and the career he follows. For the most part these are elected. Why, then, should the college student not *elect* some of his courses?

The reader may react indignantly to my comments on this question. Perhaps he will recall a course that he himself was fortunate enough to stumble or be guided into, which proved to be of lasting interest and value to him. Rare indeed is the college alumnus who does not look back fondly on at least one such course taught by a popular and talented professor who opened his eyes to a whole field of knowledge. But one cannot plan a program around the reminiscences of old grads.

When in 1885 the elective system had come into force at Harvard, President Eliot, its great exponent, conceived it as an opportunity for the student to arrange a coherent and sequential program. The idea of a collegiate education as a grab bag or cafeteria was far from his mind. He wrote, "Under an elective system the great majority of students use their liberty to pursue some subject or subjects with a reasonable degree of thoroughness. . . . Among the thousands of individual college courses determined by the choice of the student in four successive years, which the records of Harvard College now preserve, it is rare to find one which does not exhibit an intelligible sequence of studies. It should be understood in this connection that all the studies which are allowed to count toward the A.B. at Harvard are liberal or pure, no technical or professional studies being admissible." Eliot was arguing for what we would call today an academic major; his view was that with free choice the student could arrange his studies in a coherent and sequential pattern.

Since Eliot's time a number of things have happened to collegiate education in America that radically altered the complexion of the elective idea. For one thing, at Harvard and at other institutions emphasizing the elective system the students did not in fact tend to arrange their courses so as to "pursue some subject or subjects with a reasonable degree of thoroughness." For another thing, in the expanding universities across the land vocational and technical courses are increasingly offered, and new schools and colleges of journalism, agriculture, home economics, and business administration sprang up on many campuses. Cornell had been founded as an institution where "any student can find instruction in any study." By the first decade of this century, Eliot's idea came more and more to be questioned, and on the recommendation of his successor the elective system at Harvard was modified; requirements for concentration and distribution came into effect. The next stage was increased emphasis on the idea of a "general education" and on the development of patterns of requirements designed to ensure a reasonable breadth in the student's background, regardless of his vocational or professional goal, and some coherence among the courses in this pattern.

But elective courses did not disappear. Far from it. In few institutions did the requirements for breadth and the requirements for completing a "major" occupy all of the students' time. In all programs leading to a bachelor's degree, there continued to be an allotment of time to more or less "free" electives, even in schools of engineering, business, and agriculture. When one examines the A.B. program in the prestige colleges and universities today, one finds that the number of semester hours free for election ranges from 24 to as many as 60; that is, from eight to twenty 3-hour courses, or from nearly a year's to two years' work, and in many cases with little or no direct control by the institution.

Any suggestion that the area of unrestricted election be reduced is likely to meet resistance by vocal segments of the faculties. Certain courses are likely to depend heavily on free elections for their enrollments. A professor who for some years has successfully given a popular elective course is not likely to welcome any change that would bring fewer students into his lecture room. He will argue, and it will be hard to disagree, that more rather than fewer students should take his course. He will find many allies in other departments who will close ranks with him to defend the areas of free election, for these are their professional bread and butter. I am not writing cynically, but only stating one of the facts of academic life, well known to anyone who has spent much time in the strange world of higher education. Of course, the argument for free electives is not usually carried on in these terms. The appeal is usually to the spirit of free inquiry, resistance to onrushing materialism, faith in the good sense of the students, and the importance of giving a person a broadened outlook so that he may face the responsibilities of citizenship. It is hard to seem to be opposed to all these fine things, especially when one is not opposed, and more especially when they are not the issue at all.

The real issue, in considering the collegiate education of students who are preparing for a vocation or a profession, is whether as much as one to two years of collegiate work can be permitted to be spread over a wide range of subjects, in no necessarily coherent pattern, entirely at the student's choice—and yet *required* for the bachelor's degree, which each year seems to be thought more of a necessity and each year becomes more expensive. While observing the varied patterns of higher education at a good many colleges and universities in America, I have been forcibly struck by the extreme looseness of the elective system as it has developed on most campuses. Accordingly, I feel bound to point out to my lay readers—especially to the parents who are supporting their children's education, often at considerable sacrifice, and to the taxpayers who support our public institutions—that a substantial part of what they are paying for may bear no relation at all to the student's field of concentration, his future occupation, or even to the pattern of a broad general education. Too often the student's random sampling of courses is dictated not by educational values, but by the courses' convenience or their reputation for ease or liveliness.

While it would be desirable for the future teacher to elect some courses of interest outside his chosen field and the subjects studied for breadth, in most of the programs that I shall describe later there will not be room for electives, *unless* the student has earned advanced placement at entrance, or wishes to add extra courses during a regular term or a summer session. To those who would protest against such a limitation, I reply that the future teacher is becoming an educated person, an example to his students, and of all people should be expected to continue his education on his own after receiving his degree. Earlier I stated my objections to the idea that a subject can be studied only by taking a course—by the student's being physically present in the classroom. Collateral studies pursued for their inherent interest need not come out of the teacher's formal educational program but should be a part of his continuing education, his own independent reading as an adult, as with any professional person. The argument that breadth should be narrowed, or depth made more shallow, in order to make room for one or two years' worth of elective courses does not seem to me to have any force.

Current programs in specialization

Now let us turn to the question of subject specialization for the future teacher. Again, we shall begin by looking at some of the requirements now in effect, including specific programs in both a teachers college and a liberal arts college.

It would be too long a story to describe the full spectrum of requirements for concentration in American colleges and universities. One has only to turn the pages of the catalogs of the arts and sciences in almost any major university to see what wide differences there are just within one unit of an institution—quite apart from other colleges or schools of business administration, journalism, and agriculture, all offering a bachelor's degree. It may surprise some laymen to discover that among the subjects included in the major programs in the college of letters and science in a very distinguished institution are "Decorative Art," "Journalism," "Physical Education," and "Wildlife Conservation." This is not to argue that these offerings are wrongly conceived, or somehow improper. That is for the institution to determine. Such evidence (which could be duplicated in the catalogs of many large universities) is offered simply to show that possession of a bachelor of arts degree may signify a great many things indeed!

Nor, if one limits his examination to the more traditional subjects, does one find that a "major" necessarily means "depth." Very frequently the student is offered a choice between concentrating in a single subject and choosing one of a number of patterns for a broader program, such as a "field major," "group major," "general program," "interdisciplinary program." Most of these are attempts to provide for the student a broad experience within a field or related fields. Properly designed and comprehensively tested, the study of such a field could provide a valuable educational experience, but at present such programs are often too loosely arranged.

I am not challenging the concept of the broad field or "diversified major," as it is sometimes called. Indeed, the notion that the student should "know one thing well" needs definition. Moreover, the very existence of many broad programs of concentration in our most reputable institutions testifies to the belief on the part of many professors that a student may be truly educated in ways other than by the usual departmental major. After surveying 18 well-known institutions, Professor Thomas[1] points out, "At least one of the colleges denies that concentration in the conventional sense of the term is a necessary part of a liberal education, and two or three others make provisions for granting a Bachelor of Arts degree in programs which do not require a departmental concentration." A conventional major is not, then, the dependable hallmark it is often thought to be.

But this may not satisfy the persistent critic of the teachers colleges, who insists that a student will get a better grasp of a subject like English at a college of arts and sciences than at a teachers college. This is a fair challenge and deserves to be taken up in these terms. Let us compare, then, the programs for an English major in a good teachers college and a good college of arts and sciences that is

[1] *The Search for a Common Learning*, p. 299.

untainted by any professional aims. I say "good," because it would be quite possible, by choosing a weak institution in either category, to prove almost anything one might wish to prove.

Both of the institutions being compared are well known. The one is frankly a single-purpose institution, concerned with educating teachers. Its program of English studies is designed for the English "major" who is preparing to be a secondary school teacher of English. The other is a college of arts and sciences wherein the English major, in the words of the catalog, "emphasizes the study of literature as an art." I have selected for listing only those courses that are required and clearly specified. Additional elective courses in English and American literature are available to the student in both institutions.

	Teachers College		*College of Arts and Sciences*	
	Subject	*Sem. Hrs.*	*Subject*	*Sem. Hrs.*
1st Year	Drama	3	Literary analysis	6
	World literature	6		
	English composition	3		
2nd Year	American literature	6	16th & 17th century lit.	6
	Speech	3		
3rd Year	Shakespeare	3	18th & 19th century lit.	6
	Poetry	3	English, American, or	
	Fiction	3	comparative lit.	6
	Foundations of language	2		
4th Year	Survey of British lit.	3	Major works of lit.	12
	Humanities elective	2		
		37		36

The comparison is interesting. The total amount of time given to English studies is nearly the same: out of 120 semester hours, 37 or 36, roughly one-third in each case. The teachers college gives a larger proportion of this work in the first three years; the college of arts and sciences in the last three. One cannot be sure exactly what authors are "covered" in each program (since these things change yearly in most departments) but, generally speaking, there seem to be provisions in each for the main periods and genres. We are not, of course, getting behind the scenes to see how effectively and by what standards the instruction is carried out in each institution, or to examine the length and difficulty of the reading assignments. But this is not our purpose; our purpose is to discover whether the one major is in its components more "solid" than the other.

Three elements in the teachers college program seem to be lacking, or not specifically required, in that of the college of arts and sciences—American literature, foundations of language, and speech. Perhaps it could be argued that a single college course in speech is not going to help markedly a student's capacity for fluency and clarity in oral expression. But most laymen would agree that it is surprising to find that it is possible to major in English at a "good" college of arts and sciences and remain partly innocent of American literature and any real knowledge of the history and structure of the English language. I may add that many programs for English majors in this country, including some in the most reputable institutions, do not specifically require the study of the English language. However all this may be, we can see that the program in the teachers college is *not,* in comparison with that of the college of arts and sciences, deficient, thin, or lacking in what goes to make up a "good, solid major." The graduate of the teachers college could, theoretically, come up with at least as rich and meaningful an educational experience in literary studies as the graduate of the college of arts and sciences. Moreover, if we are thinking of future teachers, we will find that in addition to the program outlined above, the teachers college graduate will have had courses in "Grammar for Teachers," "The Language Arts" (oral and written English, propaganda, reading, listening, etc.), and "Literature for Adolescents." Purists may object to courses with these titles, but I can assure the objector that many a beginning teacher facing a restless class of 35 high school freshmen would be grateful for such training.

What constitutes education in depth?

For the future secondary school teacher, there is no argument about his devoting a considerable amount of time to the study of the subject to be taught. For such a person, the study in depth of a field might well be classified as special education, as is the study of science beyond the freshman year for the future doctor or the more advanced courses in physics and chemistry for the future chemist. If there were no other reason than a vocational one for a student's concentrating his efforts on one field during the college years, I might close this chapter here. But the history of college education in this country in this century shows that there is a rationale for the idea of studying a field in depth quite apart from the student's future profession or vocation, and though I must confess to a distrust of a good many high-flown statements that I have read in college catalogs, I subscribe in general to the rationale.

There is a way of stating the argument that has always appealed to me, although its validity is limited. It is this: Only through pursuing a subject well beyond the introductory level can the student gain a coherent picture of the subject, get a glimpse of the vast reaches of knowledge, feel the cutting edge of disciplined training, and discover the satisfactions of the scholarly habit of mind (so that if he becomes a teacher, he can communicate something of this spirit to others). Thousands of students each year wander through survey courses with only the shallowest knowledge of the subjects. I believe that if the student once has the experience of getting inside a subject, he is more likely to become so interested in it that he will wish to go on with it on his own (which I regard as one of the hallmarks of an "educated" person); at the same time he will be less likely to be timid in addressing himself to other complicated subjects, or to accept dogma, or to countenance nonsense on any subject.

Before suggesting programs for education in depth, I should like to jettison two mongrel academic terms, "major" and "minor." I would throw them out both in their noun and verb forms, not only because I dislike them but because they have come to be used so loosely as to have little meaning. In their place I shall use the terms "concentration" or "degree of concentration in a field or fields." As we have seen, it is risky to assume that a holder of a bachelor's degree from an American college has necessarily pursued a recognized subject in depth, or in a sequence or coherent pattern. Many of the subjects in which students concentrate are very far afield from such traditional subjects as English and mathematics, and the requirements for them are very often no more than an accumulation of a specified number of semester-hour "credits." Let me, therefore, try to be quite definite in setting forth what I would regard as a good program of concentration for the future teacher, and suggest some specific programs in English, the social sciences, mathematics, and natural science.

Here I must be quite doctrinaire, for obviously opinions differ among academic faculties themselves. As I see it, to gain anything like a coherent grasp of a subject like English or biology or mathematics, any student should complete a minimum of 12 courses, that is, 36 semester hours, or the equivalent of more than a full college year's work, including 2 or more courses on the introductory level, carried as part of the general education requirement.

For the elementary teacher, a concentration of 36 hours is about all that can be included in a four-year program, and should suffice. For students intending to be high school teachers, I suggest more than the above minimum—in many cases a total concentration of 16 courses, or 48 semester hours, again including such introductory work as may have been taken as general education. To complete an honors program in most colleges, this amount of time must usually be devoted.

Admittedly, this is a fairly stiff prescription. Not one of the "prestige" colleges mentioned earlier requires as much.[1] Nevertheless, it is quite feasible within a four-year program. As we have seen, the requirements for breadth will occupy 60 hours or somewhat less, depending on the high school preparation; but these will include at least 6 hours of introductory work in the subject in which the student is concentrating. To meet my suggested minimum amount of concentration, 30 hours (plus the introductory 6) would be needed, leaving free 30 in the total of 120; to meet the maximum amount, 42 (plus the introductory 6) would be needed, leaving free 18 hours. All of this must be approximate, since I am attempting here only to indicate what the dimensions of a field of concentration should be. In later chapters I shall try to show specifically how the hours for general education and concentration can be allocated in four-year programs for future elementary and secondary teachers.

[1] Of the 20 prestige institutions, the time for a major ranged from 18 to 42 semester hours. Free electives 24 to 68.

Let us turn from the question of *how much* concentration to the related question of *what kind*. I have already said that a program of concentration should have coherence; it should either be sequential or be capable of being tested comprehensively. To illustrate the contrast between two different fields and to show the absurdity of generalizing about "fields of concentration" as if they were all similar, we can look at a sequential subject, chemistry, and one that is not necessarily sequential, English literature.

A student concentrating in chemistry must usually begin by learning the properties of elements and compounds and by becoming familiar with laboratory manipulations, preparations, and analysis. This will be followed, perhaps by further study of analytical chemistry, and of organic chemistry; in the latter he must begin with the simpler compounds before advancing to study complex compounds: for example, proteins and the carbohydrates. Before the student goes on to tackle physical chemistry and the study of matter in the gaseous, liquid, and solid states, he should have an understanding of general physics, and it would be highly desirable for him to have at least an introduction to the differential calculus. In short, the study of chemistry is partly a matter of stepping stones followed in order.

By contrast, in the field of English literature there are essentially no stepping stones in a necessary order. The student can be introduced to the literary traditions, to genres, and to individual authors in many patterns. He might begin with a study of Shakespeare, and move on to a course in the several forms of literature. He might then spend some time on romantic, Victorian, and modern literature (not necessarily in that order), and follow this with the intensive study of two major authors, such as Chaucer and Milton. Meanwhile he may read some major critics, have courses in the novel and drama, and spend some time on the history and structure of the English language. The history of English literature will have unfolded along the way; literary forms and techniques will have become familiar in many different settings. Out of the whole, the student will—it is to be hoped—come to see a literature as the voice of a people, expressing their aspirations, their insights, and their sense of life's comedy and tragedy. Beyond this understanding he should develop the ability to handle difficult works: those that are, in Bacon's words, "to be chewed and digested." Unlike a subject like chemistry, however, the most advanced course in literature will not necessarily presuppose mastery of preceding courses. I can imagine that a student might do brilliantly in the Victorian novel without ever having read a line of Milton or of Chaucer. Therefore, the test of his total performance cannot rest on the final courses taken in a sequence, or for that matter on his performance on individual course examinations, which can do no more than measure his assemblage of facts and his grasp of a circumscribed area. Instead, the test should be a comprehensive examination, written or oral or both, occupying as many as 6 to 12 hours over two or more days, which will assess not only the student's storehouse of information but—what is more important—his grasp of the whole with its interrelated parts. For subjects like English and American literature, and history, such examinations can be adequately framed and reliably judged. They are given successfully in many honors programs, and are required of all A.B. candidates in some institutions.

These two illustrations from chemistry and English literature will, I hope, show the differences in two such fields, and also give substance to my suggestion that *either a program of concentration should be sequential, so that completion of the most advanced work ensures a grasp of what has preceded it, or it should be tested comprehensively and be capable of being so tested.* A so-called "major" that fails to meet either of these tests is in my judgment a dubious educational instrument.

Finally, I believe strongly that a properly conceived and framed program of concentration should be a beginning and not an end. It should be a sustaining process, and this is one of the tests of a liberal education. As someone has said, the diploma should not be the death mask of the educational experience. Education in breadth and depth, rightly conducted, should lead to further self-education in greater breadth and depth.

What I have tried to do in this chapter is to show what ought to be achieved and could be achieved, in contrast to what actually takes place in a good many four-year efforts in American colleges and universities. While I have been writing with future teachers in mind, there is clearly a need for wide reforms generally, as many critics and experts assure us; and if some of the above views were to be accepted as having validity on a wider scale in our scheme of higher education, I should not be upset.

I have three recommendations to make to the boards of trustees of colleges and universities and the state boards responsible for state colleges, for I have long been convinced that higher education is far too important to be left exclusively to professors. At the risk of incurring the everlasting hostility of the American Association of University Professors, I suggest that the time is more than ripe for lay boards to ask searching questions of the experts. These questions, needless to say, should be addressed to the faculties through the president and deans. Depending on the answers, the lay board may or may not decide to use its influence. The important point is that the questions should be of a kind to elicit from the faculties valid reasons for the present policy, for everyone who has had experience with college faculties knows how often policy is determined by compromises of different academic disciplines. The chemists will argue, for example, that so much time should be devoted to their subject, the professors of English so much to theirs. Rarely is there a *joint* examination of the content and aims of the two proposals. What emerges is a timetable in which so many semester hours are allotted to each of the contending parties.

When in doubt, a board should refrain from action, and under no conditions should it attempt to dictate the content of specific courses once authorized, or attempt to take a hand directly in the appointments of members of the staff. I recommend that:

13. *If the institution is engaged in educating teachers, the lay board trustees should ask the faculty or faculties whether in fact there is a continuing and effective all-university (or interdepartmental) approach to the education of teachers; and if not, why not.*

Only through such an approach can the requirements of the departments of instruction—which must be concerned with all students, not only future teachers—be coordinated with the particular needs of teacher education, both in general education and in programs of concentration.

14. *The board of trustees should ask the faculty to justify the present requirements for a bachelor's degree for future teachers*

with particular reference to the breadth of the requirements and to spell out what in fact are the total educational exposures (school and college) demanded now in the fields of (a) mathematics, (b) physical science, (c) biological science, (d) social science, (e) English literature, (f) English composition, (g) history, (h) philosophy.

15. *If courses are required in a foreign language, evidence of the degree of mastery obtained by fulfilling the minimum requirement for a degree should be presented to the board of trustees.*

6

THE THEORY AND
PRACTICE OF TEACHING

I NOW COME to a question many readers will have had in mind when they opened this volume: How about those courses in education? Do they deal with anything worth dealing with? A closely related query is: Why should the state require all teachers to take these courses? To this second question I have already given my reply. Without passing judgment either on courses in education or on courses in the arts and sciences, I have recommended that there be only *one state requirement* for future teachers. I would eliminate all course requirements by the state—all adding up of semester hours. I would have the competence of a future teacher tested by practice teaching under conditions set by the state and subject to state supervision. Beyond that I would put the responsibility squarely on the university or college for certifying that in the opinion of the institution the young man or woman is ready to enter upon a full-time teaching responsibility. The reputation of the institution would be at stake; no longer could the faculty dodge the issue "What should we require if there were no state certification rules?" They would then be forced to face up to the question of what professional information is desirable.

In the last chapter I imagined I was advising an institution that had complete freedom to experiment, and suggested what I thought might well be the academic courses in programs for teacher training. Let me now continue my role as imaginary adviser and examine the following question: Need professors of education be involved, except in training and assessing teachers in practice-teaching centers? I have already made it plain that in the state's requirements for future teachers a threefold partnership should be involved—an educational institution, a local board, and the state.

Few if any thoughtful people have denied that the art of teaching can be developed by practice, under suitable conditions. Thus, the members of the Massachusetts Board of Education, before they established the first normal school in the United States, subscribed to the statement that "No one can entertain a doubt that there is a mastery in teaching as in every other art. Nor is it less obvious that within reasonable limits this skill and this mastery may themselves be made the subject of instruction and be communicated to others." These words were written in 1838. The question then was: What is this skill and how can one communicate it to others? This question remains the hard core of the issue.

At the outset, I think we can identify four components of the intellectual equipment that would be a prerequisite to the development of teaching skill. The first I shall call the "democratic social component." The second is an interest in the way behavior develops in groups of children and some experience of this development. A third is a sympathetic knowledge of the growth of children, by which I mean far more than physical growth, of course. A fourth might be called the principles of teaching. This last is almost equally applicable to a teacher with only one pupil (the tutor of a rich family in former times) as to a person attempting to develop an intellectual skill in a group of children.

My phrase "democratic social component" may need an explanation. To understand what I mean, we must consider everything that is involved in teaching in our elementary or secondary schools. We must constantly bear in mind that the schools in every nation have been and continue to be involved in more than imparting knowledge and developing skills. They are by no means solely public institutions for transforming unlettered children into youths who understand rational discourse and can participate in such discourse. Public schools and the teachers in those schools are charged with the responsibility of developing certain attitudes. The British educators in the nineteenth century called it building character. Many of us have spoken of the task of our public schools in educating for citizenship in a free society; more recently the phrase "social responsibility" has gained currency. In most nations and in most periods, the attitudes being developed can be characterized as conservative as contrasted with revolutionary, though in some sections of this country in some periods of our history, a revolutionary overtone has been present. Among some writers on education, radical reforming sentiments have been in the forefront of their thinking without the implication of forceful political revolution.

The progressive era of Theodore Roosevelt was one such period. Reforms of political institutions were in the air. Progressive education was clearly related to progressive politics. Therefore, it is not surprising that long before the depression John Dewey wrote, "But if one conceives that a social order different in quality and direction from the present is desirable and that schools should strive to educate with social change in view by providing individuals not complacent about what already exists and equipped with desires and abilities to assist in transforming it, quite a different method and content is indicated for educational science."

What is interesting in this quotation is the reforming spirit. But there have been changes in this spirit since Dewey wrote. One hears much less in the 1960s than one heard in the 1920s about the need for social change. The great depression, the rise of totalitarianism in Italy, Germany, Japan, and Russia, followed by World War II, were all undreamed of when John Dewey wrote—not to mention hydrogen bombs, electronic computers, and space travel! Yet in spite of the truly revolutionary changes in the last quarter of a century, we all adhere to what was fundamental in the point of view of the reformers. Many today may repudiate the progressive plea for social change; but no one thinks of repudiating the premises on which this plea was based. Our social and political structure rests on an assumption that is no less than the belief that each successive generation in the United States, through the democratic process, will shape to some degree the social order. Liberals and reactionaries alike must agree that we need to develop future citizens whose actions will assure the survival of our *free* society. Call it education for citizenship or developing loyalty to the American way of life, twist it to the right or to the left—within wide limits the postulate remains.

Communists and fascists, of course, would not accept our postulate; they do not wish the survival of our open, free society. They wish, each in their own way, to construct a closed system in every nation. To insure our future, we must educate the voters of tomorrow, in whose hands vast power is placed. There is no need for such education in the Soviet system; there was no place for it in Germany in the Nazi period. Under a totalitarian regime, the citizens do not participate in the process of government; this fact simplifies certain phases of the educational process, for it enables dogmatism to replace free inquiry and purposeful discussion.

Today in free European nations, thoughtful people recoiling from the horrors of the totalitarian past are ready to admit that teachers cannot avoid having an attitude toward certain social and political fundamentals. Many Europeans are asking what we have done and are doing about teaching "democracy" in our schools and how our belief in the validity of the democratic process has affected the education of our teachers. They want to know how we seek to develop the attitude toward pupils as future citizens that I have called the democratic social component of a teacher's intellectual and emotional equipment.

The second of my four components, which has to do with the development of behavior in groups of children, is not unrelated to the first. A concern with the values inherent in a "democratic social system" has intruded itself into questions that some social scientists might say should involve only predictive generalizations based on observation or experience. At all events, *a teacher must know something about the processes by which social behavior emerges in groups of children.* Technically one ought to be able to study this process dispassionately as a problem in social psychology. In fact, however, it has proved incredibly difficult to separate this question from one of another type: "What kind of social behavior do we wish to develop?"

My third and fourth components, a knowledge of the growth of children and the principles of teaching, emerge most clearly if one notes what good schoolteachers do. Let me ask you to run through a list of such "doings." First of all, obviously the teacher disseminates information, and it goes without saying that this information should be accurate and significant. In this respect the elementary or secondary school teacher is no different from the college or university teacher, and the sources of information for both are courses in general education, school and college; courses in specialized fields; and independent study. It is not the responsibility of the professors of education to provide this information.

But the elementary teacher, and to a lesser extent the secondary teacher, must select and organize materials without the guidelines marked by university research fields; that is, he teaches "science" not "qualitative analysis," "social studies" not "history of England in the seventeenth century." Moreover, the information must be presented in a form understandable by the very young; the conceptual and verbal skill of the educated adult cannot be assumed.

The public school teacher is also expected to adjust his methods of instruction to a student group that is highly heterogeneous with respect to intellectual ability, motivation, and previous educational achievement. This means that he must select from a wide range of instructional materials those most suited to the intellectual maturity of each youngster, and this maturity may vary as much as two or three years in normal development. Where attempts are made to group children for instruction in terms of ability or achievement, the teacher may be asked to determine the group in which a particular child best fits.

The child enters the elementary school largely unsocialized, since he has had little prior opportunity to develop the simple habits on which group activity depends. While the university teacher need only *enforce* habits of restraint at least partially built before, the elementary teacher starts almost from scratch, though of course the parents are engaged simultaneously in the same task. The maintenance of discipline among the very young is therefore quite a different problem from that faced by the college teachers, and somewhat different from that of the secondary school teacher.

Moreover, few elementary or high school students have yet developed a continuing interest in any field of study. The initial development of such interests is a different task from that of providing further information to one whose interest is already aroused. And the usual elementary or secondary school student has not yet faced the necessity of choosing a vocation, which serves as a motive for more mature people.

Furthermore, the elementary and the secondary teachers must report to parents who are concerned not only with what information the child has learned but also with his progress toward socialization and with his physical and mental health. Although college deans occasionally encounter an irate parent, the insulated college professor usually knows only the anxiety and concern with which he as a parent confronts the teacher of his own children. Public school teachers, on the other hand, must know their students well.

Finally, in his contacts with parents and other patrons, the public school teacher is expected to interpret the school's efforts, to defend its program from unwarranted pressure and criticism, and to plan for curriculum changes dictated by new social conditions or new developments in the realm of knowledge. Typically he spends many hours in curriculum meetings, in policy meetings, and in case conferences concerning particular students.

From what I have written, I hope it is quite clear why I have spoken of the first two components of a teacher's equipment—the democratic social component and the concern with group behavior. I hope the meaning of my other two components—a knowledge of the growth of children and the principles of teaching—is also clear. Included in these latter two components is the necessity for understanding the processes of individual motivation (including the response of a child to his environment) and for knowing the specific ways a teacher should act to evoke from a pupil the maximum reponse.

Having identified four components of a teacher's intellectual and emotional equipment, I would like to consider a question pertaining to them that has been much debated: Is there a science of education? Whether or not the behavior of man as an individual or in a group can be studied scientifically has been discussed for more than a hundred years. The modern way of starting the argument is to ask whether the social sciences are fundamentally different from the natural sciences. My own answer is that there is no basic difference *provided* one limits the discussion to predictive generalizations based on observation and experiment.

In order to clarify this limitation, perhaps it will be useful to consider the relation of science to certain other practical arts.

There are many examples of the changes wrought in a practical art or craft by the introduction of concepts and generalizations developed in a natural science. The transformation of metal making during the period 1750–1850 by the introduction of ideas and methods from what was then the new chemistry is one example. The tremendous alterations in the diagnostic and remedial practices of the physician in the last fifty years is another. As a consequence, today the future doctor must spend a vast amount of time studying chemistry, physics, and the various branches of biology before he tackles subjects that for generations were the starting points in a medical education—human anatomy and materia medica (now altered beyond recognition).

The ancient practical arts of glassmaking, farming, and brewing have all been affected by advances in the natural sciences. Yet even today many procedures are still unrelated to scientific generalizations. Like the recipes of former times, they are based on the practical experience of skilled artisans. The same is true in medicine and surgery. We can say that practice has been modified by the introduction of theory. Or we can say we have displaced some of the predictions based on trial and error by predictions logically derived from wide scientific generalizations. And the width of the scientific predictive generalization is a measure of the advance of the science in question.

It is easy to demonstrate that scientific generalizations have a bearing on the day-to-day work of the physician or surgeon. It is far more difficult to demonstrate a similar relevance in the case of the teacher. Perhaps this is why the effort still persists in some quarters to talk in terms of developing a science of education. But there are necessarily complications involved in this effort. Like the man of affairs in politics or in business, the teacher is continually passing judgments as well as making predictions. Moreover, he is influencing those who will pass many judgments as adults. These judgments are a result of rational thinking, which starts from wide generalizations that for most people are taken as unexamined premises, some would say self-evident principles. These are the ethical principles, the moral principles, the religious principles to which so many turn to start a chain of reasoning that results in a decision to act, including the action we call passing judgment. We are thus faced with the need to treat both the disciplines that yield predictive generalizations and those that are useful where value judgments enter. In practical situations, like teaching, the two are never separable.

There is a long history of the interplay, even in the development of the natural sciences, between what may be called the deductive-theoretical approach and the inductive-empirical. Particularly in biology the influence of German philosophers was strongly on the side of the deductive-theoretical approach during the first half of the nineteenth century. One started with a wide generalization, not unrelated to theology, about the nature of the universe and then deduced specific consequences—which, it was hoped, could be correlated with observations. In relation to the study of man, those who favor the deductive-theoretical approach tend to dismiss modern educational research as trivial because it is too empirical. Which is to say, its generalizations are too narrow and are unconnected. Many proponents of the deductive-theoretical approach have considered that it is impossible to create a science of human behavior in the sense that there is a science of physiology, for example. In the field of politics, the writings of the great authors are examples of philosophical discussions of human problems; wide premises— moral, legal, and political—are examined, and their logical consequences are carefully scrutinized in the light of commonsense knowledge of human beings. Though philosophy, history, and political science have in recent years sought to analyze and explain, rather than to prescribe the "best" action, they remain largely concerned with principles that have been arrived at by the deductive-theoretical approach.

When logical arguments rest on wide premises, it is important to me to note whether those premises are part of our culture or whether they refer to predictive generalizations based on observation. There is surely a difference between examining an argument that starts with the proposition "No man shall enslave another" and examining one that stems from the principle that acids are neutralized by bases. At least this is true as a practical matter. It is beyond the scope of this study to pursue the question of the ultimate validity of ethical and legal principles.

Since I shall have occasion to refer again to the distinction between the wide premises of our culture and the predictive generalizations that have significance for education, let us look at an illustration that emphasizes the importance of this distinction. When a physician says to himself, "I ought to prescribe a certain treatment," he has in mind both his obligation under the Hippocratic oath and his knowledge of modern science. The first embodies the ancient ethical code of his profession: he must endeavor to cure. The second is composed of predictive generalizations in part based on experience but today largely based on the generalizations of branches of chemistry and biology (biochemistry, pharmaceutical chemistry, and bacteriology). The first, the ethical principle, has remained constant over the centuries; the second has changed rapidly in the last few decades. The physician who attended George Washington in his fatal illness of a throat infection felt that he ought to bleed the patient for two reasons. First, he was bound by the Hippocratic oath to do his best to cure the patient; and second, he believed with many of his fellow practitioners that if he bled the patient, his condition would improve. We continue to accept the line of argument that justifies the ethical principle, but we are confident the predictive generalization was an error.

Teachers, like physicians, think in terms of predictive generalizations as well as arguments derived from general principles. Some people would like to combine these two modes of thought and speak of a single, all-embracing science of education. The question is whether it is useful to try to cover with the word "science" a vast field of human activity directed toward practical ends. I have come to the conclusion that it is not. Perhaps it is only a question of terminology. However, I prefer not to speak of the science of engineering but of the engineering sciences. I doubt that there is or ever will be a science of medicine, yet I am sure enormous strides forward have been made in the medical sciences. Therefore, I think it would be better to discuss the academic disciplines that have relevance for the labors of the teacher than to try to talk in terms of a developing science of education. In other words, I shall examine academic disciplines—which might be called educational sciences or educational disciplines—rather than the science or the discipline of education.

What science or sciences can offer generalizations to supplement the practical wisdom of the practitioner in each of the four components I have named? Turning first to the democratic-social component, it must be borne in mind that—once it is granted that building the "democratic social component" is a function of our schools—the school becomes the object of a power struggle among groups advocating competing views of the good society. Much of the history of American education may be regarded as a history of this struggle. School people are under incessant pressure from ideological, economic, political, and other social groups to mold the schools in their interests. An understanding of the values of such groups as they bear on educational practice seems an important part of the equipment with which teachers should be provided. Skill in the analysis of propositions used in these debates is also of value. To develop this understanding and skill—rather than, as is too often attempted, to produce by indoctrination partisans of a particular point of view—should be the aim of the college or university. If I can rely on the complaints I have often heard expressed, professors of education spend too much time mouthing platitudes about what a "democratic education" ought to be and too little time teaching their students to understand, analyze, and criticize the functions that various competing social groups (including educators) would impose on the schools as conditions of "democratic" education. In short, the historian, the political scientist, and the philosopher may have much to say to the future teacher, some of which is based on the tacit acceptance of ethical principles and some on predictive generalizations based on observation and experimentation.

With respect to the second component—understanding the social behavior of groups of children, that is, children's collective behavior—historians and philosophers have been the traditional source of general statements alleged to be of value. Today, contributions come from sociologists, anthropologists, and social psychologists. The same is true, with more emphasis on psychologists, when we examine the theoretical basis for my third and fourth areas of competence: the growth of children and the principles of teaching. History, philosophy, political science, anthropology, sociology, and psychology are, then, academic disciplines that have something to say to future teachers.

The question that will come up time and again in these pages is: Can these academic disciplines really add anything to what an apprentice teacher can learn on the job from a first-rate teacher *under favorable circumstances?* No one is ready to dispense with the apprentice-master relationship that is illustrated by practice teaching and that I myself have already emphasized. The arguments turn on whether a middleman is needed, so to speak, between the professors of the relevant philosophical and scientific fields and the master teacher and his apprentice. I believe that the role of the professors of education in the undergraduate training of teachers is, at its best, that of an intermediary to bridge the ravine that separates theory and practice. If this is true, then the professors of educational philosophy, educational history, educational sociology, and educational psychology should be professors of philosophy, history, sociology and psychology who have a commitment to the public schools and their improvement.

The analogy with a biochemist in a medical school may be helpful in explaining what I mean. Because he is a member of a medical faculty, the biochemist's investigation will in one way or another be directed toward increasing that corpus of knowledge known as modern medicine. Because the generalizations of biochemistry pertain to the preparation of physicians and surgeons, the professor gives a course required of all medical students. These students, be it noted, will already have absorbed much knowledge of chemistry and biology (including some biochemistry) before entering into the study of medicine. They will all eventually, in their resident work in a hospital, enter into an apprentice-master relation with an experienced and skillful physician or surgeon. The professors in the preclinical subjects in medical school today are intermediaries between the sciences and the practice of medicine. Biochemistry, physiology, bacteriology, and pharmacology are intermediate disciplines. What is presented in the lectures and examined in the laboratories by the students has been constantly changing in this century because the professors have been in close touch with both the basic sciences and the needs of the practitioner.

The analysis I have presented of the relation of the social sciences to the education of teachers is by no means widely accepted. Objections will be raised to my presentation from two sides. First, there will be certain professors of education who wish to consider the educational process as a whole. If I read their writings correctly, my identification of components of a teacher's preparation would be unacceptable; also they might dissent from my distinction between wide premises of a cultural pattern and predictive generalizations based on observation and experiment. Such educators appear to start from a well-developed theory of education comparable, it is believed, to a theory in a natural science. The theory involves a set of generalized statements concerning "what we know about children, learning, and American culture," from which, by a process of deductive reasoning, various conclusions about curricula, school organization, and instructional processes appear to follow. The future teacher, it is assumed, can discover the elements of the theory in what are called laboratory experiences. That is to say, practice teaching is to be regarded as an opportunity "to implement theory—both to study the pragmatic value of the theory and to check with the student his understanding of the theory in application."[1]

Another group of professors (few of whom would be professors of education) might well challenge my assumption that intermediary professors are needed. Let the future teacher study the "educational sciences" in courses in which little or no attention is paid to school problems; then, equipped with this background, let him enter into a program of practice teaching—so some would say!

The advantage I would claim for my way of considering the formal education of teachers is that it enables one to answer the question raised as to the need of an intermediary, discipline by discipline. To be sure, if the general education of the future teacher is well arranged (meaning, of course, as I suggest!), helpful philosophical, political, and historical insights will be supplied by professors of philosophy, political science, and history. I assume that such professors are both reasonably informed about the schools and concerned with the bearing of their discipline on educational problems. I must say, however, that this assumption is not yet met by many of these professors.

Since, for the purposes of general education, these professors can give very limited attention to the more specialized interests of those

[1] From *School and Community Laboratory Experiences in Teacher Education*, American Association of Teachers Colleges, Committee on Standards and Surveys, published by the Association, Oneonta, N.Y., 1948.

who work in the schools, it does seem desirable for teachers to have one course taught by a professor trained as an historian, philosopher, or political scientist who has made the study of education a major interest. Such a professor is the intermediary or middleman. Sociology, anthropology, and psychology in the not too distant past were presented from a philosophical or primarily theoretical-deductive point of view; today the possibility of predictive generalizations based on observation and experiment looms on the horizon. From my appraisal of this possibility, I find an important role for the professor of educational psychology, and a somewhat less important role for the professor of educational sociology as apart from the professor of sociology.

LET US LOOK, now, at what seems to be the subject matter of the education courses that are at present required by law in all states in the union. When I began this study in September, 1961, I said more than once that I hoped I could divest myself of all my accumulated prejudices about the education of teachers except two. These were: first, that all future teachers, grades K–12, should have graduated from high school; and second, that before entering on their careers they should have taught under skillful supervision in a school. How many years should intervene between the two events and what should happen during those years was the subject of my inquiry. As the reader will have surmised by now, I have to report that almost the only characteristics common to all the institutions I have visited are exactly those that correspond to my two initial prejudices. On the variation in exposure to academic subjects I need not elaborate further. But aside from the specification of a certain number of semester hours of courses labeled education, I have found as little consensus among professors of education as among academic professors.

The minimum amount of time devoted to the professional sequence is determined by state law at present. The actual amount is far from constant throughout the United States, though I might risk the generalization that, with few exceptions, more time is devoted to the professional sequence in single-purpose state colleges than in universities, and more in both than in four-year multipurpose private colleges.

There do seem to be a few constants in professional education programs. All the programs I have examined include a study of educational psychology, at least one course in methods, and one course that treats historically or philosophically the relation of the school to society. In every institution some practice teaching is specified. But here the uniformity ends. Even in the area of practice teaching, great diversity is found in the actual provision for students. The number of clock hours of practice teaching differs from institution to institution. The minimum requirement I encountered was 90, the maximum 300. The translation of such teaching experience into academic bookkeeping is most confusing. One college, which specifies 110 clock hours, allots the same number of semester hours' credit as another, which requires 220. Therefore, when I report a range in the time devoted to practice teaching for secondary teachers from 4 to 11 semester hours, I have hardly recorded anything of quantitative significance even as a first approximation.

In an earlier[1] study of the education course requirements in 294 institutions, the range for elementary teachers was 18 to 69 semester hours, for secondary teachers 10 to 51 semester hours. In the institutions on which I have centered attention the corresponding ranges were 26 to 59 and 17 to 30. With such variation, the value of the median, of course, has no significance, though one often finds it quoted in surveys of teacher education.

As a matter of fact, the situation is even more confusing than the figures I have quoted indicate. There is a shadowy area, particularly in the program of future elementary teachers, where a course might be classified as an education course, or in an academic field of concentration, or in general education. Even in the training of secondary school teachers ambiguities in reporting can easily arise. For example, I visited a state college that announces only 15 semester hours devoted to education courses, but a careful examination of the catalogs reveals that the time devoted to practice teaching is not included. If it and several other courses my colleagues considered as "really education courses" were included, the figure is not 15 but 30 semester hours. Another complication arises

[1] *Summary of Requirements in Teacher Education Curricula Offered by Institutions Accredited by NCATE,* 1958, Washington, D.C.

from the fact that all or almost all institutions require a special methods course which may or may not involve a considerable amount of study of the subject to be taught.

One more variable is of some significance, and that is the stage at which the professional program begins. Here, I might hazard the generalization that the professional sequence is more likely to start as early as the sophomore year in single-purpose state colleges than in either universities or private colleges. However, there are exceptions to this generalization, and one of the many controversial issues among professors of education is when a future elementary or secondary teacher should be "introduced to the profession" and how. Students and teachers with whom I have talked likewise differ in their judgment as to when in the college course a future teacher should begin to have some inkling of what the career of a school teacher is really like.

In the majority of large institutions—large in terms of the number of graduates preparing to teach—the first professional course is taken in the junior year. Equally in dispute is how early in the college work a student should be exposed to some experiences in a classroom or with a child or children. I can think of a number of well-known institutions that place considerable emphasis on the importance of introducing the student to these experiences in the *first professional course,* so the student may come to understand something about the classroom by observation and something about the behavior of a child or children. On the other hand, I could identify many institutions where no such opportunities are provided until the second or third course of the sequence of professional courses. Often, but by no means always, there is a difference in respect to the point I have just raised between the program for future elementary teachers and that for future secondary teachers.

In the majority of the institutions I visited, the future teacher starts his or her sequence of professional courses by taking the same introductory courses irrespective of whether the eventual goal is to teach in an elementary or a secondary school. Sometimes the first course is a course in educational psychology, usually requiring as a prerequisite a course in general psychology; but often it is of the type I shall describe as "eclectic." Frequently the type I describe as "eclectic" carries the label "foundations of education."

Those in charge of these foundations courses often attempt to patch together scraps of history, philosophy, political theory, sociology, and pedagogical ideology. The professors are frequently not well trained in any one of the parent disciplines; certainly very few have such mastery of all the disciplines as to be able to talk about them except at a most superficial level. They are far from being the kind of intermediary or middleman professor I described a few pages back. Occasionally, to be sure, one encounters a mature scholar who has ranged so broadly and so deeply over the fields of philosophy and social science that he can organize data from many fields to give his students a clear and exciting picture of the relationships between formal schooling and other cultural patterns. If an institution has one of these rare scholars, it might wisely encourage him to offer a social foundations course. In general, however, I would advise the elimination of such eclectic courses, for not only are they usually worthless, but they give education departments a bad name. I have rarely talked with students or school teachers who had good words to say for an eclectic foundations course. Perhaps the kindest word used to describe most of these courses was "pathetic."

As an example of such an eclectic course I might cite a course entitled "American Foundations" in a large private metropolitan university. The course is described in the prospectus as follows:

> An introduction to the professional sequence. A field of study in which the student becomes acquainted with the development of the contemporary school; with the teaching profession, its opportunities, requirements, and expectations; with the beliefs and aspirations of our people as they apply to the school and other agencies; and with the fundamental problems in American education. The historical development of ideas, events, and laws are reviewed in relation to the organization, purpose, and program of today's school. Satisfies requirements for (1) American Public Education, and (2) Philosophy of Education. 4 semester hours.

One characteristic of this course and of similar courses with which I have become familiar is the very impressive list of reference books. In this particular course no fewer than 23 titles are listed under the heading "Personalities, Ideas, and Events"; the titles range from Ulich's *History of Educational Thought* to Rugg's *Foundations for American Culture*. In the third section of the course, which is entitled "Purposes of the School in Our Society," the suggested reading runs to 34 titles ranging from Counts' *Education and American Civilization* to Caswell & Foshay's *Education in the Elementary School*. Such lists are impressive indeed, but in the institutions I visited I found on inquiry that only one copy of each suggested book was available, and not by any conceivable stretch of the imagination would a student find time to read even two or three of the books listed for each section. It must be remembered that such a course is, as a rule, a one-semester course carrying three semester hours of credit.

Another sample of an eclectic course is one entitled "Introduction to Teaching" at a well-known state university. This course is even more of a potpourri, since bits of educational psychology and references to the literature on instructional methods have been stewed in. The 18 main headings of the outline of the course, each of which has two or three subheadings, will indicate the range of material covered:

1. The Challenge of Being a Teacher
2. Planning a Career in Education
3. Competencies and Certification Standards for Educators
4. Preparation for Teaching
5. Opportunities in Teaching
6. School and Community Responsibilities of Teachers
7. Learning to Guide the Growth of Pupils
8. Professional Organizations and Publications
9. Salaries of Teachers
10. Other Economic Benefits
11. Historical Development of Our Schools
12. The Development of Modern Concepts of Education
13. Community Aspects of Education
14. Purposes of Education in American Democracy
15. Problems, Issues, and Inservice Professional Growth
16. Organization and Administration of Schools
17. Financing our Schools
18. Moving Ahead

I have found little evidence that these courses stimulate a student to read either deeply or widely. Quite the contrary. The classes I have visited are far too reminiscent of the less satisfactory high school classes I have seen. The course is dominated by a textbook or a syllabus, and the instruction seems to be wedded to the dogma that a discussion must take place whether the talk is lively or the class is bored. The pace and the intellectual level seemed geared to students far less able than those in the top 30 per cent group from which we should recruit our teachers.

The eclectic courses may be said to be a conglomeration of bits of the history of American education, the philosophy of education, educational sociology, the economics and politics of the school, together with an introduction to education as a profession as well as a glimpse at the application of psychological phraseology in the observation and teaching of children. From the point of view of education, I see no reason for the existence of these courses. One suspects that they exist to meet (on paper) state requirements! Since virtually every state has differing course titles and descriptions in their requirements, one must respect the versatility of the professors of education in designing courses that they can reasonably argue meet these diversely defined requirements. I have found the type of foundations course I have described being given in institutions approved by NCATE. *I consider the existence of such courses, which is encouraged by the present certification requirements and accreditation practices, one of the arguments for the reforms I have recommended.*

Courses in the philosophy, history, or sociology of education are, unlike "eclectic" courses, intended to apply the disciplines of specific academic areas to education. But these, too, may be of limited value; the crucial question is how they are taught and by whom.

The word philosophy, as used by many professors of education, is like a thin sheet of rubber—it can be distorted and stretched to cover almost any aspect of a teacher's interest. Under the best conditions, it seems to me a course in the philosophy of education would legitimately presuppose that the students had been exposed to the basic issues of epistemology, ontology, and ethics in an introductory philosophy course required of all teachers as part of their general requirements. Such a course would not, however, have addressed itself to the problems of education. In the philosophy of education course a well-trained philosopher should turn his, and his students', attention to the problems, the language, the assumptions, and the value premises that enter into educational theory and practice. Using the new tools of the logical analysts, and demonstrating by his own behavior the philosophic impulses for comprehensiveness and clarity, the professor of the philosophy of education should train his students to think clearly and critically about educational issues, including those raised by the psychologists, other professional educators, and informed laymen. Occasionally one finds a course in philosophy of education so taught. Far more often one finds that it represents little more than the professor's attempt to indoctrinate the student with his own educational values, or to make the student vaguely familiar with the views of eminent men who have written about education, a few of whom may have sought to put their views into practice. Even if one assumes that it is important to know what these people have written about education, I doubt that the students have time to gain an understanding and appreciation of the material presented. What is most likely to be the consequence is a superficial knowledge. The same criticism may be made of some of the courses in the history of education: those that in fact, are more in the nature of histories of educational theories or philosophies.

The worst type of philosophy of education course I have encountered is one that attempts to combine a survey of a few well-known philosophies with an analysis of problems in a school. One textbook—the worst I have seen—attempts to give the student an understanding of such words as realism, scholasticism, and pragmatism by a paragraph each in the appendix. As my suggestion of a program in general education makes evident, I believe it is important for a teacher to have some appreciation of the way philosophers have tackled the problems that come under the headings of epistemology and ontology. But I am very certain that a glib attempt to summarize certain philosophers' views can only leave the future teacher with the most dangerous of misunderstandings: that he knows what he is talking about when, in fact, he does not. There are exceptions to my general condemnation of courses in the philosophy of education. Some are given by the type of person I have called an intermediary. If I were participating in faculty appointments in an institution that certifies future teachers, I should do all in my power to see to it that all who gave courses in the philosophy of education were approved by the philosophy department as well as the department or faculty of education. *Graduate schools of education should cease trying to train professors of the philosophy of education without the active and responsible participation of the departments of philosophy.* The latter should move into this field as fast as possible, though they have been unwilling to do so in the past. Well-trained philosophers who turn their attention to problems of American education have an opportunity to make a real contribution to overhauling the philosophic foundations of education, which today consist of crumbling pillars of the past placed on a sand of ignorance and pretension.

The future teacher, as I have said, would do well to study philosophy under a real philosopher. An additional course in the philosophy of education would be desirable but not essential. The same is true of a course in the history of education. Again, the professor should be an intermediary or middleman; he should be approved by a department of education and a department of history or an outside committee containing eminent historians. The explanation of the history of the schools of the United States under the guidance of a first-rate American historian would be a valuable experience for any teacher. It would strengthen his understanding of the political basis of our educational system and relate what he should have learned in his American history courses to his own professional work. Some of the material presented might be considered sociological rather than historical. If a competent sociologist is investigating social problems closely related to the schools and is ready to give a course in educational sociology, the desirability of such a course is evident. As to whether the present group of professors who consider themselves educational sociologists should perpetuate themselves, I have the gravest doubts. I would wish that all who claim to be working in sociology would get together in the graduate training and appointment of professors who claim to use sociological methods in discussing school and youth problems.

The discipline of psychology is, as I have indicated, more closely related to the work of the teacher than are philosophy, history, and sociology. As one would therefore expect, every teacher-training institution with which I am familiar includes in the program a course in educational psychology (under one name or another). In addition, a few institutions require a course in general psychology. Advanced courses in various branches of educational psychology given in summer schools are popular among teachers and are often included in graduate programs.

Many laymen and professors of academic subjects are skeptical about psychology. Those who disparage the subject can easily produce examples of trivial and even inane statements in textbooks of psychology and in particular of educational psychology. But the harsh critic must remember that in this century the word "psychology" has come to cover a vast field of knowledge. Furthermore, unlike the fields of chemistry, physics, or biology, there is relatively little separation between "pure science" and "applied science." The reason is clear. "Pure chemistry" could be defined, at least in the nineteenth century, as systematized knowledge (including wide generalizations) applicable to procedures in a laboratory. Without specifically so restricting the definition, this meant procedures dealing with relatively small amounts of homogeneous material. Applied chemistry, on the other hand, was concerned with practical operations like sugar purification, beermaking, or even the manufacture of large quantities of chemicals like sulphuric acid, soda, and quicklime. Because the materials were never homogeneous, there were many limitations to the applications of "pure chemistry" to applied chemistry.

The contrast with psychology is striking. From the beginnings right down to the present day, the applications were in the forefront. Teachers, for example, have been eager each generation to avail themselves of what psychologists were claiming as new knowledge of the human brain and its workings. Professor Boring, in his history of psychology, has written, "The most important and greatest puzzle which every man faces is himself, and, secondly, other persons." What over the years different schools of psychology have presented to the public has been "the key to the mystery, a key fashioned in the scientific laboratory and easy to use."

In a sense one might define psychology as the search for the key to the mystery every man faces—"a key easy to use." Philosophical speculation and religious dogma still provide for many persons a satisfactory key to the puzzle every man faces. Thus, even in the mid-twentieth century, psychology is bounded on one side by metaphysics. It is bounded on a second side by anatomy and physiology, and on a third side by the vast domain of commonsense generalizations about human nature. These are for the most part highly limited and unsystematized generalizations, which are the stock in trade of everyday life for all sane people. But from these generalizations a science is slowly emerging that enables us to predict to some degree the future behavior of an individual from a knowledge of the past. If one defines psychology as the area within the triangle I have just outlined, it is clear that much depends on whether one approaches the subject as a philosopher, a neurophysiologist, or a practical man concerned with human nature—an advertiser, for example, or above all an educator. If one examines the texts in general psychology used in introductory college courses, one will find material that can be classified in terms of the triangle I have drawn, though the triangle is far from equilateral; the metaphysical side is apt to be quite short! The amount of space devoted to physiological psychology—sense perception, brain construction, and nerve action—will vary with the author. But this aspect of the subject is certain to be emphasized far more in texts on general psychology than in those on educational psychology. The material in the latter falls under four major headings: growth and development, learning, personality adjustment, and evaluation.[1] In terms of my triangle, the line representing common sense marks the boundary between educational psychology and the art of teaching.

My own classification of the psychological material I have seen treated in different courses would be as follows: individual differences, child growth and development, tests and measurements (evaluation), adolescent psychology, mental health and abnormal psychology, learning theory, results of animal experimentation (Pavlov's dogs, Thorndike's cats, Kohler's apes, Skinner's pigeons),

---

[1] Hendrickson and Blair reported on 13 books which were far from uniform in *Encyclopedia of Educational Research*, W. S. Monroe, ed., a product of the American Educational Research Association (page 349). The Macmillan Company, New York, 1950.

and neurophysiology. In any introductory course, an account of psychology as a science based on experiment should include, of course, considerable space devoted to the description of animal experimentation and an evaluation of the evidence thus obtained.

If those who write and read books in psychology were not always concerned with finding the "key to the mystery every man faces" and keen to use it, a good introduction to the establishment of a new science might be presented with little or no reference to human beings. As it is, most authors make the extrapolation from animal experimentation to human behavior seem so self-evident as to blur some important philosophic and methodological issues. Having had some experience with attempting to explain to students what is involved in the advances of science, I can be sympathetic with the writers of the general texts in psychology. The focus of attention, they feel, must be not only on science but also on its applications—on what the reader is going to apply tomorrow in his day-to-day dealings with people. Yet it must be demonstrated that the statements made are "scientific," which implies careful evaluation and analysis of the evidence. Furthermore, a vast range of phenomena must be considered.

The role of psychology in the education of teachers is a subject of much controversy. This is the case not only in the United States but also in other countries. In a recent report of a joint working party appointed by the British Psychological Society and the Association of Teachers in Colleges of Education (in Great Britain), the following statement occurs:

> Child centered teaching, in the sense of teaching based on a study of learning and development in the child, forms a distinctive feature of present-day education. . . .
> . . . All this involves an understanding of the pupil's processes of maturation and learning and what he is ready for in the class situation. These topics form an important part of the subject matter of educational psychology. Although classroom techniques, observations and experiments have been and are carried out in their own right, the theoretical models and languages used to account for the results of these activities are essentially psychological. It may be that educational science will evolve its own language but it is difficult to see such a language being independent of psychological terms. Cer-

tainly at the present time nearly all its terms are psychological. . . . We should make use of psychology wherever, as a theory or through its experimental results, it appears relevant to Education. . . . More specifically it should provide students with knowledge of the major aspects of child development and the nature and conditions of classroom learning; and with certain skills in the use of tests and other devices for assessing children, diagnostic procedures, case history techniques, etc. At the same time, it should provide skill in recognizing when to call in specialist help.

In another section the authors of this report point out certain difficulties and precautions. They state:

There must always be a cautious use of psychological theory, particularly when arguing by analogy. This refers particularly to some of the more speculative suggestions emanating from learning theory based on animal studies or on human learning in situations much simpler than those of the classroom. . . . The language of psychology should be taken over with the full context of its psychological use. Often this language is taken over in a slipshod way and subsequent casual usage can see it applied in situations far removed from the originator's mind. . . . A further difficulty is in securing the effective transfer of psychological knowledge to classroom circumstances; that is, in teaching the subject in such a way as to cultivate a student's psychological insight and judgment in concrete situations.

For my part, on the basis of my observations and reading of textbooks on educational psychology, I would subscribe to what the British group has written. But by no means all American professors of education (as apart from professors of educational psychology) would agree with my emphasis on the importance of a course in educational psychology as such. Those who believe in a science of education, whose attitude I described earlier, would be particularly reluctant to accept my argument. To them the interpretation of the results of research, or perhaps even the carrying out of such research, can be left to those who are trained as "educators," not as educational psychologists.

It would be my contention that the validity of principles of psychology applicable to teaching depends on whether, from these principles, one can deduce such specific predictions as "If I (as a teacher) do so and so, such and such will probably happen" or "If he (the pupil) behaves in this or that way in situation X, he will behave in a certain way in situation Y."

What is at issue here is the applicability of the research work of psychologists in this century to what goes on in the classroom. Do the writings of psychologists help the teacher in understanding children? Are there principles of child growth and development that can be demonstrated by laboratory experience—that is, in a classroom? After listening to many arguments, eliciting the opinions of many teachers, and reading some of the textbooks used in courses in education, I have come to the conclusion that there are perhaps a few principles of psychology—as well as a considerable amount of purely descriptive material—which are relevant. They are particularly relevant to the total task of teachers for the kindergarten and the first six grades. My quotation from the British report indicates what those principles are likely to comprehend.

Despite the present limitations on the scientific aspect of psychology as applied to teachers, *I have been convinced, largely by the testimony of students and teachers, that for those who teach children, psychology has much to say that is so valuable as to warrant the label "necessary," at least for elementary teachers.* I believe that research will continue that will yield generalizations sufficiently wide as to be called scientific. As an introduction to the point of view of those concerned with the behavior of animals (including man), a general course in psychology would seem essential. One would hope for close coordination between those responsible for such a general course and those who were teaching and advancing the applied science of educational psychology.

The principal complaint I have heard from undergraduate students about psychology is that there is a great deal of duplication between what is presented in the general course and what is presented in the courses in educational psychology and sometimes in the "methods courses" (which I shall discuss later). In one institution, at least, a valiant attempt is being made to coordinate the teaching of general psychology and educational psychology. In some colleges or universities, on the other hand, those who give the two types of course are barely acquainted with one another.

Except for aspects of educational psychology that deal with the

field of tests and measurements, I am doubtful about the significance of educational psychology for the teachers in a senior high
school. I venture to question the width and solidity of the so-called
scientific generalizations that some professors of education claim
are the product of research.[1] If my conclusion is at all sound, the
role of psychology in the education of future elementary teachers
should be greater than in the education of teachers for secondary
schools.

I am aware that there exists a vast body of literature concerning
the unique problems and behavioral traits of adolescents, and
stressing the fact that American culture imposes severe strains on
many young people of this age group. Any literate adult can
scarcely avoid extensive contact with this literature. But the overwhelming proportion of students found in secondary school classrooms are stable enough in their personality structure, and are capable of learning and thinking in a sufficiently adult manner, that
the classroom teacher can rely on his general education and experience in understanding them. Remember that I have recommended
a course in general psychology for all teachers. Beyond this a school
district in whose classes a disproportionate number of disturbed
youngsters are found might well provide special instruction in adolescent psychology as part of its efforts to introduce the new teachers to the problems of the schools within the district. This is particularly true of the large cities. The time for a consideration of
many psychological and sociological factors is clearly during the
first few years of a new teacher's experience.

And now I come to a red-hot question: How about those terrible
methods courses, which waste a student's time? If the reader agrees
with my recommendations about drastic changes in state control,
he will subscribe to the idea that methods courses, like all other
courses, must prove their worth in a free competition. Yet since
one type of methods course is tied closely to practice teaching, to
which I have given a key role, I must do my best to clarify a complicated situation.

For our purposes, it may be helpful to distinguish between gen-

[1] I am here discussing the preservice education of secondary school teachers.
An experienced teacher may have sufficient insight to gain much from psychological instruction that would mislead the novice.

eral methods courses and special methods courses. While all the institutions with which I am familiar required special methods courses for secondary teachers, by no means all required a general methods course. The more one is inclined to believe in a well-developed corpus of knowledge about how to teach (a science of education, if you will), the more one is ready to accept the idea of a general methods course. Yet in none of the 27 institutions whose programs I analyzed in detail was more than one course (3 semester hours) required.

The general methods course assumes the existence of a body of predictive generalizations valid wherever a teaching-learning situation exists. It follows from this assumption that these generalizations are not dependent on variables inhering in the specific material to be taught, or on the characteristics of a particular body of students. That is to say, the material offered is assumed to be equally relevant to history, French, mathematics, and all other subjects. I fail to see where such generalizations would differ from those developed by psychologists concerned with the study of classroom learning, and taught in the general psychology course or in a basic course in educational psychology. I conclude, therefore, that such general methods courses are unnecessary and duplicate material already studied.

My judgment of special courses in the use of particular instructional techniques (e.g., audio-visual methods) is equally negative, though for different reasons. The techniques involved in such courses are likely, given the rapid advance of technology, to become quickly obsolete. And, fortunately, they can also be rather quickly learned by one who so desires. While it is useful for teachers to know the techniques and the instructional material available for use with these techniques, this material is highly specific, subject by subject, grade by grade. It seems to me, therefore, that the methods and materials can best be presented in the context of special methods instruction, which accompanies and is closely related to the actual practice-teaching situation. The expert in audio-visual methods should be available to the student who, with a specific instructional unit in mind, asks what material is available and what techniques for presenting it are recommended.

Those who maintain that a knowledge of the subject matter is both the necessary and the sufficient basis of teacher preparation have no patience with even the special methods courses. They believe that the professors of "how to teach" should be replaced by scholars from the academic fields. I know of no one who would now deny that knowledge of the field to be taught is necessary, and I note an increasing desire on the part of the professors of education to involve advanced university scholars in the analysis of curriculum and instruction in the elementary and secondary schools. But they argue, and I think wisely, that the knowledge of such experts is not sufficient. Let us test the argument with respect to a concrete problem.

Take for example the case of a distinguished physicist who comes to the conclusion that much should be done to improve the teaching of the basic principles of physics in the lower schools. He first turns, naturally, to an analysis of content in the elementary and secondary school science course that might appropriately be called physics. He should also, I think, turn to his discipline to identify the roots that he thinks should be learned by a young person starting toward a mastery of the field, so that he could say, in effect, "Here are the fundamental principles, ideas, or concepts on which physics is based, or which make up the discipline of physics, stated in the simplest form in which I can accurately define them." He might very well go on to say that these ideas should follow each other in a certain sequence.

But when one turns to the actual planning and teaching of the science course for, let us say, the fifth grade, new questions arise, which the physicist, as such, is not prepared to answer. One must ask, for example, if a given concept is too difficult to be easily mastered by a typical youngster in the fifth grade or too simple to provide a challenge for the bright youngster of that age. Here the judgment of the psychologist and the experienced teacher, who have studied and worked closely with students of this age group, must be brought in to supplement that of the physicist. If questions of vocabulary come up, again those who know the vocabulary level of the students must be heard. Moreover, since the science course is concerned with the root ideas of chemistry, biology, geology, etc., as well as physics, experts in these fields must be consulted. The market is flooded with science material—some good, some terrible; some tested, some not; some known to the university physicist, some not—from among which the elementary teacher, with too little time for a careful analysis, must select that to be used. He needs the advice of someone well acquainted with these materials.

But other problems confront the elementary or secondary school teacher, concerning which the university physicist, as such, is not prepared to give advice. He is accustomed to working with mature adults, usually of better than average intelligence; his students have developed a reasonably long attention span and have had at least sufficient motivation to elect the program in which his course is taught; and he, or his university, can expel those who don't achieve or who create intolerable discipline problems. These conditions do not exist on the elementary school level; they exist only with qualifications on the secondary level. Disciplining the attention and the energies of an overactive ten-year-old, or a rebellious adolescent held in school against his will, is simply not the same as lecturing to college seniors. The psychologists may give some clues, but the greatest assistance is apt to come from someone with long and successful experience in the kind of situation the new teacher actually faces.

We are, then, led to the logically sound, but logistically impossible, position that a panel of specialists—physicists, chemists, psychologists, audio-visual technicians, and experienced teachers—should stand at the shoulder of each new teacher planning and teaching the course in elementary science. The same line of argument could be developed with respect to the teaching of social studies, the language arts, and other fields. But it is impossible to amass such a panel to support every student being prepared to teach. The most realistic alternative that has come to my attention is the "clinical professor of education," prepared by training to understand what the other specialists have to say, and inclined to listen to them, and prepared by continuing experience in the elementary or secondary school to demonstrate in concrete teaching situations the implications of expert judgment. At the moment the potential teacher most needs all the useful knowledge he can get; that is, *when the teacher actually begins to teach,* the clinical professor must make that knowledge available through the special methods course. If my recommendation in Chapter 4 is accepted, this would be done in connection with fulfilling the certification procedure required by the state.

It is difficult to describe in a few words to the lay reader the role of methods courses in the preparation of elementary teachers. My conclusions about the proper way of combining theory and practice are presented in the next chapter. For those who do not wish to examine the subject in as much detail as is requisite in presenting a complete plan, let me make here only one remark. The usual criticism of those colleges that started as normal schools is that they devote too much time to methods courses. To a certain extent this is true; in the training of secondary school teachers, for instance, many of these colleges still require a course in general methods as well as one in special methods. My criticism of the education of elementary teachers, on the other hand, would be that far too often too little time is devoted to the right kind of methods course, though time may be wasted on courses in which practice and theory are not sufficiently combined.

On the basis of all these considerations of specific educational courses as they are now being taught, the basis of what my colleagues and I have seen, heard, and read, I can only reach one conclusion: *Professors of education have not yet discovered or agreed upon a common body of knowledge that they all feel should be held by school teachers before the student takes his first full-time job.* To put it another way, I find no reason to believe that students who have completed the sequence of courses in education in one college or university have considered the same, or even a similar, set of facts or principles as their contemporaries in another institution even in the same state.

Far from reflecting unfavorably upon the professors of education, their inability to reach consensus concerning the material to be universally required might be considered, by a friendly critic, an indication of their respect for evidence. They are well aware that to date there simply is no conclusive research proving beyond reasonable doubt the superiority of one pattern of teacher education (including general education and areas of specialization) over another.[1] Given this lack of evidence and consensus, one can only

[1] In preparing this chapter I have benefited from reading a chapter on "The Role of the Teacher in School Learning" from Prof. John Carroll's forthcom-

conclude that the time has not yet come when the educational sciences can play the same role in training teachers as the medical sciences do in training doctors. To me the conclusion (with which many professors of education agree) points clearly to the need for giving institutions freedom to experiment with different ways of training teachers. Except for practice teaching and the special methods work combined with it, I see no rational basis for a state prescription of the time to be devoted to education courses, whether or not an attempt is made to specify the content. I see even less excuse for prescription by a voluntary accrediting agency whose decisions become in one way or another assimilated by a state authority.

As we have seen, the one indisputably essential element in professional education is practice teaching. The professor of education who is to supervise this practice teaching is analogous to the person who, in some medical schools, is called a "clinical professor." Following the suggestion of Prof. Robert Bush of Stanford University,[1] I am taking the phrase and applying it to the field of education. In so doing, I remind the reader that a clinical professor of surgery is an outstanding surgeon who continues his practice and gives only part of his time to students. His status is equal to that of a professor of surgery or professor of medicine, both of whom nowadays are expected to be primarily research men. The clinical professor, on the other hand, is not expected to publish papers. His status is assured by his accomplishments as a practitioner. He keeps up to date on modern medicine, but in his contribution as a teacher the emphasis is on practice rather than theory.

---

ing book provisionally entitled *Educational Psychology and Educational Research.* Professor Carroll's treatment includes a review of published research on criteria of teacher performance and attempts to relate these criteria to patterns of teacher preparation. One problem that plagues the researchers on this matter is that to date it has proved extremely difficult to identify precisely measurable criteria of good teaching.

[1] *Professional Imperatives: Expertness and Self-Determination.* Report of the NCTEPS, Fort Collins, 1962. National Commission on Teacher Education and Professional Standards, NEA. Washington, D.C., 1962, p. 45: Prof. Robert N. Bush chapter on "Self-Determination and Self-Realization in the Profession of Teaching."

I recommend that:

16. *The professor from the college or university who is to supervise and assess the practice teaching should have had much
practical experience. His status should be analogous to that of
a clinical professor in certain medical schools.*

He might carry the title of "Professor of the Theory and Practice
of Elementary Teaching" or "Professor of the Teaching of Mathematics" (or other field). The salary should be equal to that of any
professor in the institution. There would be no junior or intermediary grades. The clinical professor must be an excellent school
teacher; he would not be expected to do research or publish papers. He must from time to time return to the school classroom as
a classroom teacher. He might *serve the college either on a part-
time basis or on a full-time basis.*

Quite apart from increasing the effectiveness of practice teaching, the acceptance of this recommendation would go far to raise
the prestige of the classroom teacher. There is an infinite amount
of talk about making teaching a profession, and constant reference
to the medical profession. But few if any universities have recognized that an excellent classroom teacher by his or her performance
merits a position as a professor at top salary. In many schools of
education, graduate courses occupy the attention of a large number
of the staff. With this graduate work is apt to go an increasing interest in research, and with this comes pressure from colleagues to
publish articles and books. For younger instructors promotion depends on publication. Thus their connection with the school classroom becomes more and more remote.

This recommendation, if accepted, would change all this. The
clinical professors need not hold the Ph.D. degree and would not
be expected to make contributions by research and writing. They
would be generally recognized as superb teachers of children or
youth and as skilled teachers of college students. Such persons
might well be given term appointments of, say, three to five years,
either taking leave from their school teaching positions or, if possible, serving both the university and the school at the same time.
They would be under an obligation to renew continually their ex-

perience in the classroom, either by serving both the university and the school at the same time or by returning to the school classroom every few years.

A special word or two about preparing secondary teachers is in order. The title I have suggested might be "Professor of the Teaching of Subject X." I did not include the phrase "Theory and Practice," which I suggested for the clinical professor concerned with elementary teaching, since I believe that there is a difference between preparing elementary and secondary teachers. There is far less theory in the latter. The "Professor of the Teaching of Subject X" should be responsible for placing the student in the proper classroom, where the classroom teacher (cooperating teacher) is an experienced skillful teacher. In addition, in the seminars during the practice-teaching period, the professor will amplify and extend what the cooperating teacher is teaching. In the sciences, a laboratory should be available for setting up demonstrations and allowing the future teacher an opportunity to become familiar with high school equipment. Current textbooks would be reviewed in each field, and if there were a revolutionary wave passing through the subject (as in the sciences and mathematics today), the clinical professor would show to his students the bearing of the new approaches on the classroom work. *Most important of all, he can and should keep the subject-matter departments in the college or university alert in regard to what a future high school teacher needs to know.* To this end, the subject-matter departments would have to go more than half way to meet the clinical professors.

Further details of when and how the clinical professor provides instruction and guidance in developing the art of teaching in a classroom are too technical for discussion in this book. Furthermore, the pattern should vary from college to college and from individual to individual. And what is essential for elementary teachers is not necessarily valid for secondary teachers. The next two chapters will make this point clear.

My recommendations in this chapter are based on two conclusions. The first conclusion is that there are certain educational sciences bearing the same relation to the training of teachers that the medical sciences bear to the training of doctors; these sciences are not yet as well developed as their counterparts in a school of medicine, but nevertheless there is a function to be fulfilled by those who may be regarded as intermediaries between the basic social sciences and the future practitioner. The second conclusion is that the induction of the teacher into a classroom through practice teaching should be under the supervision of an experienced school teacher who holds high rank as a university professor. Such a clinical professor, maintaining or renewing his classroom experience should also be in close touch with the new developments in the educational sciences, particularly with educational psychology. Something like a team approach is needed. A careful and continuing examination of the detailed programs for teacher training should be carried out by such a team, which should include subject matter specialists. Only in this way can the phrase "an all-university responsibility" come to have real meaning. In the next two chapters I shall suggest possible ways in which these basic ideas might be translated into specific four-year programs for educating elementary and secondary teachers.

7

THE EDUCATION OF
ELEMENTARY SCHOOL TEACHERS

In this and the next two chapters I shall assume that I am advising an all-university committee. To begin with, I shall outline what I suggest as a satisfactory program for the education of future elementary school teachers.

Let me start by reminding the reader of the enormous extent of public elementary education. Some 84,000 elementary schools employ about 900,000 teachers and enroll over 26 million pupils. Elementary schools vary widely with respect to size. One-, two-, and three-room schools, located mostly in rural areas, number in the tens of thousands. In these small schools, teachers teach all the elementary school subjects often at several grade levels: reading, language arts (spelling, handwriting, grammar, composition, and speech), arithmetic, social studies (history and geography), science, music, art, health, and physical education.

In cities and suburban school districts too there frequently are small schools (though seldom smaller than six or seven classrooms), but schools of twelve to thirty classrooms tend more commonly to be the pattern. In densely populated sections of large cities, elementary schools sometimes run to a hundred or more classrooms and enroll several thousand pupils. In all these schools, what is known as "the self-contained classroom" dominates and is found almost uniformly in kindergarten and the first three grades. In the self-contained classroom, one teacher is unassisted in his teaching of all subjects to a single class. However, in the upper elementary

146

grades specialists often take over from the regular classroom teacher, particularly in the fields of health and physical education, music, and art. Complete departmentalization—that is, a separate teacher for each subject—is a rare phenomenon in the kindergarten and the first six grades. Here, I am devoting my attention entirely to elementary schools embracing kindergarten through the sixth grade, and the education of teachers for such schools. Problems of grades 7 to 12 are dealt with in the next chapter.

There is without doubt a ferment among educators with respect to the conduct of elementary education. The long-standing notion of a self-contained classroom of 30 pupils taught by one teacher is giving way to alternative proposals. One of these proposals is team teaching, which, as we have seen, has advantages in orienting new teachers.

If the idea of team teaching becomes widely accepted—and many elementary school principals predict that it will—there will be places in classrooms for a wide range of instructional talent. How such schemes will work out over the years in practice remains to be seen, but team teaching seems to many the answer to the question of how to attract more of the ablest college students into elementary school teaching. The possibility of a teacher's having an opportunity to take advantage of her special field of interest is exciting.

Clearly, whether teachers of the future are to teach all subjects in a self-contained classroom or are to be specialists teaching only one subject throughout the grades is profoundly significant in considering the education these teachers are to receive. What one needs is a reliable crystal ball, for prophecy must precede planning. My guess is that, in spite of all the talk about the importance of specialists in the elementary school, *self-contained classrooms will continue to be the dominant pattern for kindergarten and the first three grades during the next ten years.* During these years, however, there will be *an increasing tendency to use specialists in grades four through six.* It follows, then, that teachers for kindergarten and the first three grades must be prepared as generalists capable of handling all the subjects appropriate for these early childhood years. Their repertoire of skills must include special competence in the teaching of reading. Because of the variety of patterns of classroom organization likely to be encountered in grades four through six, the teacher for these grades also is advised to have familiarity with a variety of subjects. But, since the demand for specialization is increasing, the teacher of these grades should also possess depth in a single subject or combination of related subjects taught in the elementary school. Many of my later recommendations depend upon these basic observations.

How are elementary school teachers now being prepared? A brief analysis of two existing programs brings many of the problems and issues involved into sharp focus. The names of the two illustrative colleges examined below are fictitious.

Two programs for the education of elementary school teachers

	Riverdale College	Lakeside College
General Education	51 sem. hours	56 sem. hours
*Academic Major	24	None
Electives	14	16
Educational Psychology, History, Philosophy, and Sociology	12	11½
Methods and Materials of Teaching	6	14
*Courses designated as Special Content Courses for Elementary School Teachers	None	18%
Practice Teaching	15	8
Total Semester Hours	122	124

* Note the contrast in these items.

My guess is that the reader, after examining the above programs, might conclude—because of the differences in regard to the academic major and the hours devoted to "special content courses"— that Riverdale is a "liberal arts college" and that Lakeside is a "teachers college." But he would be wrong. *Both are single-purpose, teacher-preparing institutions.* Both are now in the process of broadening their functions to provide bachelor's-degree programs for persons other than those planning to teach.

There is little agreement between the two in respect to general

Specific courses in two programs

Riverdale College		Lakeside College	
General Education	*Sem. Hrs.*	*General Education*	*Sem. Hrs.*
Speech	3	Intro. to College Life	1⅓
Composition	3	Literature and Composition	9⅓
Comp. and Literature	3	Drawing and Painting	2
World Literature	3	Graphics and Sculpture	1⅓
Art History & Appreciation	3	Physical Geography	2⅔
Music History & Appreciation	3	World Regional Geography	2
General Biology	3	Civic Biology and Conservation	2
Human Biology	3	Hygiene	2
Chemistry and Physics	3	Biological Science	2
Geology and Astronomy	3	Physical Science	4
General Mathematics (three additional hours are required if high school background is weak)	3	Fundamental Concepts of Arithmetic	5⅓
Western Civilization	3	World Civilization	8
American Institutions	3	Early American Civilization	2⅔
Asian Civilization	3	Later American Civilization	2⅔
Africa and Near East	3	Contemporary Social Issues	2
The Behavioral Sciences	3	General Psychology	2⅔
Senior Seminar	3		
Physical Education and Recreation (5 semesters)	No credit	Physical Education	4

Academic Major	*Sem. Hrs.*	*Academic Major*	*Sem. Hrs.*
A Major of 24 semester hours is required in an "academic area"		No major or concentration is required although some students take their 16 hours of electives in one subject.	

Electives	*Electives*
14 semester hours—*must be* in music, philosophy, speech, or foreign language	16 semester hours—may be selected from either general *or* professional education courses.

Educational Psych., History, Philosophy, and Sociology	*Sem. Hrs.*	*Educational Psych., History, Philosophy, and Sociology*	*Sem. Hrs.*
Child Development	3	Educational Psychology	2
Advanced Child Development	3	Human Development	$3\frac{1}{3}$
History and Philosophy of Education	3	Social Foundations of Education	2
Education Elective	3	Education Elective	$1\frac{1}{3}$
		Classroom Management	$2\frac{2}{3}$

Methods and Materials of Teaching	*Sem. Hrs.*	*Methods and Materials of Teaching*	*Sem. Hrs.*
Curriculum I (Social Studies, Art, Music)	2	Language Arts (including reading)	2
Curriculum II (Language Arts, including Reading)	2	Science	2
Curriculum III (Arithmetic, Science, Health, P.E.)	2	Handwriting	$\frac{2}{3}$
		Social Studies	2
		Arithmetic	2
		Music	$1\frac{1}{3}$
		Art	2
		Physical Education	2

Special Methods and Content Courses	*Sem. Hrs.*	*Special Methods and Content Courses*	*Sem. Hrs.*
(No courses of this nature are designed)		Music Fundamentals	6
		Children's Literature	$2\frac{2}{3}$
		Speech and Drama	$2\frac{2}{3}$
		Industrial Arts	$2\frac{2}{3}$
		Health of the Child	$2\frac{2}{3}$
		Nutrition	2

Practice Teaching	*Practice Teaching*
Two 8-week sessions at two grade levels in the senior year.	One 12-week session at one grade level in the senior year.

education: art history and appreciation in Riverdale, drawing and painting in Lakeside; human biology in Riverdale, hygiene in Lakeside; general mathematics in Riverdale, fundamental concepts of arithmetic in Lakeside.

There are equally striking differences in regard to electives and academic majors. Riverdale restricts electives to the humanities (music, philosophy, speech, foreign language); Lakeside permits selection from either general or professional education courses. Riverdale students will graduate with a concentration of 24 semester hours in an "academic area"; Lakeside students acquire at most only 16 semester hours, provided they concentrate all their electives for this purpose.

There are differences in professional education. Riverdale stresses child development and the history and philosophy of education. Lakeside has only half as much child or human development but adds courses in educational psychology, educational sociology, and classroom management.

Before discussing other differences in professional education, I digress for a moment to discuss a segment of the curriculum that is unique to the education of elementary school teachers and about which there is considerable controversy. The expectation that elementary school teachers will teach all or several subjects raises the problem of how best to provide these teachers with the requisite background of content and methodology. One position is that a "good general education" is sufficient. However, we have seen that general education includes almost everything and anything, and it is unlikely that a general education curriculum, whatever its content, would provide, for example, a course in children's literature, which both elementary school teachers and teachers of teachers say is needed. Certainly, a general education curriculum would not provide a course in the teaching of reading. Courses such as children's literature, industrial arts, and health of the child, prescribed in the Lakeside curriculum, are termed "special content courses for teachers" in that they would not be provided if the institution did not seek to educate elementary school teachers. In addition to these courses for elementary school teachers, there is a cluster known as "special methods courses." Very often these special methods courses cover both the content of an elementary school subject and the problems of teaching the subject. Consequently, it is extremely difficult to distinguish between "special *content* courses" and "special *methods* courses," and so they can be conveniently lumped together as "special content and methods courses" for elementary school teachers. These are professional courses designed to do a rather specific job.

Riverdale devotes only six semester hours to courses in methods of teaching, organizing them into three "curriculum" courses. By contrast, Lakeside requires more than twice as much attention to "methods" courses, specifying eight courses, each devoted to a subject commonly taught in the elementary school. In addition, Lakeside specifies six courses in the "special methods and content" category, whereas Riverdale specifies none, on the assumption, apparently, that all content needed for teaching in the elementary school is provided in general education, in special methods courses, or, perhaps, in the secondary and elementary schools.

In regard to practice teaching, however, Riverdale requires a third more in time and assignment and at two grade levels rather than one. Probably it is assumed at Riverdale that much of the special content and methodology needed by an elementary school teacher can be learned in the actual business of teaching as a practice teacher. Conversations with members of the faculty at Riverdale confirmed this assumption.

One other significant difference between the two institutions is not apparent in the listing of courses. The faculty at Riverdale argued that the general requirements for teachers should be the same as for doctors, lawyers, or business people, with as little specialization as possible, even though Riverdale claims to be a single-purpose, teacher-preparing institution. On the other hand, the faculty at Lakeside, also a single-purpose, teacher-preparing institution, admitted that the teaching of many general education courses is colored by the assumption that their students are to be teachers.

The foregoing example of two significantly different curricula at two institutions bearing the same label testifies to the difficulty of generalizing. Much current criticism of and debate over the education of teachers is conducted at the level of slogans—for example, the frequent and passionate articles about "those terrible teachers colleges." To be constructively critical about the education of teachers in the United States, one must examine specific courses and what goes on in them.

The vast majority of elementary school teachers complete their preparation for first employment in four years (eight semesters).

In the past in some states many teachers assumed full-time responsibility following two years of college. However, in one way or another such teachers were urged to take courses on an in-service basis, and large numbers thus obtained the bachelor's degree several years after they had been teaching on a full-time basis. One might consider such an arrangement an on-the-job completion of a four-year program. However, few elementary school teachers now begin their work without a bachelor's degree.

A review of the four-year program in 11 state and 9 private universities, 11 state colleges, and 4 private colleges demonstrates (Appendix I) that diversity is the rule. There is no uniform pattern. In the 35 institutions I just mentioned, the time devoted to general education ranges from 39 to 90 semester hours; the time allotted to what might be called professional courses (except special methods and practice teaching) ranges from 11 to 29 semester hours. Special methods courses make up from 12 to 36 hours, and the time devoted to practice teaching (in terms of semester-hour credits) ranges from 5 to 14. Nevertheless, a few similarities can be found. All institutions offer at least 3 semester hours in educational or child psychology, and all, of course, provide for practice teaching. Almost all require some special content and methods courses in arithmetic, social studies, science, language arts (including reading), physical education, music, art, and crafts. All institutions preparing elementary school teachers, it would appear, make some effort to provide special content and methodology directly related to the curriculum of the elementary school and what these teachers are expected to do.

Thus, approximately half of the four-year curriculum is devoted to courses considered to be general education. The content of these courses varies for elementary school teachers, just as it does for all other students in four-year college curricula. There simply is no basis for concluding that the so-called general education of elementary school teachers is better or worse than the general education of other college students.

Judging from my observations, most prospective elementary school teachers "major" in elementary education, spending one or two of the four years in professional courses, including special content, methods, and practice teaching. But a much smaller group manages to build a "major" of 24 or more semester hours in a field other than education, and a few concentrate sufficiently to meet the full graduation requirements of an academic department. One has great difficulty in determining course content from titles and, therefore, in classifying courses or in equating them from institution to institution.

Members of my staff and I talked to hundreds of students preparing for elementary school teaching in the institutions visited. They were frank and specific in their evaluation of courses. Some of these judgments have already been reported. The eclectic introductory course covering a smattering of topics—job opportunities in teaching, certification requirements, professional ethics for teachers, the evolution and organization of American schools, and so on —finds few friendly voices among the student body. Students were somewhat less critical of the courses in educational psychology but frequently complained that these were far removed from classroom practice. Students were more enthusiastic about child development and methods courses, although a significant proportion believed that the latter could be improved through eliminating duplication, and that both types of course should be more effectively related to practice. Their comments about practice teaching ranged from "helpful" to "great," and they frequently mentioned the ability and readiness of both college supervisors and cooperating classroom teachers to provide the practical help needed in beginning actual teaching.

In the section that follows, I summarize briefly where my observations, discussions, and study have brought me with respect to the education of elementary school teachers. My present point of view is presented in a series of conclusions and recommendations, with supporting arguments. The chapter concludes with a sample four-year curriculum for elementary school teachers.

FOUR YEARS OF COLLEGE are adequate for the breadth and depth of education needed for teaching in elementary schools, assuming that two of the four college years are devoted to a general education more or less like that suggested earlier. The remaining two years are sufficient for the concentration of studies and professional preparation recommended below. Consequently, the general education previously proposed, and included in the sample program appearing later in this chapter, is my *recommended program of general education for all elementary school teachers.* If one insists on more free electives, then a five-year continuous program will result. I am convinced, however, that such a prolongation before the teacher takes his first job is unnecessary and unwise. My second conclusion is that the professional education of teachers for kindergarten and the first three grades should be differentiated from the professional education of teachers for grades four, five, and six.

There are several reasons for this conclusion. As I have talked to elementary teachers, I have become convinced that a rather special type of person is interested in teaching very young children, and that the preparation of these individuals requires more concern with child psychology as well as a broader academic program. Furthermore, the self-contained classroom is more likely to persist in the three lower grades than in the three upper grades.

The following recommendation is addressed to the trustees, president and members of the faculty of colleges and universities engaged in the preparation of elementary school teachers.

17(a). *The program for teachers of kindergarten and grades 1, 2, and 3 should prepare them in the content and methodology of all subjects taught in these early school years. Depth in a single subject or cluster of subjects is not necessary.*

17(b). *The program for teachers of grades 4, 5, and 6 should provide depth of content and methods of teaching in a specific subject or cluster of subjects normally taught in these grades with only an introduction to the remaining elementary school subjects.*

Unquestionably there is a body of material worthy of inclusion in the education of elementary school teachers, but in many institutions, there is a considerable amount of duplication and repetition. To remedy this situation I make three suggestions. *First, the total time allocated to courses in special content and method, frequently amounting to almost two semesters, should be reduced to the equivalent of one semester's work.* Actually, the program that I suggest in the following paragraphs will require the student to take the equivalent of one semester's work (16 semester hours) in this area. *Second, these courses in special content and method should be taken in the student's senior year and should be taken concurrently with actual experience in an elementary school classroom.* This "laboratory" experience in a classroom should involve the student almost continuously in observation, participation as a teacher's assistant, and a period of practice teaching. The practice teaching should include several weeks of full-time responsibility for the conduct of a classroom under the guidance of an experienced elementary school teacher. *Third, these courses in special content and method should be taught by a team of clinical faculty members whose own education and teaching experience qualify them in both the content and the methodology of the specific subject.* The work of these specialists should be coordinated so as to reduce to a minimum any duplication in the elements of methodology common to the various content areas. The courses themselves need not conform to the traditional pattern of academic organization. That is, they need not meet three days a week for a semester, for example. In fact, they might better be organized in a series of two- to three-week intensive "workshops" strategically arranged to realize the maximum benefit from the student's actual experience in a classroom—i.e., the laboratory experiences that are suggested above.

BECAUSE GOOD READING INSTRUCTION is of the utmost importance in elementary schools, I feel compelled to say a word about this area before specifying more completely the remainder of special content and methods courses. I have found that by no means all the colleges we visited required a specific course in teaching reading. For example, out of 35 institutions only 19 required such a course, and where the course was required, the credit given ranged from 2 to 4 semester hours. This is barely adequate for teachers of grades four, five, and six and entirely inadequate for teachers of kindergarten and grades one through three. *I suggest a minimum of three semester hours in the teaching of reading for all elementary school teachers and twice this amount for teachers of kindergarten and the lower three grades.*

The initial three-semester-hour course in the teaching of reading, which would be required of all prospective elementary school teachers, should include as a minimum of instruction: 1) A view of the entire elementary school reading program in all grades and an acquaintance with a wide variety of texts and other instructional materials for all levels; 2) a thorough grounding in the basic reading skills and the extension of these basic skills into the upper-grade reading program; 3) an opportunity for the prospective teacher to concentrate in some depth on the reading program of either the primary or upper grades; and 4) an opportunity actually to try teaching some or all of these reading skills to a group of children (the laboratory experience mentioned above).

For upper-grade teachers this would be the extent of their formal undergraduate preparation in the teaching of reading. For kindergarten and lower-grade teachers an additional three-hour course would be required. This second course should deal primarily with the identification and the correction of reading problems. Again, students taking the course should have ample opportunity actually to work with children who are learning to read. The prospective teachers would thus *learn about and actually use* diagnostic and remedial techniques prior to assuming their first full-time teaching positions. I have actually visited such courses during my travels around the country, and I was impressed by the importance of providing this valuable experience for future teachers.

IN MY SUGGESTED PROGRAM, lower-grade teachers must in 10 semester hours consider the following areas of study: arithmetic, children's literature, social studies, science, art, music, health, and physical education. It is easy to see that it would not be possible to take a course in each of these areas. In fact, it would be best not to have a separate course in each. Because of the nature of young children, I am convinced it is vital for lower-grade teachers to be able to relate these many subjects one to another in their daily classroom programs. Therefore, the future teacher's introduction to these subjects might also be handled in an "integrated" course covering the total curriculum of the lower grades and taught by a team of clinical professors who are experienced teachers at this level.

The suggested organization of such courses for upper-grade teachers is a more complicated problem for two closely related reasons.

First, many upper-grade teachers are not required to teach all subject areas (art, music, and physical education are often handled by specialists, for example). Second, I suggested earlier in this chapter that upper-grade teachers should specialize in one field. The question then arises: Do all upper-grade teachers need to be introduced to the special content and methods of *all* the traditional elementary school subjects? And further: If they are to be so introduced, are the 13 semester hours remaining in the program sufficient for such an introduction?

In my many conversations with prospective elementary school teachers of the upper grades, I found that they often think of themselves as teachers of science or of arithmetic or of social studies and are loath to take courses dealing with the teaching of art, music, physical education, or subjects other than those closely related to their special interests. One can sympathize with such a point of view, but while I suggest upper-grade teachers should develop a special teaching field, I am convinced that all elementary school teachers must have at least an introduction to the teaching of all subjects commonly taught in the elementary school. For this reason, I suggest for upper-grade teachers a series of "workshops" arranged during the senior year, devoting varying amounts of time to *all* elementary school subjects. In this manner the 13 semester hours remaining could be allocated as follows: the equivalent of 3 semester hours in the upper-grade teacher's major field of concentration, and the remainder allocated to the other elementary school subjects. I consider this amount of instruction sufficient for upper-grade teachers.

Table I below combines the suggestions and conclusions presented above. It provides for a four-year program with essentially no free electives. This four-year curriculum includes both the breadth of education required and the necessary special knowledge essential for the elementary teacher. As I shall explain later, further formal professional instruction of an elementary teacher is more profitable if it comes after a year or two of teaching experience. At this point I only wish to point out that there is much confusion about a so-called five-year program for elementary teachers. A five-year program is sometimes interpreted to mean (a) four years of college without any education courses, plus one

TABLE I:

A proposed curriculum for the education
of elementary school teachers

Summary		Semester Hours
General Requirements		60
Concentration		30
Professional		30
	Total	120

General Requirements: (See Chapter 6)

The English Language	6
Western World's Literary Tradition	6
History (at least one half other than American)	9
Mathematics	6
Philosophy	3
Science (physical and biological studied consecutively)	12
Economics, Political Science, Sociology, and Anthropology	9
Introduction to General Psychology	3
Fine Arts (art or music)	6
Physical Education (non-credit)	—
	60

Concentration (See Chapter 5) 30

Professional Sequence (30 semester hours, most of which will be in the senior year)

(1) Course in child growth and development, with extensive laboratory experiences; year-long study of children in many settings (3 semester hours' total credit for one class meeting plus laboratory experiences each week, perhaps in the junior year).

(2) Course in history, philosophy, or sociology of education (3 semester hours, perhaps in the junior year).

(3) Courses in the teaching of reading accompanied by regular laboratory experiences (minimum of 3 semester hours for teachers of grades 4, 5, and 6; minimum of 6 semester hours for teachers of kindergarten and the first three grades).

(4) A series of intensive workshops in the content and method of elementary school subjects (including a special methods course in the field of concentration for upper-grade teachers) with course work differentiated for lower and upper elementary grades in line with differing demands of these levels of teaching. (Maximum of 13 and 10 semester hours for prospective teachers of upper and lower grades respectively.)

(5) Year-long laboratory experiences accompanying course work above and including at least 8 weeks of practice teaching, involving a minimum of 3 hours daily in the classroom (8 semester hours).

further year of work of a professional nature, (b) five consecutive years in which general and professional work are carried on simultaneously, (c) four years of combined general and professional education followed later by the equivalent of a year's work accomplished over a period of years.

What I am suggesting here amounts to the third interpretation (c), that is, a four-year program with advanced study coming later if so desired. The other two (a and b) provide for the luxury of a year of free electives *before* a teacher begins his first teaching job. I am convinced that it is a luxury and is, for some students, quite unwise. My interviews indicate that many future elementary teachers, unlike prospective high school teachers, have manifested keen interest in teaching early in their lives. A wait of five years before attaining this goal seems to me unduly long. The sooner such students have the full responsibility of a classroom, the better for them.

Table I summarizes my proposed curriculum for the education of elementary school teachers. The reader will recall that the course and credit estimates are designed merely to suggest what might be necessary for most students to achieve the level of understanding in each field that I consider desirable.

The 30 semester hours labeled "Concentration" in the above table should be distributed differently according to whether students are being prepared to be teachers for grades K-3 (Recommendation 17a) or for teaching in grades 4–6 (Recommendation 17b). For the first group the 30 hours should be distributed over three fields, namely, English, social studies, and mathematics; the mastery of these subjects should be tested by a comprehensive examination. For the second group, preparing to teach in grades 4, 5, and 6, the 30 hours should be devoted to the study of one of the following: English, mathematics, social studies, science. Together with the time devoted to one of these subjects as part of the general education program, this will mean a total concentration of 36 hours in one field. Again, a comprehensive examination in the field of concentration is desirable.

My program must be interpreted in light of the discussions in the previous chapters. If the reader disagrees with my diagnosis of the role of theory and practice, he may well disagree with the conclusions summarized in Table I. Though I consider a course in the philosophy, history, or sociology of education highly advisable, I do not believe these courses are essential. The reader will remember that I consider such courses worth while only if the professors involved are competent as judged by the standards of the academic discipline they seek to apply to education. If competent professors are not available, such courses should not be offered. On the other hand, I consider courses in educational psychology, including child growth and development, to be essential. In making this distinction I do not mean to imply that the courses in educational psychology I have observed are better taught than those in the history or the philosophy of education; there exist both good and bad courses in all these disciplines. Just as the educational historian must be first of all an historian, so must the educational psychologist be first of all a psychologist, with a continuing interest in educational problems. But I do believe that for the elementary school teacher the psychological instruction is essential.

Let me return now to the term "laboratory experience," which refers to both the observation of children and the practical activity in the classroom carried on in conjunction with professional instruction. Those who believe there is a rapidly developing total science of education place particular emphasis on the word "laboratory." Whether or not one approves of including such laboratory experiences in the teacher education curriculum, it seems clear that the future elementary teacher has much to learn that can be learned only in the elementary school classroom. What is learned by direct observation embraces far more than the principles of teaching. It includes an understanding of how children develop, singly and in groups. Therefore, without entering into a long argument about what might be called scientific, I conclude that the effectiveness of education courses is substantially increased when accompanied by appropriate "laboratory experiences." *I would argue that all education courses for elementary teachers (with the possible exception of courses in philosophy or sociology or history) be accompanied by "laboratory experiences" providing for the observation and teaching of children.* To some limited extent the use of film and television can take the place of direct classroom observation.

I have already presented my case for requiring all teachers to prove their competence during a period of practice teaching. Such practice teaching is to be done in close cooperation with the school board and under conditions approved by state officials; the university or college professor responsible is to be a clinical professor. He is to be responsible for arranging the teaching experience and, together with the cooperating teacher, for assessing the competence of the student. It is perhaps necessary to emphasize that practice teaching serves a dual purpose: it is an essential part of the teacher's training and a critical point for examining and attesting to his competence. I therefore recommend:

18. *All future elementary teachers should engage in practice teaching for a period of at least 8 weeks, spending a minimum of 3 hours a day in the classroom; the period must include at least 3 weeks of full responsibility for the classroom under the direction of a cooperating teacher and the supervision of a clinical professor.*

The amount of practice teaching I am prescribing would carry 8 semester hours of credit.

ONE MATTER OF SERIOUS IMPORT for small colleges seeking to prepare elementary school teachers is the number of professors needed to do the job described on the preceding pages. One might argue that there should be a specialist in each area of professional instruction enumerated earlier. At the other extreme, one could take the view that a specialist in elementary education, himself experienced in elementary school teaching, could provide the needed instruction in *all* courses and supervise the laboratory experiences. I found precisely this situation in some of the institutions visited. In spite of the valiant job being done by some of these overburdened individuals, what I saw on the whole convinces me that a one- or two-man staff in elementary education is completely inadequate. No staff of only two persons, no matter how well trained or energetic they might be, could meet the varied responsibilities that a clinical and an intermediary professor must be prepared to handle.

I conclude that the equivalent of three to four professors constitutes a bare minimum. Such a minimum staff might be put together in a variety of combinations. Let us assume, first, an historian (or philosopher or sociologist) devoting half his time to the courses in education and half time to teaching outside the field of education. An educational psychologist devoting at least half time is essential. These two half-time professors constitute one. Let us assume, next, a full-time clinical professor specializing in teaching reading and other language arts, devoting half his time to these courses and half to the supervision of practice teaching. Finally, let us assume another full-time clinical professor specializing in science and mathematics who would devote half his time to these courses and half time to supervision of practice teaching. The equivalent of another clinical person, actually several part-time persons, still would be required to handle content and methods in the remaining fields. What I am talking about here is the *bare minimum* number of professors needed. The instruction in these areas would occur in short-term workshops that could be taught by regular faculty members from other departments in the college, or by highly skilled elementary school teachers of these subjects who could be brought in on a consultant basis. One needs, then, at least the equivalent of one intermediary professor and two or three clinical professors to maintain an adequate program for the professional education of elementary school teachers.

I recommend:

19. *Those responsible for financing and administering small colleges should consider whether they can afford to maintain an adequate staff for the preparation of elementary school teachers. Unless they are able to employ the equivalent of three or four professors devoting their time to elementary education, they should cease attempting to prepare teachers for the elementary schools.*

Two other alternatives are open to small colleges wishing to maintain elementary school teaching programs for its students and yet unable to maintain this minimum staff. The first alternative is to join forces with a neighboring college or university. We found one highly satisfactory arrangement where a small college for women conducted a joint teacher-education program with a coeducational university located nearby. A second, and more likely, alternative is to enter into an informal cooperative arrangement with a university offering a fifth year or master-of-arts-in-teaching program. Such arrangements now exist in all sections of the country. Many of the universities involved in the master-of-arts-in-teaching program apparently could quadruple enrollments without straining their resources.

An institution that graduates annually 25 or more future elementary teachers should be able to support the minimum-sized staff. Where fewer students are involved, the problem of financing becomes serious. In theory the public institution can turn to the taxpayers; in theory the private colleges can turn to the interest on its endowment. In practice the private college more often than not depends for its finances largely on tuition fees. Therefore, I question whether the institutions that now graduate fewer than 25 elementary teachers a year should continue to attempt to prepare elementary school teachers. Table II, which is based on the number of teachers graduated in 1962, provides some interesting figures. Out of some 35,000 elementary school teachers prepared annually in the 16 most populous states, only 2,452 come from institutions that graduate fewer than 25 a year. If all these institutions were to cancel their *elementary* programs, the supply of teachers would be diminished by only 7 per cent. Eleven public colleges and 165 private colleges would be affected.

The consequence of adopting a similar policy *for the nation as a whole* would mean the dropping of the elementary education program from 35 public colleges and 291 private colleges, and the decrease in the number of elementary teachers by some 7 per cent. Such a loss, in my judgment, would not be serious. I doubt if most of these small institutions are adequately preparing elementary teachers because of the limitations imposed by their inability to maintain a faculty of sufficient size and diversity to offer the many courses that are demanded. These colleges, the prospective elementary school teachers attending them, and the children of the nation would all be better off if these inadequate programs were discontinued. A workable solution to this serious problem can be provided by the continued growth of fifth-year programs of the M.A.T. type in institutions with adequate faculties and by cooperative arrangements between small colleges.

Number of elementary teachers prepared in "large"
and "small" programs by control of institution

16 MOST POPULOUS STATES—1962

	"Small"— 1 to 24 Students			"Large"— 25 or more Students		
	Insti- tutions	Teachers Prepared	Per- centage	Insti- tutions	Teachers Prepared	Per- centage
Public	11	157		148	23,708	
Private (Ind.)	52	735		47	3,162	
Private (Church)	113	1,560		118	6,405	
Total	176	2,452	7	313	33,275	93

	"Small"— 1 to 49 Students			"Large"— 50 or more Students		
	Insti- tutions	Teachers Prepared	Per- centage	Insti- tutions	Teachers Prepared	Per- centage
Public	27	729		132	23,136	
Private (Ind.)	73	1,427		26	2,470	
Private (Church)	189	4,189		42	3,776	
Total	289	6,345	18	200	29,382	82

Who pays the bill for the training of teachers?

16 MOST POPULOUS STATES —1962

	Elementary Teachers		Secondary Teachers		All Teachers	
	Number	Per- centage	Number	Per- centage	Number	Per- centage
Public Expense	23,865	66	34,411	65	58,276	66
Private (Ind.) Expense	3,897	11	7,589	14	11,486	13
Private (Church) Expense	7,965	23	11,063	21	19,028	21
Total	35,727	100	53,063	100	88,790	100

8

THE EDUCATION
OF SECONDARY SCHOOL TEACHERS

IN THIS CHAPTER, continuing in my role as an adviser to an all-university committee, I shall concern myself with the education of secondary teachers. I shall divide the chapter into two parts. In the first I treat of the education of teachers of English, social studies, mathematics, general science, physics, chemistry, and biology. In the second I discuss the education of teachers of foreign languages, music, art, and physical education. Much of what follows is based on my answer to the question "Is there a science of education?" and on my appraisal of practice teaching. As far as practice teaching is concerned, I shall have little to add to what I have already written.

Part I: English, social studies, mathematics, science

We are living in a period of change in regard to many aspects of education. The ferment in secondary education is no less than that in the elementary field. Four developments are noteworthy. First, the rapid introduction of new methods and materials, particularly in physics, in chemistry, in biology, and in mathematics; second, the increasing tendency to push down into the lower grades the teaching of material once thought proper only for the higher grades; third, the introduction in some high schools of college work in the 12th grade by means of the advanced placement program; fourth, the increasing use of television, team teaching, and some form of programmed instruction. All these developments have had and will continue to have their impact on the education of secondary school teachers.

It goes without saying that an adequate preparation in the subject to be taught is essential for the secondary school teacher. Everyone subscribes to such a statement, but people differ radically on what the word "adequate" means. First of all, *a decision must be made as to whether the institution is to certify any given graduate in more than one field.* At present in many colleges and universities, secondary school teachers are graduated with a "major" and a "minor." Some state requirements encourage such an arrangement. However, the difficulties of providing adequate practice-teaching experience in two fields are considerable. I have found not only difficulties but dissatisfaction among college students. Since the practice teaching is to be the essential step in assessing a future teacher's capabilities, it would be necessary to have two prolonged periods of practice teaching if a secondary school teacher were to be certified by the state in two fields.

Aside from these considerations, I believe it is impossible to study two academic fields in sufficient depth in four years. I therefore recommend that:

20. *An institution should award a teaching certificate for teachers in grades 7 to 12 in one field only.* The fields would be as follows: social studies, English, mathematics, physics and chemistry combined, and biology.

I recognize that in making this recommendation I am going contrary to established custom in many institutions. The argument in favor of certifying a teacher in two or more fields is that the small high school cannot afford a separate teacher for each subject. In *The American High School Today* I wrote at length about the necessity to consolidate small high schools. Throughout the nation, in thousands of small high schools with small staffs, teachers must be utility infielders with the capacity to teach at least two, often three, and sometimes four different subjects. This fact has had an important effect on the preparation of secondary school teachers. There are still many small schools in which the science teacher will teach chemistry and physics in alternate years and fill in his schedule with general science, biology, and mathematics. The social studies or

English teacher will take one or two foreign language classes, if foreign language is offered at all.

The result of this situation has been *that certification requirements and teacher education programs have been geared to the employment conditions in the small schools.* If teachers must teach more than one subject, it is clear that their preparation in any one area cannot be as deep as it would if they were to teach just one subject. Many institutions require teaching majors and teaching minors with the dubious assumption that a teacher needs to be less well prepared in his second field, or minor. A common program consists of 30 semester hours for a major and 18 semester hours for a minor, or 10 courses in one subject and 6 in another.

The assumption that secondary teachers ought to be prepared to teach at least two different subjects needs careful examination *state by state.* In 1952 the enrollment in the median size public secondary school was 175; in 1959, just seven years later, the figure had jumped to 278. Whereas in 1930 only 25 per cent of the schools had enrollments over 200, by 1959, 60 per cent of the schools enrolled more than 200 students. Secondary schools are becoming larger, and this fact has important implications for teacher education.

Another important factor is the increase in the number of six-year high schools (grades 7 through 12 inclusive). More pupils attend six-year high schools than any other kind, and these schools outnumber all other kinds of secondary school in the nation. Many of these schools are in rural areas and represent efforts to consolidate several small systems organized in 8-year elementary and 4-year secondary schools. The purpose of this consolidation is to provide a better program with specialist teachers at minimum expense for grades 7 through 12. Actually, 61 per cent of the small high schools are six-year schools, and they enroll 75 per cent of all students attending the small high schools. This means that only 7.5 per cent of the secondary students in the whole nation are in small high schools (with fewer than 90 students in the senior class) that are not six-year schools. The importance of the six-year school is that it obviates the need for utility infielders by adding more grades, thereby increasing the likelihood that a specialist can spend all his time on one subject—mathematics or English, for example. This fact balances the smaller number of students in each grade. Because of these continuing efforts to eliminate small four-year high schools, I doubt that in many states there is any necessity for teachers who can teach two or more subjects in grades 7 to 12.

It can be argued that factors other than school size are involved. I have heard it said that there will always be a need for at least a few teachers to take classes in subjects other than their specialty because teacher schedules, even in large schools, never come out exactly even. Often there is an extra class in social studies, for example, that must be picked up by a teacher whose major might be in another field. Or so the argument goes. Moreover, shifting student enrollments may mean that whereas in one year there are two geometry classes, in another year there may be four such classes. The shifting of enrollments, combined with a low staff turnover, obviously presents problems, and a school district cannot always find a teacher who fits exactly the vacancy within the staff.

I readily admit it is unlikely that there will ever be a time when *all* high school teachers can teach solely in their fields or subjects *the nation over.* But I am convinced that with more attention paid to hiring policies, better teacher assignments, and more imaginative scheduling by principals, the number of those teaching in more than one field in high schools of sufficient size could soon be reduced to zero. In short, the progress of school consolidation (Appendix H) precludes the necessity to educate new teachers in more than one subject area in many states. In fact, if no new teachers are prepared in more than one field, the shortage of teachers so trained and the corresponding increase of specialists would, in all probability, hasten the development of larger schools.

Having presented my case for a single teaching field, I must now emphasize that the content of such a field must correspond to the needs of the secondary school teachers. This means that each subject-matter department must have a close liaison with the high schools. The clinical professors are the people who should provide such liaison. Here let me only point out that I have found institution after institution in which most, if not all, the members of a subject-matter department (English or chemistry, for example) were totally unfamiliar with what was going on in the schools and couldn't care less. Academic faculties almost invariably specify the courses to be taken in a field of concentration in such a way that their graduates can proceed in the same field to graduate study leading to a Ph.D. More often than not, such a pattern of studies is *not* suitable for a future high school teacher.

Before I illustrate the point I have been making, let us consider how much time should be devoted to courses given by professors of education. The question will be raised: Would it not be better to eliminate some or much of this work, and increase the time devoted to a subject field, or even bring in an elective or two? In answering this question, I should like to return to the distinction I made earlier between what is *essential* and what is *desirable*. In so doing, I assume the present state-erected protective tariff wall, which protects the professors of education, has been destroyed. If not, then the question is academic in a double sense. The only question then is the parceling out of the number of hours specified by the state among the various professors of education. (Appendix J summarizes the professional education requirements for secondary school teachers in 27 institutions which my staff and I visited.)

The reader may recall my negative judgment about introductory courses that I have labeled as "eclectic." If I were arguing as a member of a faculty about the course offerings for either elementary or secondary school teachers, I should vote for the elimination of such a course. My vote would be the same if the course were labeled "social foundations." I recognize that an argument can be made for a future teacher in our public school system having some understanding of the history of our American schools, but unless a competent *historian* is available to give a course on the subject, I would rather let the teacher acquire information by extra reading on the basis of the general education course in history than by exposure to most of the social foundations courses I have seen. The same line of reasoning holds, I believe, in regard to a philosophical and sociological approach to school problems. In short, I would hope that in any institution educating teachers a course in the history of American education, philosophy, or sociology—designed for the future teacher—would be available. While I think exposure to such courses is highly *desirable,* I would not class such an experience for future secondary school teachers as absolutely *essential.*

When it comes to psychology, I am of two minds. If I were advising an all-university committee, I should be inclined to question in detail the person who was proposing to give the course in educational psychology. Many institutions have the same course in psychology for all future teachers, elementary or secondary. In a few colleges and universities, on the other hand, one does find a separate course on child growth and development for future elementary teachers. I would follow this second pattern. In reviewing the courses on educational psychology in a previous chapter, I expressed the opinion that the educational psychologists (using this phrase in its widest sense) had more relevant scientific information for future elementary teachers than for secondary teachers. However, I should put in the category of "essential" some knowledge of tests and measurements. Such knowledge might be provided in connection with the special methods course and practice teaching, or it might be given in a course in educational psychology. As for learning theory, I humbly submit my opinion that at the present time this phase of educational psychology is not sufficiently developed to warrant more attention for secondary teachers than that given in a good course in general psychology required as part of a general education.

To sum up my suggestions, the amount of time devoted to the professional sequence would vary from a minimum of 12 to a maximum of 18, depending on the resources available in the institution; of these hours, 9 semester hours would be the credit for the time spent on special methods and practice teaching.

How MUCH TIME should be devoted to the specialized academic work? And how should this time be distributed? One can only hope to answer these questions subject by subject. First, let us consider the preparation of the high school teacher in social studies. It must be pointed out that a major in history is no guarantee of adequate preparation. The program must include work in at least economics, geography, and political science in addition to history, and preferably anthropology and sociology as well. Since American history is taught in all, or nearly all, American high schools, it is clear that the future social studies teacher must include a study of this subject. My own prejudice is strongly in the direction of recommending that all future social studies teachers for grades 7 to 12 *complete* a program of studies approximately as given below.

General education, including 9 hours in history,
   3 hours of sociology and anthropology,
   3 hours of political science, 3 hours of economics,
   and 3 hours of general psychology   60
Educational psychology   3
Philosophy or history or sociology of education   3
Further history   33
Further political science   3
Further economics   3
Geography   6
Practice teaching and special methods   9
                                        ―――
                                      120

What is important is the level of competence, *not* the number of semester hours. I would argue strongly for a comprehensive examination in the senior year.

It may be argued that there would be alternative programs for social studies teachers in which, for example, a field of concentration of economics, geography, and political science would occupy more time than in the outline I have given. To anyone who raises this objection I would reply by pointing out that the general education program I have suggested provides a broad base on which to build. If the teacher wishes to become better acquainted with economics or political science, he can do so by reading, and by further study. If he or she wishes to obtain a master's degree, the way is open for much more formal work. What I have outlined seems to me to correspond to the realities of the demands on a beginning teacher. The certification of the competence in subject matter and the guidance of the student will depend on the structure of the university. It would seem reasonable to expect that all the disciplines involved shall be represented on whatever body fulfilled these functions.

For the teacher of English, let me assume that, as with the social studies teacher, there will be a comprehensive examination, and let me turn to the question of the inadequacy of a conventional major. One might suppose that an adequate major or concentration in English for the A.B. degree in a college with the liberal arts tradition should be more than enough for the high school teacher. Indeed, such a major may provide enough hours of study, but the level of competency in different areas is another matter. On the advice of highly competent persons in the field, I have been persuaded that a future English teacher should have studied not only British and American literature in some depth but also the structure of the English language, and modern grammar; in addition, he should have given some time to familiarizing himself with adolescent literature, with reading problems, with speech and drama, and to composition at the advanced level. Yet many a major in English in our best colleges and universities may have omitted some of these studies. Indeed, the omission may be quite in order if the graduate is not going to be a high school teacher.

Obviously, what is essential is a close cooperation between the professors of English and the clinical professor in charge of the methods course and practice teaching. The same is true in every field and needs no further underlining.

For teachers in the field of mathematics, let us see what the Mathematical Association of America recommends. In January, 1961, its committee suggested for level III (high school mathematics) 11 three-semester-hour courses based on a high school "preparatory course." Since 6 hours of mathematics in the general education program would reduce the time required for the field of concentration to 27, there is ample time left (33 hours) for professional courses and for free electives if one so desires.

It might indeed be possible to meet the requirements for level IV (which prepares the person to teach elements of calculus, linear algebra, and probability) since this course of study would require approximately 54 hours, of which 6 would be in the general education program. But the Association itself suggests that preparation for teaching level IV should be completed in a master's program, and I am inclined to agree with them. The problem is that, while 8½ full-year courses could be fitted into a four-year program, the student would be likely to encounter difficulties because of the sequential nature of the subject. That is, he could not take two mathematics courses simultaneously if his understanding of one were to depend upon prior mastery of the other. Thus in this field, I would not recommend that the student sacrifice courses in educational philosophy or sociology or history to make room for extra "major" courses; it would be better, perhaps, for him to include selected courses in these areas, and to add extra physics or chemistry. Such a program might be then as follows:

	Semester Hours
General education, including 6 hours of mathematics, 12 hours of science, and 3 hours of general psychology	60
Educational psychology	3
Philosophy or history or sociology of education	3
Physics or chemistry	6
Field of concentration (mathematics)	39
Practice teaching and special methods	9
	120

The reason for including physics or chemistry would be to enable the future teacher to start from a level of competency in planning a fifth-year program. The amount of science in the four-year course, including the general education requirement, would total no less than 18 hours, which is more than many high school teachers can now boast but far too little to qualify them for teaching a science in high school. Yet the temptation to use mathematics teachers to teach science is great, for the number of students who elect physics and chemistry is relatively small. There will be many a superintendent who will insist that a teacher must be qualified to teach both science and mathematics. Let us examine this demand.

Because it is unlikely that a person will have the opportunity to teach only physics or only chemistry, some combination of subjects must be chosen. Let us consider first a combination of mathematics and physics. If one eliminates the study of the philosophy or history or sociology of education, one can write a program of 48 hours of physics and mathematics in addition to the 6 hours in mathematics and the 6 hours in the physical sciences in general education. If 27 hours are taken up by the mathematical preparation (as recommended by the mathematicians), this leaves 21 hours for physics on top of the 3 hours in general education; but no chemistry above the 3 hours in general education would be available. Considering the close connection of the two fields today, I should hesitate to suggest a program for a future physics teacher that includes so little chemistry. Therefore, I should not want to endorse such a combination, and I doubt the need for it.

Physics and chemistry seem to me to go together better than either does with mathematics. Let me now turn to consider such a combination. The program might look something like the following:

	Semester Hours
General education, including 6 hours of mathematics, 6 hours of physical science, and 3 hours of general psychology	60
Additional mathematics, or history or philosophy or sociology of education or educational psychology	6
Chemistry	21
Physics	24
Practice teaching and special methods	9
	120

(The total physical science, including that in general education, would be 51 semester hours.)

In such a case the secondary school teacher might graduate without benefit of a course in the philosophy or history or sociology or psychology of education. However, I have already said it does not seem essential that every senior high school teacher should have studied with a philosopher, an historian, or a sociologist in the field of education. Considering the importance of thorough subject-matter preparation and the paucity of teachers of physics and chemistry, I would recommend that an institution certifying a teacher in both physics and chemistry should do so on the basis of the kind of program I have just outlined.

The amount of time devoted to the two physical sciences in my outline is, I admit, barely adequate, and one would expect the teacher to study either or both subjects in his fifth-year work. Those who feel my sights are too low are invited to examine the table on p. 53 which indicates how little preparation many individuals who are now teaching science actually have. The reader should also recognize the difficulty of persuading any person majoring in either physics or chemistry to go into high school teaching instead of into research or college teaching. In institution after institution, I found

that no physics teachers and few chemistry teachers had been prepared in the last five years. A student concentrating in either of
these fields, unless he is a failure, is almost invariably determined
to become a professional physicist or chemist. The best chance of
attracting able students into the field of high school teaching of
physics or chemistry is to show the possibility in a combined field.

Biology is widely offered and enrolls so many high school students that I see no reason for combining a field of concentration in
this subject with another science. Of course, the biologists themselves would without doubt recommend an additional 6 or 9 hours
in physical science (probably chemistry) over and above the 6
hours in general education. This would result in a program like that
outlined for level III of mathematics; in detail, it might look as
follows:

	Semester Hours
General education, including 6 hours of biology, 6 hours of physical science, 6 hours of mathematics and 3 hours of general psychology	60
Educational psychology	3
Philosophy or history or sociology of education	3
Additional physical science	9
Biology	36
Practice teaching and special methods	9
	120

How much difficulty in staffing teacher-training institutions
would these programs impose? In a university or large college, there
would be little difficulty. The problem of what to do in a small
college is another story. In the preceding chapter I recommended
a staff of three professors of education as a minimum for any institution attempting to train elementary school teachers. And I
suggested that unless a heavy endowment was available, my recommendation raised grave doubts about the wisdom of a small college's
attempting to educate elementary teachers. Unless year in and
year out at least 25 were graduated, I did not see how the salaries
of the professors involved could be justified. In fact, I might have

the same doubts about a college with a graduating class of elementary teachers numbering fewer than 50. The situation as to training secondary school teachers in the academic subjects is somewhat different. The difference is evident if one compares the programs I have suggested in this chapter and in the preceding one.

The first concern of any institution educating secondary school teachers is, of course, the quality of the instruction in the subject-matter field and, closely related, the standards maintained. More than one small college with a liberal arts tradition is vulnerable at this point. The second concern is the quality of those who supervise practice teaching. The third is the facilities for practice teaching. The fourth is the understanding of school problems by the academic department. The fifth is the quality of those who offer courses in educational philosophy, history, sociology, and psychology.

I have recommended that the courses in the philosophy and history and sociology of education be given (if they are given at all) by a philosopher, an historian, and a sociologist. Therefore, in a small college that follows my recommendations, there might be no need for the appointment of anyone carrying the title of professor of education. But as I made plain earlier, any purely academic professors undertaking such an assignment would need to devote much time to a study of the schools and their problems. A special psychologist to give instruction in educational psychology would probably be required in addition to the person giving general psychology. The real difficulty, however, enters when one considers what I believe to be essential in regard to the supervision of practice teaching. One clinical professor (The Professor of the Teaching of Subject X) should be available for each of the fields in which the institution certifies a teacher. With certain exceptions, it is *not* satisfactory for one person to try to give the special method courses and supervise practice teaching in several fields. (A combination of physics, chemistry, and possibly biology might be tolerated, but *not* mathematics and science.)

I therefore recommend that:

21. *Every institution awarding a special teaching certificate for secondary school teachers should have on the staff a clinical professor for each field or combination of closely related fields.*

The reasons for this recommendation are obvious. Yet there are difficulties I admit. Very few institutions, large or small, graduate each year as many as 25 students in a secondary field other than English or social studies. It would be financially impossible in many institutions to employ a sufficient number of clinical professors. But it must be remembered that what happens all too often today in even the best institutions is that the practice teaching is supervised by *someone from the college who has never taught the subject in a secondary school.* This is analogous to suggesting that a surgeon be trained in a hospital under the supervision of someone who has never performed an operation! Those who are involved in supervising practice teaching are apt to be long on theory but so woefully short on practice as to make their relation to the cooperating teacher one of a theoretician to a practitioner. Under such circumstances the seminar on methods is usually unrealistic.

The difficulties in staffing are not insuperable in many cases. The clinical professor need not be full-time. As I indicated earlier a joint appointment with a high school may be the best solution, but the salary paid by the college should be *at the rate of a full professor.* If the proper person is not available locally, he would have to be found in another community. Supervisory professors are now expected to travel by car to a number of schools.

Quite frankly, I should imagine that a number of small colleges I have visited would not be able to find or support clinical professors in certain fields in which year in and year out only one or two students were preparing to teach. Similarly, many small colleges are unable to make satisfactory arrangements for practice teaching. In such cases the institution should abandon the practice of training teachers in the fields in question unless a combination of colleges can provide adequate facilities. Giving up the program does not necessarily mean that no one from that college could enter teaching in the abandoned fields. The general education program, the course in educational psychology, and the courses in the philosophy and history of education might be available. *If the academic major were arranged with the needs of the high school in mind,* arrangements could be made with another institution for the special methods seminar and the practice teaching. At the most, another semester of work would be required.

If my recommendation as to state certification were adopted, I should think a number of small colleges now training very few teachers in certain fields would give up the idea of certifying their graduates for teaching in these fields. They would do better to make arrangements for one semester's work with a larger or more fortunately situated institution that had established a state-approved practice-teaching situation.

Part II: Foreign languages, art, music, and physical education

The teachers of the four fields listed as the title of this section have more in common than one might at first assume. Unlike the teachers of English or mathematics or social studies, they may be called on to teach their specialties in any grade. To be sure, historically the foreign language teacher has taught in the high school. But in recent years more and more school systems are introducing the study of a modern foreign language in the lower grades. Whether or not such a procedure requires a foreign language teacher as apart from the elementary classroom teacher is a debatable question, since some who put their faith in the use of television believe that there is no need for a foreign language specialist in the lower grades. But others disagree. At all events, few school systems wish to employ a person to teach French or Spanish only to elementary classes. And a good language teacher is able to teach the same language starting at any grade level and carrying the instruction through the 12th grade.

Similarly, the music teacher or the art teacher must be prepared either as a specialist to be brought into an elementary class to take over from the classroom teacher or to provide instruction in an elective course in high school. And while the instructors in physical education are as a rule closely bound to the secondary schools, they too may be asked to give instruction at least on a supplemental basis in the lower grades.

Another characteristic of all four fields is the present somewhat undefined nature of the task that confronts the teacher. Instruction in foreign languages is in the process of being revolutionized by the so-called oral-aural method. The revolution is far from complete. (It is still possible to find schools in which the new methods are used in the lower grades and the older methods in high school. In such circumstances the advantages of the new methods are not likely to be realized.) Even the aim of the foreign language teacher has changed. The old arguments for the conventional course in a modern or ancient language are rarely heard today. These arguments led to the type of situation, all too common a decade ago, in which a high school student started either Latin or a modern language in grade 9 or 10 and carried forward the study for only two years before shifting to a second language. Such exposure, which leaves no lasting impression on the pupil, was justified by the same line of reasoning that led to the development of the "scrambled language course" (a little French, a little Latin, a little German all in one year!) which, happily, has all but disappeared. Whatever the arguments were, the real motive seemed to be that if an adult could say he or she had once studied a foreign language, his or her prestige in some circles was enhanced. Now that the purpose of studying a foreign language is clearly recognized as that of obtaining something approaching mastery, the task of the teacher is clear-cut. But the change in objective has not yet been accomplished all over the United States, and this fact complicates the problem of teacher training.

If the answer to the question "Why study a foreign language?" has not been clear-cut over the last fifty years, the answers to similar questions about art and music have been even more uncertain. And even the justification of physical education has shifted with the shifting times. Fifty years ago, body building through formal exercise with dumbbells, Indian clubs, and chest weights was in order. Ten years ago, however, one could hunt in vain for such equipment in a school gymnasium: the emphasis was on sports. Today the emphasis is still on sports, but the pendulum is swinging toward a renewed emphasis on body building.

The American public and the professional educators, then, are still a bit uncertain as to why instruction should be provided in art, music, foreign languages, and physical education. This uncertainty is reflected in the amount of time allotted to these subjects in the schools and in the varying practice as to the optional nature of the work. In a sense all four fields are in competition. In only a few of the schools I have visited are the teachers of all four satisfied with the positions accorded to their specialties.

The increased emphasis since Sputnik on science and mathematics is believed to have reduced the amount of time spent by the average or better-than-average student on art and music. While the study of foreign languages has to some extent benefited from the new surge of popular interest in academic work, the revolutionary changes in method have left the teachers somewhat insecure. Physical education as a required subject one period a day five days a week obviously takes time away from music and art, as do the academic subjects. Therefore, a certain tension exists, to put it mildly, among the proponents of all these fields.

As I have talked to the teachers and professors active in the four areas I am here exploring, I have become impressed with an attitude something like an inferiority complex that seems to arise out of the lively competition for the high school student's time and interest. One consequence of this attitude in the case of art, music, and physical education has been an attempt to gain respectability by adopting the phraseology and the symbols characteristic of the faculties of arts and letters, such as listing with a course number "Football Fundamentals," "Advanced Basketball," and "Textiles I and II." The consequences are most ridiculous in the graduate programs to be considered in the next chapter. The terms in which the undergraduate programs are described, however, reflect the same tendency. All this seems to me a pity. In each case a level of competency would seem to be relatively easy to define, and once it is defined, a student's success or failure in meeting the level could be demonstrated through proficiency examinations.

In the field of languages, the Modern Language Association of America has developed, over the last ten years, proficiency tests for teachers and advanced college students. The test as now used takes about four hours and has several parts. The speaking tests "involve reading aloud to test pronunciation, stress, accent, and intonation. . . . The reading tests are designed to measure sensitivity to style, shades of meaning, and comprehension of the message. The writing tests include various devices such as reconstructing paragraphs and interlinear correction of error." [1] To a layman these portions of the

---

[1] Wilmouth H. Starr and others, *Modern Foreign Languages and the Academically Talented Student*; report of a conference sponsored jointly by the

test would seem to measure the degree of mastery of the language and to be of the first importance. For he is probably all too familiar with high school teachers who do not have anything approaching a mastery of the foreign language they are teaching as a *spoken* language. To be sure, a modern foreign language differs from all the other subjects taught in high school in that achievement can be defined in terms of an absolute standard. The standard is the language as spoken and written by a well-educated native of the nation. No similar self-evident criteria are to be found in other areas. Therefore, it seems to be no accident that proficiency tests have been developed and *accepted* in the United States in the case of a modern foreign language. The specter of a state or national "syllabus," so feared by Americans (but accepted as a matter of course in Great Britain), does not raise its ugly head.

There are three other parts of the proficiency test developed by the Modern Language Association; the "Applied Linguistic tests," the "Culture tests," and "Professional Preparation tests." These three parts test not proficiency in the language, but mastery of an arbitrarily agreed-on body of knowledge. One might or might not agree that every future teacher should be required to make a high score on these portions of the test. I am quite prepared to accept the experts' view that today (as contrasted with yesterday) the linguist has something important to say to the future teacher and that the teacher should have some knowledge of the culture of the country in question. I have the greatest doubts, however, as to the possibility of preparing a paper-and-pencil test that will measure "the examinee's ability to control the methods most likely to produce competency" (the stated aim of the Professional Preparation test). I should prefer the judgment of the supervisor of the practice teaching. However, even with this reservation I am ready to recommend enthusiastically to all colleges and universities training foreign language teachers that they use this proficiency test to determine who is to be certified as a teacher. The counting of semester hours should be scrapped.

If the score on the proficiency examination determines whether or

National Education Association Project on the Academically Talented Student and the Modern Language Association of America. Foreign Language Program, 1961.

not the candidate is certified, then the issue of whether a graduate of a four-year course should be certified in more than one language is easily settled. Let the proficiency tests provide the answer. How the proficiency is acquired is surely of minor significance. As for practice teaching, assessment of the future teacher in teaching one language will provide sufficient evidence. If a clinical professor has competence in several languages, he may be able to supervise several fields. Otherwise except for a possible combination such as French and Spanish, separate professors in each language would be in order.

IN ART, MUSIC, AND PHYSICAL EDUCATION a satisfactory teacher must be a competent performer. By no means every young person even with high intelligence has the capacity to develop the skill in question. And the capacity or lack of it can usually be determined quite early in a youth's development. Music affords the best example. Musical talent manifests itself at an early age, and unless it is developed during the school years, there is extremely little likelihood of a person's becoming an accomplished performer on an instrument during college. The implications of this fact for the education of music teachers are obvious. A test of developed musical skill should be a prerequisite for admission to a program training music teachers. In other words, the professional training starts before the future teacher enters college. Artistic talent, like musical talent, can and should be identified and encouraged while the future artist is very young. And it is obvious that some of the skills in sports demanded today of the physical education teacher would be manifest in high school. In all these fields, the development of a certain degree of competency should be the prerequisite for admission to a teacher-training program.

In an earlier chapter I emphasized my belief that the education of teachers in college depends in large measure on the high school preparation. In the areas of music, sport, and art, since skills are to a considerable extent developed on an extracurricular basis by high school students, the *total youthful experience* must be considered in establishing the level of attainment demanded for admission to the teacher-training programs. Admission should depend on the demonstration of a high level of performance. Those who fail should be directed to the teaching fields that do not require such highly developed skills. Thus, it is during the pre-college years that the future teachers of modern foreign languages, of music, of art, and of physical education must receive the basic training on which their competence as teachers eventually depends.

If one accepts the views presented in the preceding paragraphs, there will be little difficulty in suggesting a four-year program for training teachers in art or music or physical education or *one* foreign language. I assume that half the four-year course will be taken up with general education. I further assume practice teaching will be carried out under the supervision of a clinical professor and in a situation approved by the state. I am inclined to think that a course in educational psychology would be highly desirable. A course in the philosophy or history or sociology of education is also desirable.

I shall not attempt to formulate a suggestion as to the number of media in which an art teacher should have competence—opinions differ. Nor shall I endeavor to make a similar judgment about the number of instruments on which a future music teacher should be able to perform. To be an effective orchestra leader would appear to require many more hours of study than can be accommodated in a four-year program; graduate work is clearly indicated.

I do not see how it would be possible for a teacher of music to combine with his specialty sufficient knowledge of another field to be competent to teach in it. I am of the same opinion in regard to art and physical education but for somewhat different reasons. But first let me formulate my conclusions in this recommendation:

22. *An institution offering programs in art or music or physical education should be prepared to award a teaching diploma in each of these fields without grade designation; institutional programs should not attempt to develop competency in more than one field in four years.*

The demands on the music teacher for competency in music are so heavy in terms of time that the problem of "major" and "minor" is hardly likely to arise. If the art teacher is to have competency in several media as well as a good knowledge of the history of art, again there will be insufficient time for a second field. Physical education is different. There is far less uniformity of opinion on the amount of time required for developing the requisite "physical skills and applied techniques." Also, colleges and universities differ on the number of hours that should be devoted to such subjects as applied anatomy, kinesiology, the physiology of exercise, and health and hygiene. Furthermore, the academic bookkeeping involves decisions on the number of credits that should be allowed for work on the playing field under such titles as "Football Fundamentals," "Advanced Baseball," and "Track and Field." One could argue that all the sport skills should be developed in the afternoons on an extracurricular basis, leaving ample lecture and study time for such a subject as mathematics or biology or general science. To argue thus, however, would be to take a position so extreme as to be revolutionary.

I am prepared to argue strongly *against a combination of physical education with any other field*. Teachers of physical education are today suspect because superintendents and principals of high schools have far too often required them to teach academic subjects that they have hardly studied in college; moreover, they are subject to so much public pressure in their role as coaches that they are often forced to neglect their classroom work. Therefore, in the interest of this branch of the teaching profession, I suggest the door should be firmly closed against such practices. The institutions and the state, through the approved practice-teaching program, should certify teachers of physical education or physical education and hygiene but *not* physical education and mathematics or similar combinations. The physical education teacher will also be a coach, either intramural or interscholastic, and to my mind should be. He therefore has two important functions to fulfill, and this should be sufficient.

Because the physical education teacher is likely to be a coach and because of the high visibility of the coaching staff, the road to administrative positions is open and attractive. I understand that not a few superintendents and high school principals are former physical education teachers. Considering the mores of American society, I am surprised that there are not more. The future is likely to be like the past in this respect. Unless there is a change in the direction of this trend, I conclude that *the physical education teacher should have an even wider general academic education than any other teacher.* If I were charged with suggesting a four-year program, I would require more than the 60 semester hours of general education I have outlined earlier. I would add another 9 or 12 semester hours in the social sciences, the humanities, or in science. Taken together with the time I have allotted for general education, this would mean a concentration of some 21 hours in one area. The suggestion resembles that which I have made for elementary teachers, except that, for the physical education teacher, I would urge the suitability of other fields of concentration, particularly the social sciences. More likely than not, the man preparing to be a physical education teacher is, perhaps unconsciously, preparing to be an educational administrator. He needs to start early on a course of wide reading in the humanities and the social sciences.

9

CONTINUING AND IN-SERVICE
EDUCATION OF TEACHERS

As I HAVE ALREADY REPORTED, a secondary school teacher graduating
from a college or university after a prescribed four-year course can
be certified by the institution as eligible for full-time employment
by a local school board in almost every state. In all states, a four-
year course regarded as satisfactory by the state, if successfully
passed, confers the same status on an elementary teacher. However,
in some states, the teacher, after assuming the first position, is
required by law to continue his or her formal education. In all or
almost all states, the salary schedules set by many if not all school
boards are such as to induce teachers to continue their formal
education. For example, there are boards that automatically increase
a teacher's salary each time he has obtained three hours' credit by
passing a course either during the school year or in the summer—
irrespective of what the course is about. This practice can be most
objectionable; take, for instance, the case of a teacher of German
who moves to a slightly higher salary bracket by taking and passing
a course in driver education. Such a ringing up of cash-register
credits, course by course, seems an odd procedure to a foreign
visitor, or for that matter to many American citizens who hear of it
for the first time. No other country has such a practice; no other
occupation or profession in the United States operates in such a way.
What are the reasons for this widespread scheme?

For many years in many states, a large proportion of the teachers
had never completed a four-year college course. As the bachelor's

187

degree assumed more and more importance in the public mind, it was natural for school boards to pay higher salaries to college graduates than to those without a college degree. But with the spread of part-time adult education, it became possible for teachers without a bachelor's degree to obtain one by attending summer school or afternoon and evening classes. Even today in many states, a considerable number of elementary teachers are slowly accumulating academic credits that will yield them a bachelor's degree and thus higher pay.

The intent of teacher groups and school boards has no doubt been to find ways of rewarding meritorious teachers with salary increments that go beyond those attached to mere seniority. Attempts to measure teaching merit, however, have not yet proved clearly valid, and teacher groups have violently resisted proposals to adopt a merit system. One suspects they would oppose any system that defined merit in such a way that particular teachers would almost certainly be denied access to the "meritorious" category.

As an alternative to some kind of merit-rating system, the teacher groups have argued that willingness to take additional college courses is evidence that a teacher is at least highly motivated and eager for self-improvement; such motivation, they assume, is prima-facie evidence of merit, though it may simply provide evidence that they want more money. But because of the characteristic American confidence in taking formal courses, it has been possible to convince most school boards and state legislators that a teacher simply *must* be better by virtue of having been exposed to more instruction. Given the varying standards of American colleges, this route to "merit" is open to all and is therefore consistent with the egalitarian sentiment of organized teacher groups. Despite their constant charge that the American Federation of Teachers (AFT) has a "trade union" rather than a "professional" bias, the NEA affiliates have been as adamant as has the AFT in opposing any kind of salary schedule except one based on length of training and experience. Though I do recommend additional work beyond the bachelor's degree for most teachers, I must express my dissent from the position that the mere accumulation of further college credits provides evidence that a teacher deserves a raise in salary.

If the holder of the bachelor's degree is to receive a higher salary because he or she holds that degree, it seems only natural that the holder of a master's degree should receive still another increment. And for the most part they do. It is only a small step further to equate increase in pay with the completion of a portion of the journey toward the master's degree, or the accumulation of the 30 semester hours of credit necessary for the degree even if the degree itself is not attained. Therefore, today one finds a bewildering complexity of arrangements relating the salary schedule to degrees and earned credits beyond the bachelor's degree and the master's degree.

Without attempting to disentangle cause and effect, it must be pointed out that for at least fifty years, private institutions in the large metropolitan areas have been doing a land-office business as a consequence of the development of the tradition I have just described. One need only look at the scheduling of the classes to understand the special position of education courses. In few urban colleges of education or faculties of education are the majority of the courses scheduled in the morning or early afternoon, as are most classes in the faculties of letters and sciences, or medicine. One need only note the vast number of education courses given in the afternoon, evening, and Saturdays by the private metropolitan institutions to realize that the part-time instruction of teachers may be a highly profitable undertaking. (It is true that a few arts and sciences courses may also be given on the same schedule in institutions with a large part-time enrollment.) It is an open secret that, at least in the past, a considerable share of the net income earned by schools of education has found its way into the general university budget.

Now, there is nothing wrong with one branch of a private university having a budget that is heavily in the black; I know of at least one famous law school that earned a surplus for many years and financed buildings out of the funds thus accumulated. However, one can hardly dodge the fact that something approaching a vested interest has been created by this situation. From the point of view of the budget, if enrollment of teachers in the afternoon and evening courses should markedly decrease, more than one faculty of education in a metropolitan institution would be in serious trouble. I have long believed that schools of education, if not adequately supported by the state, should have sufficient endowment so that they need not depend on tuition from in-service education courses. Citizens who criticize schools of education might well devote their efforts to raising endowments that would place such schools on as solid a financial base as the better schools of engineering enjoy.

In some metropolitan areas, the courses I have been discussing are offered by state and municipal public institutions. Often, these institutions, like the private ones, charge fees, and the income from this source is by no means negligible. Frequently there is competition between several different types of institution in the same area.

Even when fees are not charged, the vested interest in continuing afternoon or evening courses is almost as great in the publicly supported institutions as in the private, though the cash nexus may be less evident. Legislative appropriations for teacher education are closely connected with enrollment, and if the courses taken by in-service teachers should disappear, there would not be enough instructional work in many faculties to justify the size of the staff that is now supported. Thus professors and administrators in both private and public faculties of education would be less than human if they did not feel that in-service education of teachers is an essential element in the entire American picture.

Let us look at the types of course involved. They may be roughly divided into the following groups: (1) professional education courses somewhat similar to those required or recommended for undergraduates but at a more advanced level (e.g., the philosophy of education, social foundations, educational psychology), (2) methods courses, such as courses in how to teach reading, (3) courses in psychology or education concerned with special problems of the classroom, such as a course in the instruction of the mentally retarded, or the unusually gifted, or the physically handicapped child, (4) courses leading to a master's or doctor's degree in such special fields as curriculum planning, guidance, administration (at the principal's or superintendent's level), (5) academic courses. On the graduate level, just as in both professional and academic collegiate work, the multiplicity of courses is astounding. One large and famous New York City private institution lists no fewer than 600 courses open to teachers who will enroll, pay the fee

($40 per credit hour), and devote a few hours in the late afternoon to attending the lectures and doing the required work. Another rival institution offers even more courses on the same basis. Lest I appear to be criticizing only the professors of education for the multiplicity of their courses, let me emphasize to the uninformed that such a multiplication is an academic American disease. The basis is very simple though rarely stated frankly: professors love to lecture on their own pet subjects.

The arguments for in-service education on a part-time basis during the school year are usually threefold. First, the teacher should continue to grow intellectually; second, the teacher is never adequately prepared in a four-year course and further preparation is desirable; third, a teacher needs to be kept up to date regarding new developments. The arguments I have heard against the present scheme are again threefold. First, the teacher is too tired to do justice to work, and if the teacher has extra time, he might well devote it to preparing more adequately for the next day's teaching task; second, all too often the teacher elects not the course that might actually assist in developing his capacities as a teacher, but rather the course that is most likely to yield credit with the minimum effort or the course that heads him toward an administrative career; third, the whole scheme actually works to tempt the better teachers, who take courses in educational administration, out of the classroom.

From my experience talking to many teachers, I am convinced that taking courses is in danger of becoming an occupational disease. As one teacher said to me, "I just love taking courses. I wish I could keep on taking courses all my life." Discussing this subject in a summer school with more than one group of teachers who were purring with pleasure at their continuing education, I felt as if I were talking to opium smokers who were praising the habit of which they had long since become the victims.

This is not to imply that I would prohibit teachers from taking additional formal course work. I do, however, seriously question the present practice of so relating salary to further course work that the teacher is bribed into taking whatever course happens to be available on a late afternoon or evening during the months when he is engaged in full-time teaching. I think it desirable to

make a distinction between courses taken as part of a well-conceived program during summer session, or during a period of academic leave from teaching, and those taken in late afternoon or
Saturday mornings as a part-time job of one already fully employed.
The latter are of two types: "on campus" and "extension" courses.
The extension courses are given "off campus" by a professor de-
clared by the educational institution to be competent to give the
course. If the lecturer is a regular member of the institution's staff,
he is likely to receive extra pay for the extra work, which may involve an automobile trip of a hundred miles or more. The lectures
may be given in a schoolhouse many miles from the university that
offers the course, and there may, or may not, be an "extension center" in which library facilities have been assembled. In those states
where there are well-established extension centers, the question of
whether the course is really an on-campus rather than an extension
course is a matter of semantics.

In the course of my journeying around the country, I have often
heard the standards in these extension courses severely criticized.
"Here is where the real scandal is," I have been told. And it is not
without amusement that I have heard more than one person connected with a *public* institution warn me against the offering of
private universities—and vice versa! Actually, I have discovered no
way of getting statistics about these extension courses and little
evidence beyond gossip as to their quality. However, within the
profession the suspicion is rife that some, if not many, of them are far
below standard. And because of this suspicion, I suppose, the number of credits, out of a total of 30 toward a master's degree, that
can be "rung up" by taking extension courses is commonly limited
to about eight. *There is often, however, no limit to the number of
extension courses that can be counted toward an increase in pay.*

Attending a summer school has been a popular practice of teachers for well over half a century. And many well-known universities
have done all they could to develop outstanding summer schools.
During July, 1962, I visited four summer schools in New York (outside New York City), Wisconsin, Colorado, and Ohio. I have also
had experience teaching in the Harvard Summer School, first in the
1920s as a chemist, and later, in the 1950s, as one attempting to
promote his ideas about the teaching of science. I am, therefore,

somewhat familiar with the advantages and disadvantages of summer-school work. Compared with afternoon or evening on-campus lectures during the school year, summer-school instruction, I believe, is usually far superior. My own prejudice has been reinforced by the almost unanimous opinion of the teachers with whom I have discussed this problem. Not only is the student (the teacher on a vacation) more ready and able to devote time and effort to studies, but the out-of-class discussions with other teachers and the opportunity to read on a leisurely basis are of great value. I have become convinced that attendance at summer school may be so refreshing and exhilarating an experience as to warrant its being repeated quite often throughout the teacher's career. I believe this is particularly the case with elementary teachers.

If one compares the courses listed in summer-school catalogs with the listing of extension courses or the on-campus courses given in the afternoon, evening, or Saturdays (and thus available to teachers on the job), it is clear that in the summer schools there is a better opportunity for the secondary school teacher to take advanced courses in his special field, for example, history or mathematics. There is divergence among summer schools in the extent to which teachers avail themselves of this opportunity, but I must record that as far as my limited sampling has any validity, by no means a majority of the returning secondary school teachers are studying subject matter. I am frank to say I think this is a pity. At least one of the deans of a School of Education with whom I talked had the same feeling and was doing what he could to direct secondary school teachers into studying more deeply in their academic fields during the summer. But he found that the lure of the courses that lead to a master's degree in administration and guidance, and thus out of the classroom, was too strong. I am sure a similar situation exists elsewhere. However, by no means all the blame rests with the education faculty for its alluring courses in administration. *Far too often the academic departments fail to provide even in the summer school enough courses of the kind a teacher needs.* There is a challenge here to which academic professors should respond.

There is a wonderful uplifting sound to a proclamation that a state has raised the standards of teacher education by requiring that in the future all teachers must eventually earn a master's degree. But when one examines this and similar proclamations that have been common in the last five years, a sense of uneasiness soon develops. First of all, can the rules be enforced in practice? I believe they cannot. Admission to a graduate school either of arts and sciences or of education usually requires an undergraduate record considerably better than the record required for graduation from college in the same institution. That is, a student with a C average may be graduated and certified to teach; but the same student would be denied admission to the graduate school. Obviously, then, an institution may be sending out to teach in the public schools men and women who cannot be admitted to the master's degree program in the same institution, at least not under the usual procedures.

There is another difficulty with the master's degree for teachers as it is usually administered. For example, a certain summer-school course that an elementary teacher might take with profit cannot count toward a master's degree. Why? Because the faculty has decided it is too elementary. An amusing illustration was afforded by my conversation with a professor of music concerned with graduate work for high school music teachers. "An orchestra leader," he explained, "might have completed his undergraduate work with a sufficient degree of competence on the trumpet and trombone but with no acquaintance with the oboe or clarinet. In the summer he should start on these instruments, but such work," he said sadly, "would not count for a master's degree." "What, is there a hierarchy among instruments?" I asked. "Oh, no," he replied, "but beginning work on any instrument cannot be counted for a master's degree." So I suppose the future orchestra leader improved his trumpeting instead of learning to play new instruments.

A common example of the same problem has been often called to my attention. A teacher of science in grades 6 or 7, who as an undergraduate majored in chemistry and physics, feels a real need for more knowledge of geology and astronomy. The freshman or sophomore courses offered in the summer appear to be just the thing. But at present in most universities, they are considered too elementary to count for a master's degree.

This phenomenon could be illustrated by a virtually inexhaustible supply of examples, but further illustration at this point seems to me unnecessary. Instead I shall here issue dogmatically a set of radical recommendations, and then in my justification of them illustrate further the present highly unsatisfactory state of affairs regarding continuing in-service education of teachers.

I recommend that:

23. *School boards should drastically revise their salary schedules. There should be a large jump in salary when a teacher moves from the probationary status to tenure. Any salary increments based on advanced studies should not be tied to course credits earned (semester hours), but only to the earning of a master's degree, based normally on full-time residence or four summer sessions in which the program is directed toward the development of the competence of the teacher as a teacher. Such a salary increment should be made mandatory by state law.*

With respect to the first part of this recommendation, I know that it is common practice in at least certain states to provide a trial period for the young teacher. However the arrangement may be expressed in words, in practice this can mean that for a period of two or three years the new teacher is being appraised. At the end of the trial period there is not the slightest obligation on the part of the school board to employ the teacher. If the decision is made to employ, then the position should be regarded as permanent up to a fixed retirement age, subject to removal for cause through established procedures. From what I have observed, the trial period might well be longer than is usual, say as much as four years, and the salary jump between the two grades—with and without tenure—very much larger than any I have noted. I feel that such arrangements, if duly publicized in the community, would go a considerable way toward meeting the complaints of some laymen about treating all teachers alike without regard to competence. Under the conditions I am suggesting, there would be two salary schedules based on demonstrated ability. One would be for the junior teachers, so to speak, applicable for the first four years. The second would be for the senior teachers on permanent appointment, and the difference between the two schedules should be very large. In short, more attention should be paid to rewarding those who have proven themselves during the probationary period. The tenure laws in many states would have more meaning if the salary increase given to a teacher appointed to a permanent position were far greater. Morale of the experienced teacher would be strengthened. The career teacher who manifests a desire to remain would be rewarded.

Once again I venture to draw on my own experience, admitting freely the danger of arguing by analogy. I can only place in evidence the considerable disturbance about tenure and promotion in more than one university in the 1930s (including my own), which quieted down only after a clear-cut distinction was made between appointments with and without tenure. I think school boards and superintendents might profit by examining the personnel procedures in some colleges and universities, recognizing that in school-teaching the period without tenure must be shorter than in higher education.

In colleges, universities or school systems, a scheme such as I have outlined will be successful only if in fact those on trial are fairly appraised. A two-salary schedule for junior and senior teachers makes sense only if the senior teachers (those with tenure) are in fact those whose competence has been clearly manifest. And who is to judge? First of all, *not* the school board collectively or individually. Second, *not* the superintendent alone. These negatives are easy to state but nevertheless important. On the positive side, clearly the principal of the school in which the teacher is teaching should carry a heavy share of the responsibility. But in addition, some arrangement should be formalized by which assistant principals and certain senior teachers—for example, heads of departments—should share in the recommendations.

So far as the second part of the recommendation is concerned, the emphasis should be placed on the development of a program directed toward increasing the person's competence as a teacher. The mere accumulation of credits, without respect to their bearing on the teacher's actual work, should not be counted. Nor should a classroom teacher who earns a master's degree in such fields as guidance and administration be rewarded by an increase in salary; if and when he obtains a position as a guidance officer or an administrator, he will then receive an increment in salary.

If, however, the teacher is to be encouraged to further his education during summer sessions and periods of leave during the academic year, some financial assistance is needed. Recommendations 24 and 25 are designed for this purpose:

24. *School boards or the state should provide financial assistance so that teachers may attend summer school after enrolling in a graduate school for the purpose of completing a program of the type stated in Recommendation 23.*
25. *School boards should provide leave of absence with salary for a full-time semester residence at a university to enable teachers to study toward a master's program, provided this program is designed to increase the competence of the teacher; state funds should be available for this purpose.*

Many of the graduate offerings for teachers are, as I have suggested, not adequate for the purposes of the kind of master's-degree program I am recommending. For this reason I have spelled out what I believe should be involved in a recommendation to the universities:

26. *The graduate schools of education or their equivalent (in universities organized without such separate degree-granting schools) should devise a program for increasing the competence of teachers as teachers with the following characteristics:*

   (1) *It should be open to any graduate of the same institution in the same field of endeavor (e.g., elementary education, secondary school social studies, etc.).*

   (2) *Courses should be allowed for credit toward the 30 semester hours whether or not the courses are of an elementary nature, provided they are clearly courses needed to increase the competence of the teacher.*

   (3) *No credit toward the degree should be given for extension courses or courses taken on campus while the teacher is engaged on a full-time teaching job.*

   (4) *Passing of a comprehensive examination should be required for the master's degree, as is now the case in some institutions.*

   (5) *The summer-school sessions should be arranged so that*

four summer residences will complete the degree requirements, or two summers plus one full-time semester residence.

(6) If the offering in the arts and sciences is not wide enough to provide meaningful work in the summer session (as it would not be in some state colleges), arrangements should be made for the transfer of credit from a university summer school with a good offering of courses in subject-matter fields.

(7) For elementary teachers, the degree should be master of education in elementary education; for secondary teachers, master of education in English (or science, or social science or modern languages or mathematics).

My insistence that only those courses taken during summer sessions or periods of academic leave should count toward the master's degree for which a substantial salary increment is allowed needs some defense. Remember, I have not urged that teachers be denied the opportunity, now widely utilized by people in all walks of life, to use their leisure time taking courses they consider worth while. I respect those desires which lead a teacher to an evening course, whether it be on the "great books," "the secondary school curriculum," "social psychology," or "watercoloring." Nor do I deny that in certain urban centers a conscientious teacher *might* put together a pattern of evening courses that would constitute a master's degree program well conceived to advance his competence as a teacher. I do think it rarely happens, however.

But salary policy, which I am here discussing, tends to determine the general path teachers follow in securing their continued education. Those who make this policy must decide which of two possible paths is likely to prove superior. The first path leads through a series of late afternoon and evening courses. These courses may well be chosen because they are offered at a convenient time and place; unfortunately, they are sometimes chosen because they make little demand on the teachers' intellectual and emotional energies. They are attended by teachers whose day's work has already placed an incredible strain on these resources, and the time and energy devoted to the course must often be subtracted from that needed for the work of ensuing days. The courses offered are usually those designed to attract the largest possible number of teachers and rarely if ever include advanced academic courses in the areas of a teacher's specialization. The second path leads to a set of courses designed by the teacher and his university adviser for his specific purposes. These courses are attended by people who have the leisure of summer session or academic leave to devote full time to their studies and who because they are full-time students, have access to libraries and laboratories, and time to use them. They should include advanced courses in the academic fields the students teach; at least there is far greater possibility that such courses will be available in summer schools than in the afternoon and evening arrangement.

Granted that there is some value to the first path; the second seems to me clearly superior. I therefore urge the public to adopt policies that will encourage teachers to take this latter route. Such policies include both financial support for the teacher as he walks up the path, and a substantial salary increment when he reaches its end.

I am aware that my recommendations will not be universally welcomed. Many professors of education will find them obnoxious, because in effect they eliminate the premium on taking courses in education on campus or on an extension basis during the school year.

An entirely different set of persons will object to my recommendations for the master's degree because they "lower standards." I would answer that, with the great diversity among institutions in their grading policies, the word "standard" as applied to grades has long since lost meaning. I would further say that the faculties of education have, for the sake of appeasing their critics in the faculty of arts and sciences, adopted academic policies designed for a quite different purpose. I would *not* advocate a general lowering of the entrance requirements for a graduate school of arts and sciences or argue for the acceptance of freshmen or sophomore courses in a master's program. The M.A., for the future Ph.D. holder in an academic field, represents a step in a process of education only distantly related to that of the teacher endeavoring to increase his or her competency. As in the case of the employment of clinical professors, it is high time the faculties of education shook off the self-imposed shackles of academic traditions borrowed from faculties of arts and sciences. The layman might note in passing that the first degree in law, although usually a postgraduate degree, is a *bachelor's* degree. But law faculties have traditionally gone their own way, rather contemptuous of the academic red tape of their colleagues in arts and sciences.

There will be some professors of the conventional academic subjects who would wish to prescribe the content of the program for the master of education degree and perhaps rule out all education courses. And I am frank to state that at one time during the past two years I was of just such an opinion. But I have been convinced by my talk with teachers that for all teachers, or almost all, some formal courses in methods and psychology are desirable—some but not many. I should let each institution frame its own program and announce it, and have free competition among institutions as to the quality and relevance of what is demanded. Surely each program must to some degree be tailored to the individual teacher's undergraduate background. Furthermore, the programs will differ, subject by subject. If I were advising a university, I should urge it to adopt the type of four-year program I have already described, and then to arrange for teachers with experience to be given such additional instruction on the graduate level as I shall now set forth field by field.

I believe an experienced elementary school teacher can profit from advanced instruction in the teaching of reading, arithmetic, and science, and in child psychology. If he is teaching in a slum school, I would advocate that some time be spent on sociology and those aspects of political science and economics that bear on school problems and urban conditions. A considerable portion of time (perhaps one-third) might well be used to amplify and deepen the teacher's knowledge of English, history, science, or mathematics, depending on which of the four fields was chosen as an undergraduate area of concentration.

Assuming that a teacher of grades 7 to 12 had been granted a teaching certificate in a single field, his master's program might include further work in psychology, the study of history and philosophy of education, and a seminar on methods. I would suggest that a major portion (say two-thirds) of the time be used either to develop the competency required for handling advanced-placement work in his special field, or in preparation to teach in another field. As I indicated in the last chapter, there will be for some time to come many teachers prepared by some institutions to teach in two fields. Such persons can make good use of summer-school work to complete their otherwise inadequate study of the subjects they are teaching. In designing master's programs, an institution should attest to the adequacy of preparation in one or two fields, using essentially the standards of competence I suggested in the last chapter. A teacher in grades 7 and 8 might well benefit from the further study of child psychology and a seminar on methods designed for junior high school teachers.

A second or third foreign language, together with a seminar in methods and perhaps some psychology, would seem appropriate fields of study for the teacher of foreign languages. For the teacher of music, the equivalent of another full year's work will not be too much to secure the mastery of additional instruments and musical theory needed by one who teaches both vocal and instrumental music. In the case of the teacher of art, I doubt if the instruction in this field at the graduate level is sufficiently developed to warrant further time devoted to the improvement of skills. The equivalent of a major in art history together with psychology might be considered. More often, I should imagine, the art teachers would like to use an academic year or four summers to develop on the basis of the general education courses the equivalent competence in English or social studies that is required for a teaching diploma in grades 7 to 12.

I am far from impressed by what I have heard and read about graduate work in the field of physical education. If I wished to portray the education of teachers in the worst terms, I should quote from the descriptions of some graduate courses in physical education. To my mind, a university should cancel graduate programs in this area. If the physical education teacher wishes to enter into a research career in the field of physiology of exercise and related subjects, he should use the graduate years to build on his natural science background a knowledge of the physiological sciences that will enable him to stand on an equal footing with the undergraduate major in these sciences.

In appraising the above guidelines, the reader must keep in mind the premises on which the suggested four-year program of earlier chapters was based. Sixty hours was allotted to general education in a prescribed program, with no free electives except for students who succeeded in "examining out" of some required courses; the aim was to insure that the graduate would have had a considerable exposure, either in college or in high school, to the following subjects: English composition, literature, history, economics, political science, psychology, mathematics, biology, physics, and chemistry. I am well aware that there is little chance of the adoption of such a program by any academic faculty. Those who enter teaching with the usual type of four-year program may be lacking in the broad academic background that would be provided by the program I have proposed. Therefore, in drawing up the programs for the master's degree in education I have just recommended, the faculty of each institution should think in terms of the *total* five-year exposure to academic and professional courses.

As I have noted, the argument for a five-year program for teachers is based in some quarters on the premise that at least four full years of academic work are necessary. For a long time, in the state of California a secondary school teacher has been required to complete five years of preservice education for the provisional certificate. The Fisher Bill, recently passed, has incorporated this feature. This legislation should not, in my judgment, serve as a model for other states.

I hope it will not serve as a model; yet I am very much afraid it will. Two slogans are popular. The first, that "a teacher should be first of all a liberally educated person," usually means that a teacher should take all the academic courses the professors can persuade the state to require. And if all graduates of a liberal arts faculty are to be considered "liberally educated persons," it is important to remember that they include graduates with a major in physical education. The second slogan, more often stressed by the educational establishment, is that "a teacher doesn't have status unless his college preparation is at least five years." The weight of these two slogans is considerable; I fear many states will enact legislation requiring a continuous five years of college for all teachers before they can enter the classroom.

As far as adequate preparation for teaching on the elementary or secondary school level is concerned, I am certain that four years are enough, provided first, that an adequate high school preparation is assured, and second, that the subjects studied are adequately distributed among general education, an area of concentration, and professional education.

If a fifth year is required by state law, I believe the New York State arrangement—in which the teacher returns after some experience to a program based on this experience as well as on his previous pattern of education—is the best. On balance, however, I am against a state's *requiring* a fifth year for either elementary or secondary teachers. I am in favor of a large salary increment to induce teachers to attend four summer sessions and obtain the kind of master's degree I have been describing.

My own arguments for more study in summer schools, or in full-time residence after the first degree and *after* experience in actual teaching, rest on the teacher's need for help in improving his teaching. Much of the work in methods and in psychology is almost meaningless when given to undergraduates. The same material has meaning when it is presented to a teacher after he has struggled with the problems of a classroom. Hence, the amount of professional education in the undergraduate program should be cut to the bone, and opportunities should be provided in graduate summer sessions for continuing such work.

One of the most distressing experiences I have had during the course of this study is to realize how "course-bound" is the average American college graduate. Among the many things our professors of arts and sciences have failed to accomplish is the inculcation of the idea that vast fields of knowledge and culture are wide open to anyone who can and will read. How often have I heard the remark "I wish I had had more of a liberal education." And this was said by teachers who were attending afternoon lectures and summer-school sessions, primarily to accumulate credits in professional courses. I wish no one receiving a bachelor's degree would carry away the belief that his alma mater has "educated" him. The well-educated man or woman of the future must be primarily a self-educated person. And self-education requires years and years of reading, and a desire to learn.

To return to the California pattern, it is only fair to repeat that the issue between four-year and five-year continuous programs turns on the value one attaches to free electives. And if a parent feels that an extra year to enable the future teacher to wander about and sample academic courses is worth the cost, I should not be the person to condemn this use of money. But I would, as a taxpayer, *vigorously protest the use of tax money* for a fifth year of what I consider dubious value. Nevertheless, many young people choose to spend four years in academic programs that allow considerable free election of courses before the student decides on a career; and there are graduates of four-year academic colleges who wish to teach in our schools but are not prepared to do so. I have chosen my words carefully and *not* written "but cannot meet state certification requirements," for I have already proposed certain drastic changes in state requirements. *In so doing, I have made it clear that an A.B. in mathematics or chemistry or English, let us say, who has had no introduction to the realities of schoolteaching, should not be hired by a local board.* Nevertheless, it is important that there be roads into schoolteaching for such people. Let us see what they are at present.

I had a share in opening one such road at Harvard, which took the form of a program in education conducted entirely on the graduate level. In the 1950s similar approaches were developed in other institutions. It is impossible in a few words to summarize the many different types of master's (or M.A.T.) programs of a similar sort now in operation. What is important is the recognition that such fifth-year post-baccalaureate programs are an entirely different breed of cat from the fifth-year programs I have been describing in this chapter.

In a recent book *The Education of the Secondary School Teacher*,[1] Ernest Stabler gives an extensive report on M.A.T. programs. He reports that "between 1951 and 1957 the Fund for the Advancement of Education granted an average of four million dollars a year to teacher education, a good share of which was channeled to 5 M.A.T. programs." He goes on to say, "In 1959 the Fund directed eleven million dollars toward achieving a major break-

---

[1] Ernest Stabler, ed., *The Education of the Secondary School Teacher*, Wesleyan University Press, Middletown, Conn., 1962.

through in the education of teachers, and again the M.A.T. and similar programs were on the grant list."

I have visited institutions in which one or more "post-baccalaureate programs for training teachers" (the best phrase I can think of) have been in operation for some years. Many are heavily subsidized, and provide a way of earning one's way to a first certificate through part-time teaching. The students are carefully selected, and the relations between the institution and the school system may be unusual and excellent. This is particularly true where the student has a part-time teaching job and is called an "intern." (But the word "intern" must be watched with care; it has several meanings and, like "team teaching," is in danger of becoming a magic phrase.) One university, which trains no teachers at the undergraduate level, has made arrangements with some thirty academic colleges to admit their graduates to the program. In the course of ten years some 1,300 teachers (both elementary and secondary) have been thus trained. In terms of the quality of the teachers, it may well be that this and similar procedures have done much to raise the level of teachers' competence. But that such arrangements are quantitatively of little significance is shown by the fact that 1,300 is only about 0.1 per cent of the total number of teachers educated in the United States in the ten-year period.

Prof. W. H. Cartwright, in reviewing fifth-year programs of the master-of-arts-in-teaching type, has said, "Fifth year programs of this type . . . have justified the hopes of those who were responsible for their development. Such programs will continue to serve the schools. . . . Fifth year programs will not and should not become the principal route to teaching careers. . . . Fifth year programs, such as those considered in this article (the M.A.T. and related types) will serve the schools and society best by preparing as teachers, college graduates who have superior academic records, personalities which give promise of success in teaching, and a genuine desire to teach but who have not fulfilled minimum professional requirements to teach, including student teaching."

THIS CHAPTER might have been entitled "On-the-Job Education of Teachers." I have up to this point considered only those courses that are arranged by an institution of higher learning and that, in one way or another, are connected with the degree-granting function of the college or university. One may designate such activities as in-service education. But, as is the case so often in the literature on education, a set of words may have a variety of meanings. Once again, therefore, I warn the layman on this matter of terminology. For example, in a comprehensive review of teacher education published in 1960 by Dean Lindley Stiles of the School of Education of the University of Wisconsin and collaborators, the section on in-service education is largely devoted to a report on fifth-year and other postgraduate programs. On the other hand, the Fifty-Sixth Yearbook of the National Society for the Study of Education, which is entitled *In-Service Education,* is centered upon "planned programs in some contrast to the various activities in which teachers and others might independently engage in order to improve themselves." [1] In-service programs of local school systems and those under area, state, regional, and national auspices are discussed in some detail.

Planned programs in in-service education are, in the judgment of the yearbook committee, essential to adequate professional improvement of school personnel. A theme that runs throughout the volume is stated by one of the contributors as follows: "Experimentation has shown that lasting improvements in professional practices of teachers may be brought about by encouraging and assisting them to make a cooperative attack on professional problems of common concern." What the contributors are writing about is the many ways in which groups of teachers may come together to discover problems of joint concern. The auspices under which such study groups or "workshops" are formed are many. So, too, are the ways in which the work of the group may be financed and the extent to which neighboring colleges or universities may be involved. The nature of the problems will also vary. In recent years, interest in the new mathematics or a new type of course in chemistry or physics may be the focus of one group. Sociological problems may be the center of attention of another.

I have no doubt that school boards should endeavor to stimulate

---

[1] *In-Service Education.* Fifty-sixth yearbook of the National Society for the Study of Education. University of Chicago Press, 1957.

the kind of in-service education that is not tied to course credits but is a group attack on a matter of mutual concern. Professors of both education and academic subjects should be brought into the undertaking at the taxpayer's expense. To give only one example, if there are several high schools in a system, all the biology teachers might be brought together to discuss the three types of new biology courses. Out of such a discussion might well develop a decision on which type should be adopted. Or if the decision was left to the individual teacher, at least he would know what the others were doing. Another example would be a seminar on some of the sociological problems involved in teaching in slum schools. In this connection I recommend that:

27. *To insure that the teachers are up to date, particularly in a period of rapid change (as in mathematics and physics), a school board should contract with an educational institution to provide short-term seminars (often called workshops) during the school year so that all the teachers, without cost to them, may benefit from the instruction. Such seminars or workshops might also study the particular educational problems of a given school or school district. (No credit toward salary increases would be given.)*

Small school districts are clearly at a disadvantage in providing the kind of in-service education I am recommending. Therefore, arrangements organized and financed by the states may be in order. At least one state, New York, has already established institutes in several fields and can claim priority over the Federal government. At the national level the kind of in-service education I have in mind is that provided by the National Science Foundation Institutes. These Institutes provide a few weeks of intensive instruction by professors in the various sciences, who attempt to bring small and carefully selected groups of teachers up to date in their scientific fields. Similarly, the foreign language institutes, financed under the National Defense Education Act, have been of great importance in improving the competence of foreign language teachers, particularly in regard to the spoken language. *The use of summer institutes for bringing teachers up to date in a subject-matter field has been perhaps the single most important improvement in recent years in the training of secondary school teachers.*

Though there are obviously many difficulties connected with the details of such arrangements, I believe these efforts are of first importance. I would venture to suggest that if my recommendation abolishing credit for afternoon and evening courses were adopted, the in-service education of the planned-program type would become increasingly popular and significant. Some of the professors now busy giving afternoon and evening courses on a formal basis would be free to be hired as consultants by school systems. In this capacity they would work most effectively with the groups of teachers who were holding a seminar largely of their own choosing on topics which to them had vital bearing. Such a use of the intellectual resources of the faculties of education of our metropolitan universities would seem to me more likely to be fruitful than the present arrangement, by which hundreds of lecture courses must be manned.

10
CONCLUDING OBSERVATIONS

I BEGAN THIS VOLUME by introducing the reader to a long-standing quarrel among educators. I close by collecting in one chapter my recommendations, whose acceptance I believe might end the quarrel. If my findings are correct, neither side in the conflict has developed as coherent and consistent a position as the battle cries would lead the hearer to expect. In any discussion about the idea of a liberally educated man, one encounters differences of opinion as to what this expression means; and there is a great variety of programs reflecting these diverse opinions. A cynic might be tempted to define a liberal education as a four-year exposure to an experience prescribed by a group of professors, each of whom has prime allegiance to his own academic discipline. The programs in many institutions seem to have been developed not by careful consideration of a group but by a process that might be called academic logrolling. (I am not unfamiliar with the bargaining between departments when it comes to dividing up a student's time.) In any event, one finds a complete lack of agreement on what constitutes a satisfactory general education program for future teachers. As to the education in a specific field which the college student expects to teach, there is a far greater degree of unanimity. But about the amount of time to be devoted to such studies in college and the level of competence to be demanded, opinions differ.

When one examines the courses in education, one finds almost as much confusion as exists in general education. Here the cynic might well say that the professors are jealous of their share of the student's time but are ill prepared to use it well.

Academic professors and professors of education are in complete agreement only on one point: that practice teaching, if well conducted, is important. Aside from practice teaching and the accompanying methods course, there is little agreement among professors of education on the nature of the corpus of knowledge they are expected to transmit to the future teacher.

In view of the great diversity of opinions and practices to be found in the leading institutions, I conclude that neither a state authority nor a voluntary accrediting agency is in a position to specify the amount of time to be devoted to either academic or educational courses. What is needed is on the one hand for the state to allow freedom for institutions to experiment, and on the other for the academic professors and professors of education in each institution to take joint responsibility for the reputation of their college or university in training teachers.

Recognizing that the 27 recommendations distributed throughout various chapters of the book may be difficult to recall, I have arranged them in five categories according to the persons most likely to be involved in bringing about their adoption.

GROUP A. RECOMMENDATIONS REQUIRING ACTION EITHER BY A CHIEF STATE SCHOOL OFFICER, A STATE BOARD OF EDUCATION OR A LEGISLATURE.

1. Certification requirements

For certification purposes the state should require only (a) that a candidate hold a baccalaureate degree from a legitimate college or university, (b) that he submit evidence of having successfully performed as a student teacher under the direction of college and public school personnel in whom the state Department has confidence, and in a practice-teaching situation of which the state Department approves, and (c) that he hold a specially endorsed teaching certificate from a college or university which, in issuing the official document, attests that the institution as a whole considers the person adequately prepared to teach in a designated field and grade level.

5. Programs of practice teaching

The state should approve programs of practice teaching. It should, working cooperatively with the college and public school authorities, regulate the conditions under which practice teaching is done and the nature of the methods instruction that accompanies it. The state should require that the colleges and public school systems involved submit evidence concerning the competence of those appointed as cooperating teachers and clinical professors.

6. State information service

State Departments of Education should develop and make available to local school boards and colleges and universities data relevant to the preparation and employment of teachers. Such data may include information about the types of teacher-education programs of colleges or universities throughout the state and information concerning supply and demand of teachers at various grade levels and in various fields.

7. Assignment of teachers by local boards

The state education authorities should give top priority to the development of regulations insuring that a teacher will be assigned only to those teaching duties for which he is specifically prepared, and should enforce these regulations rigorously.

10. Certification reciprocity among states

Whenever a teacher has been certified by one state under the provisions of Recommendations 1 and 2, his certificate should be accepted as valid in any other state.

GROUP B. RECOMMENDATIONS INVOLVING APPROPRIATIONS BY STATE LEGISLATURES.

4. State financial responsibility for practice teaching

The state should provide financial assistance to local boards to insure high-quality practice teaching as part of the preparation of teachers enrolled in either private or public institutions.

12. Loan policy for future teachers

Each state should develop a loan policy for future teachers aimed at recruiting into the profession the most able students; the requirements for admission to the teacher-training institutions within the state should be left to the institution, but the state should set a standard for the recipients in terms of scholastic aptitude; the amount of the loan should be sufficient to cover expenses, and the loan should be cancelled after four or five years of teaching in the public schools of the state.

GROUP C. RECOMMENDATIONS REQUIRING ACTION BY A LOCAL SCHOOL BOARD, EITHER ACTING ALONE OR IN CONJUNCTION WITH STATE ACTION.

3. Cooperating teachers in practice teaching

Public school systems that enter contracts with a college or university for practice teaching should designate, as classroom teachers working with practice teaching, only those persons in whose competence as teachers, leaders, and evaluators they have the highest confidence, and should give such persons encouragement by reducing their work loads and raising their salaries.

11. Initial probationary period of employment

During the initial probationary period, local school boards should take specific steps to provide the new teacher with every possible help in the form of: (a) limited teaching responsibility; (b) aid in gathering instructional materials; (c) advice of experienced teachers whose own load is reduced so that they can work with the new teacher in his own classroom; (d) shifting to more experienced teachers those pupils who create problems beyond the ability of the novice to handle effectively; and (e) specialized instruction concerning the characteristics of the community, the neighborhood, and the students he is likely to encounter.

23. Revision of salary schedule by local boards

School boards should drastically revise their salary schedules. There should be a large jump in salary when a teacher moves from the probationary status to tenure. Any salary increments based on advanced studies should not be tied to course credits earned (semester hours), but only to the earning of a master's degree, based normally on full-time residence or four summer sessions in which the program is directed toward the development of the competence of the teacher as a teacher. Such a salary increment should be made mandatory by state law.

24. Financial assistance to teachers for study in summer schools

School boards or the state should provide financial assistance so that teachers may attend summer school after enrolling in a graduate school for the purpose of completing a program of the type stated in Recommendation 23.

25. Leaves of absence for further education of teachers

School boards should provide leave of absence with salary for a full-time semester residence at a university to enable teachers to study toward a master's program, provided this program is designed to increase the competence of the teacher; state funds should be available for this purpose.

27. In-service education of teachers

To insure that the teachers are up to date, particularly in a period of rapid change (as in mathematics and physics), a school board should contract with an educational institution to provide short-term seminars (often called workshops) during the school year so that all the teachers, without cost to them, may benefit from the instruction. Such seminars or workshops might also study the particular educational problems of a given school or school district. (No credit toward salary increases would be given.)

GROUP D. RECOMMENDATIONS REQUIRING ACTION BY THE FACULTIES, ADMINISTRATIVE OFFICERS AND TRUSTEES OF AN INSTITUTION ENGAGED IN EDUCATING TEACHERS FOR THE PUBLIC ELEMENTARY AND SECONDARY SCHOOLS.

2. Collegiate or university responsibility

Each college or university should be permitted to develop in detail whatever program of teacher education it considers most desirable, subject only to two conditions: first, the president of the institution in behalf of the entire faculty involved—academic as well as professional—certifies that the candidate is adequately prepared to teach on a specific level or in specific fields, and second, the institution establishes in conjunction with a public school system a state-approved practice-teaching arrangement.

13. The all-university approach to teacher training

If the institution is engaged in educating teachers, the lay board trustees should ask the faculty or faculties whether in fact there is a continuing and effective all-university (or interdepartmental) approach to the education of teachers; and if not, why not?

14. Requirements for collegiate or university teacher-education programs

The board of trustees should ask the faculty to justify the present requirements for a bachelor's degree for future teachers with particular reference to the breadth of the requirements and to spell out what in fact are the total educational exposures (school and college) demanded now in the fields of (a) mathematics, (b) physical science, (c) biological science, (d) social science, (e) English literature, (f) English composition, (g) history, (h) philosophy.

15. Foreign language preparation

If courses are required in a foreign language, evidence of the degree of mastery obtained by fulfilling the minimum requirement for a degree should be presented to the board of trustees.

16. The establishment of "clinical professors"

The professor from the college or university who is to supervise and assess the practice teaching should have had much practical experience. His status should be analogous to that of a clinical professor in certain medical schools.

17. Basic preparation of elementary teachers

(a). The program for teachers of kindergarten and grades 1, 2, and 3 should prepare them in the content and methodology of

all subjects taught in these early school years. Depth in a single subject or cluster of subjects is not necessary.

(b). *The program for teachers of grades 4, 5, and 6 should provide depth of content and methods of teaching in a specific subject or cluster of subjects normally taught in these grades, with only an introduction to the remaining elementary school subjects.*

18. Practice teaching for elementary teachers

All future elementary teachers should engage in practice teaching for a period of at least 8 weeks, spending a minimum of 3 hours a day in the classroom; the period must include at least 3 weeks of full responsibility for the classroom under the direction of a co-operating teacher and the supervision of a clinical professor.

19. Adequate staffing of small colleges training elementary teachers

Those responsible for financing and administering small colleges should consider whether they can afford to maintain an adequate staff for the preparation of elementary school teachers. Unless they are able to employ the equivalent of three or four professors devoting their time to elementary education, they should cease attempting to prepare teachers for the elementary schools.

20. Single field diploma for secondary school teachers

An institution should award a teaching certificate for teachers in grades 7 to 12 in one field only.

21. Clinical professors in institutions educating secondary teachers

Every institution awarding a special teaching certificate for secondary school teachers should have on the staff a clinical professor for each field or combination of closely related fields.

22. Teaching diploma for art, music and physical education teachers

An institution offering programs in art or music or physical education should be prepared to award a teaching diploma in each of these fields without grade designation; institutional programs should not attempt to develop competency in more than one field in four years.

26. Master's degree programs

The graduate schools of education or their equivalent (in universities organized without such separate degree-granting schools) should devise a program for increasing the competence of teachers as teachers with the following characteristics:

(1) It should be open to any graduate of the same institution in the same field of endeavor (e.g., elementary education, secondary school social studies, etc.).

(2) Courses should be allowed for credit toward the 30 semester hours whether or not the courses are of an elementary nature, provided they are clearly courses needed to increase the competence of the teacher.

(3) No credit toward the degree should be given for extension courses or courses taken on campus while the teacher is engaged on a full-time teaching job.

(4) Passing of a comprehensive examination should be required for the master's degree, as is now the case in some institutions.

(5) The summer-school sessions should be arranged so that four summer residences will complete the degree requirements, or two summers plus one full-time semester residence.

(6) If the offering in the arts and sciences is not wide enough to provide meaningful work in the summer session (as it would not be in some state colleges), arrangements should be made for the transfer of credit from a university summer school with a good offering of courses in subject-matter fields.

(7) For elementary teachers, the degree should be master of education in elementary education; for secondary teachers, master of education in English (or science, or social science or modern languages or mathematics).

GROUP E. CONCERNING VOLUNTARY ACCREDITING AGENCIES.

8. Composition of NCATE

The governing boards of NCATE and the regional associations should be significantly broadened to give greater power to (a) representatives of scholarly disciplines in addition to professional education, and to (b) informed representatives of the lay public.

9. Function of NCATE

NCATE and the regional associations should serve only as advisory bodies to teacher-preparing institutions and local school boards. They should, on the request of institutions, send in teams to study and make recommendations concerning the whole or any portion of a teacher-education program. They should, on the request of local boards, evaluate employment policies. They should provide a forum in which issues concerning teacher education and employment are debated.

If I were to try to characterize in two words the conclusion of my study, these words would be "freedom" and "responsibility." The state should allow each college and university the maximum degree of freedom to develop its own program. Each institution should assume the maximum degree of responsibility for those graduates it certifies as being competent to teach. In the chapters dealing with the preparation of elementary and secondary teachers and in-service education, I have suggested the kinds of programs I have in mind when I refer to an institution's certifying the specific competence of a future teacher. Yet these chapters are not to be taken as blueprints of the one and only way of preparing classroom teachers. Rather, they are submitted as evidence of my contention that teachers can be adequately prepared for initial employment in four years. There may well be alternative programs which would be as good or better.

What I have been arguing for in essence is a competition to see which institution will quickly earn a high reputation for preparing well-trained teachers. Once free competition becomes possible in any state, there will be every reason for the academic professors and the professors of education in each college or university within that state to join hands to enhance the reputation of their particular institution. Before that day arrives, however, laymen will certainly have to enter into the fray in many states, and public opinion must be aroused. Yet in any such endeavor the quarrel among educators must not be made more bitter; the goal is not victory for either side but mutual respect and complete cooperation. Thus while this volume is a call for action, it is also a call for reconciliation. Once the quarreling educators bury their hatchets, the layman may put his present worries aside. That united efforts to prepare better teachers would result in better schools requires no argumentation; that the nation would be the beneficiary of such a revolution is a self-evident proposition.

APPENDICES

APPENDIX A

1. Institutions Visited, Alphabetically by State and Type

Total Institutions: 77[1]   Total States: 22[2]

(* Institutions visited personally by J. B. Conant: 52)

Type of Institution	Code Letter	Number Visited
State University	a	(22)
Private University	b	(24)
State College or State Teachers College	c	(16)
Private Liberal Arts College	d	(8)
City University of New York	e	(1)
City College	f	(2)
County College	g	(1)
Private Teacher Education College	h	(3)

Institutions by State

California:

* San Fernando State College, San Fernando	c
* San Francisco State College, San Francisco	c
* Stanford University, Palo Alto	b
* University of California at Berkeley	a
* University of California at Los Angeles	a
* University of Southern California, Los Angeles	b

Colorado:

* University of Colorado, Boulder	a

Connecticut:

Yale University, New Haven	b

Florida:

* Florida Agricultural and Mechanical University, Tallahassee	a

[1] These institutions prepared one-fifth of the students expecting to complete certification requirements in the United States in 1962.

[2] 73 per cent of the students expecting to meet teacher-certification requirements in 1962 were prepared in institutions in these 22 states.

Institutions by State	*Code Letter*
* Florida State University, Tallahassee	a
* University of Florida, Gainesville	a
University of Miami, Coral Gables	b
University of South Florida, Tampa	a
Georgia:	
Atlanta University System	b
Emory University, Atlanta	b
University of Georgia, Athens	a
Illinois:	
* Chicago Teachers College, North, Chicago	f
* Chicago Teachers College, South, Chicago	f
National College of Education, Evanston	h
* Northwestern University, Evanston	b
Roosevelt University, Chicago	b
* University of Chicago, Chicago	b
* University of Illinois, Urbana	a
Indiana:	
* Ball State Teachers College, Muncie	c
Indiana University, Bloomington	a
Purdue University, Lafayette	a
* St. Mary's College, South Bend	d
* University of Notre Dame, South Bend	b
Iowa:	
Coe College, Cedar Rapids	d
Cornell College, Mount Vernon	d
* Drake University, Des Moines	b
* Grinnell College, Grinnell	d
Massachusetts:	
Boston University, Boston	b
Harvard University, Cambridge	b
State College at Boston	c
State College at Salem	c
Michigan:	
Central Michigan University, Mount Pleasant	a
* Michigan State University, East Lansing	a
* University of Michigan, Ann Arbor	a
* Wayne State University, Detroit	a

Institutions by State	*Code* *Letter*
Minnesota:	
* Carleton College, Northfield	d
* St. Olaf College, Northfield	d
* University of Minnesota, Minneapolis	a
Missouri:	
* Washington University in St. Louis	b
New Jersey:	
* Montclair State College, Upper Montclair	c
* Paterson State College, Wayne	c
New York:	
Bank Street College of Education, New York	h
* Brooklyn College, New York	e
* Fordham University, New York	b
* New York University, New York	b
* State University College, Albany	c
* State University College, New Paltz	c
* Syracuse University, Syracuse	b
* Teachers College, Columbia University, New York	b
North Carolina:	
Atlantic Christian College, Wilson	d
* Duke University, Durham	b
East Carolina College, Greenville	c
Fayetteville State Teachers College, Fayetteville	c
* North Carolina College at Durham	c
* St. Augustine's College, Raleigh	d
* University of North Carolina, Chapel Hill	a
Ohio:	
Kent State University, Kent	a
* Ohio State University, Columbus	a
Pennsylvania:	
* Indiana State College, Indiana	c
* Temple University, Philadelphia	b
* University of Pittsburgh, Pittsburgh	b
Tennessee:	
* Fisk University, Nashville	b
* George Peabody College for Teachers, Nashville	h
* Vanderbilt University, Nashville	b

	Code Letter
Institutions by State	
Texas:	
Southwest Texas State College, San Marcos	c
University of Texas, Austin	a
Virginia:	
* Richmond Professional Institute, Richmond	c
* University of Richmond, Richmond	b
Washington:	
* Central Washington State College, Ellensburg	c
* University of Washington, Seattle	a
Wisconsin:	
Racine-Kenosha County Teachers College, Union Grove	g
* University of Wisconsin, Madison	a

Students Completing Certification Requirements—1962
in Institutions Visited by J. B. Conant and Staff

State	Total Prospective Teachers Graduated in 1962[A]	Prospective Teachers Graduated in 1962 from Institutions Visited by Staff	Total No. of Institutions Preparing Teachers	Institutions Visited by Staff
California	9,224	2,794	46	6
Colorado	2,931	490	9	1
Connecticut	1,791	54	16	1
Florida	2,296	1,727	12	5
Georgia	2,037	589	26	3
Illinois	5,913	1,201	52	7
Indiana	4,245	2,914	33	5
Iowa	2,952	503	27	4
Massachusetts	4,099	1,277	51	4
Michigan	7,712	4,037	24	4
Minnesota	4,265	909	24	3
Missouri	3,606	253	28	1
New Jersey	3,112	867	18	2
New York	9,571	3,259	80	8
North Carolina	4,302	1,538	33	7
Ohio	7,231	1,467	49	2
Pennsylvania	9,211	1,331	81	3
Tennessee	2,906	296	35	3
Texas	7,605	847	49	2
Virginia	2,150	162	32	2
Washington	2,718	924	15	2
Wisconsin	4,163	498	51	2
22-State Total	104,040	27,937	791	77
U.S.A.	142,547	. . . . .	1,150	. .

[A] NEA figures

Of the 104,040 teachers prepared in 1962 in the 22 states listed, J. B. Conant and his staff have visited institutions that graduated 27,937, or 27 per cent of the total.

Of the estimated 143,000 teachers prepared in the entire country in 1962, J. B. Conant and his staff have thus visited institutions that graduated 27,937 prospective teachers, or 20 per cent of the total.

APPENDIX B: PART I
Facts About the 16 Most Populous States

State	Total Population 1960	Public School Enrollment 1962–63	Classroom Teachers 1962–63			Teachers Prepared 1962			Teacher-Training Institutions 1962
			Elementary	Secondary	Total	Elementary	Secondary	Total	
New York	16,782,304	2,943,167	67,065	60,714	127,779	4,362	5,209	9,571	80
California	15,717,204	3,755,000	80,500	49,500	130,000	5,294	3,930	9,224	46
Pennsylvania	11,319,366	2,059,411	40,413	37,442	77,855	2,989	6,222	9,211	81
Illinois	10,081,158	1,889,746	51,317	26,753	78,070	2,325	3,588	5,913	52
Ohio	9,706,397	2,082,134	48,019	31,887	79,906	2,825	4,406	7,231	49
Texas	9,579,677	2,291,279	52,963	36,758	89,721	2,605	5,000	7,605	49
Michigan	7,823,194	1,791,921	39,121	30,119	69,240	3,250	4,462	7,712	24
New Jersey	6,066,782	1,159,283	31,127	19,815	50,942	1,343	1,769	3,111	18
Massachusetts	5,148,578	943,189	20,381	17,248	37,629	1,888	2,211	4,099	51
Florida	4,951,560	1,093,941	22,453	19,274	41,727	955	1,341	2,296	12
Indiana	4,662,498	1,028,988	22,174	17,555	39,729	1,464	2,781	4,245	33
North Carolina	4,556,155	1,140,281	28,047	11,558	39,605	1,476	2,826	4,302	33
Missouri	4,319,813	857,620*	21,687*	10,866*	32,553*	1,344	2,262	3,606	28
Virginia	3,966,949	905,740	20,501	14,925	35,426	572	1,578	2,150	32
Wisconsin	3,951,777	767,115	19,429	12,043	31,472	1,873	2,290	4,163	51
Georgia	3,943,116	991,125	21,822	12,670	34,492	739	1,298	2,037	26
TOTAL	122,576,528	25,699,940	587,019	409,127	996,146	35,304	51,173	86,476	665
U.S. Total	179,323,175	38,836,610	889,012	622,239	1,511,251	54,499	88,048	142,547	1,150
% of U.S. Total Represented by 16 States	68%	66%	66%	66%	66%	65%	58%	61%	58%

* 1961–62 data

PART II
Statistics on 16 Most Populous States*

	A	B	C	D	E	F	G
California	620	111.2%	9.8%	$7,050	86.4%	$516	$42.72
Florida	218	98.6	6.7	5,450	62.9	347	13.37
Georgia	398	22.6	3.0	4,637	51.8	298	13.34
Illinois	131	59.4	21.9	6,360	84.5	526	15.79
Indiana	32	45.6	11.3	6,150	74.1	405	28.17
Massachusetts	208	48.7	22.2	6,075	68.2	465	5.88
Michigan	163	50.6	15.5	6,444	78.4	447	30.60
Missouri	122	27.1	15.8	5,289	73.0	405	10.69
New Jersey	222	53.6	21.1	6,308	78.8	556	8.73
New York	706	38.0	22.6	6,950	74.1	645	10.77
North Carolina	180	25.0	1.4	4,975	57.4	297	15.86
Ohio	203	59.7	14.8	5,750	72.4	422	16.05
Pennsylvania	290	23.8	23.5	5,660	78.0	464	7.63
Texas	279	51.7	6.5	5,300	60.6	379	18.18
Virginia	169	41.7	6.4	4,950	51.9	335	14.83
Wisconsin	59	44.2	25.8	5,650	92.3	467	20.86
National Average	137	44.6%	13.6%	$5,735	70.6%	$432	$19.50

A: Size of State Department of Education Professional Staff July, 1960.

B: Percentage of Change in Public Elementary and Secondary School Enrollments, 1952–53 to 1962–63.

C: Nonpublic School Enrollment as Per Cent of Total Enrollment in Elementary and Secondary Schools, 1959–60.

D: Estimated Average Salaries of Classroom Teachers in Public Schools, 1962–63.

E: High School Graduates in 1962 as Per Cent of Eighth Grade Enrollment in 1957–58.

F: Estimated Current Expenditure for Public Elementary and Secondary Schools per Pupil in ADA (Average Daily Attendance), 1962–63.

G: Expenditures for State Institutions of Higher Education per Capita of Population, 1961.

* Source for all columns except column A: *Rankings of the States, 1963,* Research Division, National Education Association.

Source for column A: U. S. Department of Health, Education, and Welfare, Office of Education.

Appendix C

State-by-State Summary of the Number and Percentage of Institutions and the Number and Percentage of Teachers Prepared, According to Control of Institutions in the 16 Most Populous States—1962

THE FOLLOWING STATISTICS are based on reports from 594 teacher-preparing institutions in the 16 most populous states. These institutions comprise 90 per cent of the 665 teacher-preparing institutions in the 16 states and 52 per cent of the 1,150 teacher-preparing institutions in the entire United States.

These statistics include an estimated 35,727 potential elementary school teachers and 53,063 potential secondary school teachers, or a total of 88,790 students who met certification requirements in 1962.

These institutions and potential teachers represent a substantial sample of all institutions and all potential teachers in the United States. The size of the sample is illustrated in the table immediately below.

	Nationwide as Reported by NEA	16-State Sample	% Sample Is of National Total
Teacher-Preparing Institutions	1,150	594	52
Elementary Teachers Prepared—1962	54,499	35,727	65
Secondary Teachers Prepared—1962	88,048	53,063	60
Total Teachers Prepared—1962	142,547	88,790	62

226

	ELEMENTARY		SECONDARY		TOTAL			
	No. of Insts.	No. of Tchrs.	No. of Insts.	No. of Tchrs.	No. of Insts.	% of Insts.	No. of Tchrs.	% of Teachers
California								
Public	17	4,084	17	2,923	17	40	7,007	76
Private (Ind.)	8	524	7	573	8	19	1,097	12
Private (Church)	15	663	15	383	18	41	1,046	12
TOTAL	40	5,271	39	3,879	43		9,150	
Florida								
Public	3	536	3	851	3	25	1,387	60
Private (Ind.)	6	329	6	363	6	50	692	30
Private (Church)	3	90	3	127	3	25	217	10
TOTAL	12	955	12	1,341	12		2,296	
Georgia								
Public	10	480	9	915	10	41	1,395	67
Private (Ind.)	4	53	5	116	5	21	169	8
Private (Church)	9	278	9	241	9	38	519	25
TOTAL	23	811	23	1,272	24		2,083	
Illinois								
Public	8	1,393	8	2,694	8	15	4,087	57
Private (Ind.)	11	482	18	774	19	34	1,256	18
Private (Church)	26	859	26	971	28	51	1,830	25
TOTAL	45	2,734	52	4,439	55		7,173	
Indiana								
Public	4	741	4	1,990	4	15	2,731	65
Private (Ind.)	2	65	4	147	4	15	212	5
Private (Church)	14	534	16	695	19	70	1,229	30
TOTAL	20	1,340	24	2,832	27		4,172	
Massachusetts								
Public	10	981	10	887	11	24	1,868	45
Private (Ind.)	16	451	16	711	19	41	1,162	28
Private (Church)	11	451	16	665	16	35	1,116	27
TOTAL	37	1,883	42	2,263	46		4,146	
Michigan								
Public	7	2,456	7	3,674	7	30	6,130	82
Private (Ind.)	2	27	3	100	3	13	127	2
Private (Church)	13	541	13	704	13	57	1,245	16
TOTAL	22	3,024	23	4,478	23		7,502	
Missouri								
Public	8	924	7	1,628	8	33	2,552	70
Private (Ind.)	2	159	2	235	2	8	394	11
Private (Church)	13	261	13	413	14	59	674	19
TOTAL	23	1,344	22	2,276	24		3,620	
New Jersey								
Public	6	993	7	1,234	7	41	2,227	74
Private (Ind.)	2	122	4	150	4	24	272	9
Private (Church)	5	228	6	287	6	35	515	17
TOTAL	13	1,343	17	1,671	17		3,014	
New York								
Public	15	3,630	18	3,644	18	28	7,274	65
Private (Ind.)	14	683	19	1,992	22	34	2,675	24
Private (Church)	11	492	23	753	24	38	1,245	11
TOTAL	40	4,805	60	6,389	64		11,194	
North Carolina								
Public	10	968	10	1,667	12	36	2,635	63
Private (Ind.)	1	27	1	142	1	3	169	5
Private (Church)	19	481	21	868	20	61	1,349	32
TOTAL	30	1,476	32	2,677	33		4,153	

| | ELEMENTARY | | SECONDARY | | TOTAL | | | |
	No. of Insts.	No. of Tchrs.	No. of Insts.	No. of Tchrs.	No. of Insts.	% of Insts.	No. of Tchrs.	% of Teachers
Ohio								
Public	9	1,685	9	2,884	9	18	4,169	56
Private (Ind.)	9	230	10	430	10	21	660	9
Private (Church)	23	1,071	29	1,533	30	61	2,604	35
TOTAL	41	2,986	48	4,447	49		7,433	
Pennsylvania								
Public	15	1,762	15	3,792	15	21	5,554	60
Private (Ind.)	13	554	25	1,190	26	35	1,744	19
Private (Church)	23	690	32	1,266	32	44	1,956	21
TOTAL	51	3,006	72	6,248	73		9,254	
Texas								
Public	17	1,645	18	3,451	18	37	5,096	67
Private (Ind.)	3	130	4	325	4	8	455	6
Private (Church)	25	838	27	1,254	27	55	2,092	27
TOTAL	45	2,613	49	5,030	49		7,643	
Virginia								
Public	10	393	11	934	11	42	1,327	62
Private (Ind.)	3	38	3	149	3	12	187	9
Private (Church)	9	141	12	495	12	46	636	29
TOTAL	22	572	26	1,578	26		2,150	
Wisconsin								
Public	10	1,194	11	1,643	11	38	2,837	74
Private (Ind.)	3	23	6	192	6	21	215	6
Private (Church)	12	347	12	408	12	41	755	20
TOTAL	25	1,564	29	2,243	29		3,807	

The following table summarizes the information presented on the preparation of teachers in the 16 most populous states.

Total Number and Percentage of Institutions and Number and Percentage of Teachers Prepared, According to Control of Institutions—16 Most Populous States—1962

| Control | ELEMENTARY | | | | SECONDARY | | | | TOTAL | | | |
	No. of Insts.	%	No. of Tchrs.	%	No. of Insts.	%	No. of Tchrs.	%	No. of Insts.	%	No. of Tchrs.	%
Public	159	32	23,865	66	164	28	34,411	65	169	29	58,276	66
Private (Ind.)	99	20	3,897	11	133	25	7,589	14	142	24	11,486	13
Private (Church)	231	48	7,965	23	273	47	11,063	21	283	47	19,028	21
TOTAL	489	100	35,727	100	570	100	53,063	100	594	100	88,790	100

APPENDIX D
Supply and Demand of Teachers

I HAVE BECOME more and more skeptical of overall figures that purport to give the annual supply and demand figures for the entire United States. The order of magnitude is, of course, quite clear. In 1962, about 143,000 graduates of our colleges and universities were prepared to teach; 55,000 were prospective elementary school teachers, 88,000 were ready for secondary schools. At present approximately 890,000 elementary teachers are responsible for 25.3 million pupils, and 620,000 secondary teachers are teaching 13.5 million pupils. It is important to note that the ratio of elementary teachers to secondary teachers now employed is about 3 to 2, while the ratio of those graduated and prepared to teach in 1962 was 5 to 8 in favor of secondary teachers. This would seem to indicate that on a national basis we are failing to educate a sufficiently high proportion of elementary teachers.

Calculations for the future are uncertain for many reasons. At present it is estimated that only 70 per cent of those prepared for secondary teaching and 84 per cent of those prepared for elementary teaching actually take a job. Therefore, the actual crop of new teachers annually may be nearer 106,000 than 143,000. On the other hand, a considerable number of former teachers or those prepared some years ago enter the classroom each year. Whether in the future a larger or smaller fraction of potential teachers in each year's graduating class will actually teach is a question no one can answer. Still another consideration involves the ratio of women to men teachers. In the elementary schools at present only 15 per cent of the teachers are men; the staffs of the secondary schools (on a national basis) are about equally divided between men and women.

Before long the total number of boys and girls of college age will be much larger than at present, as a result of the increased birth rate immediately after World War II. For the period 1964–70, the number in any one age group (18 years, for example) will be 3.4 million plus or minus 10 per cent. If one wished to recruit an equal number of men and women from this group for both elementary and secondary schools and set the goal at, say, 200,000 (which is high as compared with today), it is clear that about 7 per cent of each age group would be needed. Whether this could be the 7 per cent who were the most able intellectually is quite another story. By no means all the top 15 or 20

229

per cent of the high school students in terms of scholastic aptitude finish high school, let alone four years of college. The projections of the E.T.S. (Educational Testing Service) indicate that in the period between 1964 and 1970, those graduating from college may number 650,000 to 700,-000, or about 20 per cent of the age group. Unless conditions change greatly, these college graduates in terms of intellectual competence will represent a far wider spread. Probably many will be, in national terms, near the bottom of the first half of the graduating high school class. At all events, the attraction of the learned professions of law, medicine, and college teaching, as well as business, engineering, theology and other vocations will lead many of the most able men and some of the women into other careers than schoolteaching.

Whatever the total supply of teachers may be, however, it is clear that they will not be distributed equitably from state to state, and that there will be differences in the number of pupils assigned to each teacher in different states. The issue of class size thus becomes a crucial one in determining whether there is a shortage or a surplus of teachers. I have elsewhere suggested a ratio of 50 professional workers for each 1,000 pupils. Such a ratio would mean (after one subtracts the administrators, supervisors, library specialists, guidance counselors, etc.) about one classroom teacher for each 25 pupils. This figure is not far from the national average (1 to 25.7) in the fall of 1960.

Such suggestions as mine are speculative and are based on the assumption that there will be no revolutionary shifts in teaching practice or in the use of technological devices to replace teachers. My own suggestions are also based on the assumption that the teachers would be expected to spend considerable time reading student essays and other written work. Obviously this assumption is more valid for some subjects and grade levels than for others. From the standpoint of hard research, it must be said that the issue of class size warrants further experimentation. As one recent writer[1] has pointed out:

> For two generations experiments have been conducted dealing with class size. Many of these have demonstrated that a small class is better than a large one. Many other experiments have demonstrated that a small class is not better than a large one. Perhaps in no aspect of education has the experimental evidence been more confused than in the matter of class size. Part of the difficulty has been in the inadequate statement of the problem. Clearly, a class of 20

---

[1] Harold F. Clark. *The Cost and Quality in Public Education*, Syracuse University Press, Syracuse, 1963, pp. 44–45.

pupils will cost more than a class of 30 on a per pupil basis. What will be done with money saved? Will the funds be put into equipment? Would a class of 20 students with little equipment exceed in quality one of 30 with many thousands of dollars' worth of equipment? It is possible to find experiments claiming to justify almost every conceivable class size. In recent years there are teachers who make a strong case for very large classes, with heavy expenditure on technological aids for certain kinds of subject-matter teaching. Although the evidence is far from clear, it is highly probable that the desirable size of a class does vary greatly, depending upon the quality of the teacher, the subject to be taught, and especially on the adequacy of the technological facilities available. Few if any classrooms in the formal school system have been equipped with anything approximating the optimum technological facilities available to aid the teacher. Few if any classrooms in the formal school system have been equipped with anything approximating the optimum technological conditions for learning. When this is done, it is highly probable that it will be necessary to conduct the class size experiments again. It is also highly probable that such changes will make possible a great rise in the quality of education.

On a nationwide basis, the average student-teacher ratio, as of the fall of 1960, was 25.7 to 1. But individual states show marked deviations from this average. By way of illustration, let us look at the supply and demand picture in the 16 most populous states. The following table (figures based on the student-teacher ratios presented in the NEA Research Division's *Rankings of the States*, Washington, D.C., 1962, p. 26) indicates the classroom teacher-student ratio (Column A), the public elementary and secondary school enrollment (Column B), and the number of teachers (Column C) in the 16 most populous states in 1960. Column D indicates the number of teachers that would have been required if the national average of 25.7 pupils per classroom teacher had been maintained in each state in 1960. Column E expresses either the state's oversupply or undersupply of teachers according to the 25.7 ratio.

An examination of these statistics reveals that the range of teacher supply in these states extends from the high point of New Jersey, with one teacher to 22.8 students, to the low of North Carolina, with only one teacher to 29.4 students. These figures indicate how difficult it is to discuss teacher supply and demand meaningfully in national terms.

Just a few examples indicate the impact of class size upon the teacher supply and demand picture in a given state. If North Carolina with the

State	A Student- Teacher Ratio 1960	B Public School Enrollment 1960	C No. of Teachers 1960	D No. of Teachers If 25.7 National Ratio	E Supply and Demand Status
California	28.1	3,301,750	117,500	128,473	−10,973
Florida	26.3	985,461	37,470	38,345	− 875
Georgia	28.4	924,108	32,539	35,958	− 3,419
Illinois	24.2	1,793,026	74,092	69,768	⊕ 4,324
Indiana	28.1	1,029,444	36,635	40,056	− 3,421
Massachusetts	23.6	837,092	35,470	32,572	⊕ 2,898
Michigan	26.3	1,660,635	63,142	64,616	− 1,474
Missouri	27.4	846,495	30,894	32,938	− 2,044
New Jersey	22.8	1,056,073	46,319	41,092	+ 5,227
New York	23.3	2,768,040	118,800	107,706	+11,094
North Carolina	29.4	1,094,194	37,242	42,576	− 5,334
Ohio	26.5	1,890,325	71,333	73,554	− 2,221
Pennsylvania	26.1	1,958,935	75,055	76,223	− 1,168
Texas	26.7	2,186,596	81,895	85,082	− 3,187
Virginia	25.9	823,335	31,789	32,036	− 247
Wisconsin	25.0	725,000	29,000	28,210	⊕ 790

highest ratio (29.4) had the same low pupil-teacher ratio as New Jersey (22.8), the former in 1960 would have required 10,749 additional teachers. In other words, North Carolina in 1960 would have had to increase its public school teaching force by almost 30 per cent.

If California with a 28.1 ratio were to provide a comparable student-teacher ratio to New Jersey, California in 1960 would have been required to provide an additional 27,314 teachers, a hefty 23 per cent increase in the supply of teachers. To match even New York's 23.3 ratio, California in 1960 would have required the substantial addition of 24,-206 teachers.

In this context, it is also clear that the unresolved controversy concerning the relationship between class size and teaching effectiveness is of paramount concern. If we assume that a national ratio of 25.7 to 1 is desirable, then 11 of the 16 most populous states in 1960 had an undersupply of teachers. But in the absence of evidence bearing directly on the importance of class size, such a judgment would be based on an arbitrary assumption.

So far, however, we have been speaking of the supply of teachers without respect to the intellectual abilities of those involved. One wishes that all elementary and secondary school teachers could be chosen from among the academically talented. Some critics of American education seem to suggest that if we would only copy the English system of education, we could recruit our teachers from the top 10 to 15 per cent of the age group, and could then redesign our teacher education programs on the British model. The important thing to note about this proposal is that it involves abandoning our commitment to educating most of our youths to the age of eighteen and a considerable portion to the age of twenty. The contrast between the English and the American systems is interesting.

In England the elementary and secondary school teachers *are* recruited from the top 10 to 15 per cent of an age group in terms of academic ability *as determined by English methods.* What happens in that country is that at age 11+ those who are educated at public expense are sorted out by an examination (often of a type very similar to our scholastic aptitude tests). Something like 20 per cent (on a national basis) are enrolled in grammar schools. Many drop out of the schools during the 7- or 8-year course. At the age of 15 or 16, most of the grammar school students take a series of examinations called the General Certificate of Education examination (GCE) at what is known as the "o" level. To be eligible for university work or admission to a teacher training college, a minimum of five such examinations must be passed. Later at age 17 or 18 or even 19, the more ambitious students will take the "A" level examinations. At each level an essay type of examination is used and is based on a syllabus. The degree of specialization required for honors on the "A" level is far too great to satisfy many English critics of their system.

Those who wish to be elementary teachers apply for admission to a training college, of which there are many related in groups to a university. Most of the students are in residence. The course is three years in length (it has recently been expanded from two) and not drastically different from that of the last two years of some programs I have observed in the United States, except that the ratio of pupils to professors is more favorable; and this, together with the high quality of students, enables much of the instruction to be given on a tutorial basis. Secondary school teachers must be university graduates and may or may not study an additional year in a professional education program.

All the university students and all the students in the training college receive substantial support from the government with due allowance for family income. The numbers involved by American standards are small

About 264,000 teachers are now employed in what we would call public schools (about 31,000 in the English "public schools," which are independent). In 1961–62 some 14,000 finished the training college course (4,000 men, 10,000 women), and in addition something like 5,000 university graduates took up the career of teaching (largely in the grammar schools and secondary modern schools).

It will be recalled we are training something like 140,000 teachers annually as compared with 19,000 in England or about seven times as many, whereas there were only about five times as many children born in the United States in 1950 as in England (3.6 million as compared with 672,000). I estimate the ratio of total population between the ages of 5 and 18 as about 1 to 4. The reasons for the large discrepancy (four- or fivefold as compared to sevenfold) are in part due to the fact that schooling continues in most states to age 17 or even 18, while in England the number continuing full-time education beyond age 15 is small. These youths are enrolled in the grammar schools or the secondary modern schools. In a report in 1960 (the Crowther Report) a committee advocated the raising of the school-leaving age from 15 to 16. To do this, however, would require an expansion of the teaching staff by some 20,000. To raise it to 17, which would still be less than the average school-leaving age in the United States, would require about another 20,000 teachers. It is estimated that the nation needs 20 per cent more teachers than it has; thus there is already a shortage. This means that classes are in fact much larger than is thought desirable. Therefore, the government is unable to increase the years of schooling at public expense at present because of the bottleneck of the supply of teachers, which in turn reflects the limited facilities of the training colleges. The point is of interest to Americans primarily because it underscores the fact that we are so heavily engaged in training teachers because we are so heavily engaged (as compared to other nations) in providing schooling for our youth aged 15 to 18.

In many ways the recruitment of teachers for our secondary schools is in competition with the recruitment of professors for our colleges and universities. And here again a comparison with England is significant. We are providing full-time education for approximately half an age group through age 20 (in our two-year colleges), and one-sixth of an age group through age 22 (in our four-year institutions). In England, since there are no equivalents of our colleges, only some 7 to 10 per cent of an age group require teachers or professors beyond age 18. Our total teaching staff (teachers plus professors) must, therefore, be almost of a different order of magnitude (in terms of the size of the population) from that of England, or indeed, any European nation. The reader needs hardly to be cautioned against comparisons that might be made between English and American methods of educating teachers. Both nations face serious problems in recruiting and training teachers, but the problems are as different as the history of education in the two lands.

Returning to the situation in the United States, if one notes that we graduate from college a total of around 415,000, assuming that this number is made up of our most talented youth, and notes that only one-third of them now prepare to be teachers, he might reach a most optimistic—though erroneous—conclusion: there must be a substantial pool of highly talented youth who could be recruited for teaching. From this judgment, the inference has been drawn by more than one writer that if school-teaching could be made more attractive, entrance into teacher training programs could be made highly selective. We might then look forward, so it is argued, to recruiting all our teachers from even the top 10 per cent of our youth in terms of intellectual ability.

Behind many such statements lies the assumption that the 15 to 20 per cent of an age group (i.e., all youth of a given age) who now graduate from college are the 15 or 20 per cent who are most able in scholastic terms. A number of studies have shown that any such assumption is very far from being correct. In terms of intellectual ability the college graduates of the United States cover a range corresponding to at least half and perhaps two-thirds of the age group. The research data on this point are consistent with my estimate, based on my visits to schools and colleges during the last seven years.

We now have available fairly reliable estimates made for the National Science Foundation. The study entitled "The Duration of Formal Education for High-Ability Youth" (NSF 61-36) was concerned with the retention in school and college of two groups of talented students: "(1) that comprising the ability range characteristic of the upper 30 per cent of high school graduates; (2) that comprising the ability range characteristic of the top 10 per cent of such graduates." The basis of selection of these groups was mental ability as measured by test scores. The conclusions from this study are highly significant for anyone exploring the question: How far down in academic ability must we go in order to obtain enough teachers for all our schools? Let me say at once that this question should really be answered state by state. The data are not available, however. What follows is a rough estimate on a national basis.

Table 13 of the NSF study is reproduced on page 236. This table gives the expected proportion of 17-year-olds in 1955 expected to graduate from college through full-time study. Section A concerns the total

Proportion of 17-year-olds in 1955 expected to graduate from college (through full-time study)

	Total	Male	Female
A. Total group			
Percentages of—			
(a) Age group graduating from high school	63	59	66
(b) High school graduates entering college	46	56	36
(c) College entrants graduating from college	55	57	52
(d) Age group graduating from college	16	19	12
B. Upper 30 per cent in mental ability			
Percentages of—			
(a) Age group graduating from high school	89	87	91
(b) High school graduates entering college	66	77	55
(c) College entrants graduating from college	65	67	62
(d) Age group graduating from college	38	45	31
C. Top 10 per cent in mental ability			
Percentages of—			
(a) Age group graduating from high school	91	89	93
(b) High school graduates entering college	76	88	65
(c) College entrants graduating from college	70	72	67
(d) Age group graduating from college	48	56	41

age group and need not be considered here except to note that the approximately 16 per cent of the total age group projected to graduate from college in 1960 is less than the actually reported figure of 415,000 [16 per cent of 2,260,000 (age group) would equal but 361,000].

Let us concentrate attention on Section C, which gives the calculations for the top 10 per cent of the high school graduates. The very last figure at the right on the bottom line of the table records the estimated percentage of the top 10 per cent of women who presumably graduated from college in 1960. The figure is 41 per cent. In other words, 59 per cent of our most talented girls were lost to vocations requiring college graduates. When one keeps in mind that these estimates concern the most intellectually able 10 per cent of the women in a high school graduating class, the figure of 41 per cent is shocking. Perhaps more shocking is the corresponding figure for men, namely, 56 per cent, since one might be inclined to attribute the large dropout rate for women to the fact of early marriage. At all events, simple arithmetic shows that in 1960, in an age group of approximately 2.2 million, only something like 45,100 women (0.41 × .10 × 1.1) and 61,600 men (0.56 × .10 × 1.1) of the top 10 per cent in ability graduated from college. This is about half the number of women who are prepared to teach (100,000) and about 21,000 more than the men who were trained as teachers (40,000). However, other professions presumably were drawing heavily on this same group. The total who received the doctorate and professional degrees in law, medicine, theology, and engineering in 1959 was 70,000. This number alone is somewhat larger than the 10 per cent pool of men! Clearly, as long as the losses between school and college and during college for the 10 per cent group are what they were a few years ago, it is out of the question to talk of recruiting teachers from the top 10 per cent of the high school graduating class.

Let us now examine the situation as regards those whose scholastic aptitude corresponds to that of the top 30 per cent of the graduating class on a national basis. Section B of the table gives estimates for the upper 30 per cent as previously defined. Only 31 per cent of the age group in this category of women (or 9 per cent of the total age group of women) will have graduated in 1960. The number is approximately 100,000 (.31 × .30 × 1.1). For men a similar figure is about 198,500 (.45 × .30 × 1.1). If the 70,000 men entering other professions comes from this same group, as well as the 40,000 men preparing to be teachers—a total of 110,000—there is not much to spare for those who wish to enter various other occupations directly on graduating from college. Since by no means all women who graduate from college are prepared for teaching, *it is clear that in many institutions many of those graduated as teachers must have scholastic aptitudes well below that of the top 30 per cent of the graduating high school class on a national basis.* This corresponds to my observations on the intellectual level of the bottom portion of the class preparing to be teachers in certain institutions.

Thus, at present, it cannot be hoped that all students preparing for teaching careers will be individuals superior in academic ability. Nevertheless, as a goal for the future, I believe it would be desirable to recruit teachers from the top 30 per cent group. If this goal seems rather optimistic, it is nevertheless worthy of consideration.

By 1974 with the larger total age group (about 3,800,000 as compared with 2,200,000 for those graduating from college in 1960) and with the trend toward lower attrition rates for the more able, *it is entirely possible that all the teachers graduating might come from the 30 per cent category.* For example, if 60 per cent of the age group of both men and women graduated from college, there would be about 684,000 graduates in the 30 per cent category. From this number one ought to be able to recruit 150,000 women and 60,000 men, a 50 per cent increase over the present output of teachers. The 60 per cent figure would be a consequence of holding nearly all the 30 per cent group in school and cutting the losses between school and college.

Several points deserve emphasis. First, an inspection of the above Table and the data on the NSF study shows that if one hopes to obtain all teachers from those who have scholastic aptitude characteristics of the upper 30 per cent of the high school graduates (on an national basis), certain steps must be taken. These involve the reduction in the attrition rate during school, the increase in the number of able students (particularly women) entering college, and the decrease in the dropout rate in college. When one considers that at present only something like half of all the girls in the 30 per cent category who graduate from high school enter college, one sees where the bottleneck really is as far as women teachers are concerned. When one realizes that now only about 45 per cent of the entire age group of men in the 30 per cent category graduate from college, one sees that we have here a bottleneck in the supply not only of teachers but of engineers and members of other professions as well.

The figures for 1974 in the preceding paragraphs are 684,000 men and women college graduates in the 30 per cent category. This number is much larger than that we estimated for the 1960 college graduates (298,500). Whether the number will prove large enough will depend on (a) the competition of other professions and business in the case of men, and (b) the demand for men and women elementary and secondary school teachers. There is every reason to believe a state-by-state analysis would reveal large differences. Anyone who has traveled around the United States knows how widely the attrition rates vary from community to community and from state to state. Thus I must warn the reader against taking too seriously figures he may read about the supply and demand of teachers on a *national basis*. These have been used here only because reliable state-by-state figures and forecasts are not yet available.

APPENDIX E

State Educational Structure as of May, 1963
(16 Most Populous States)[1]

State	Pop. Rank 1960	Method of Selecting State Board			No. of Members	Term of Office	Method of Selecting Chief State School Officer			Term of Office	Salary as of January, 1963
		Elected	Appointive	Other			Elected	App. by St. Bd.	App. by Gov.		
California	2		X		10	4	XN			4 yrs.	$22,500
Florida	10			XA	5A		X			4 yrs.	17,500
Georgia	16		X		10	7	X			4 yrs.	17,500
Illinois	4		D				X			4 yrs.	20,000
Indiana	11		X		19C	4	X			2 yrs.	18,000
Massachusetts	9		X		9	9		X		POB*	25,000
Michigan	7		D†				X			2 yrs.	17,500
Missouri	13		X		8	8		X		POB*	19,750
New Jersey	8		X		12	6			X	5 yrs.	24,500
New York	1			XB	13	13		X		POB*	28,875
North Carolina	12		X		13	8	X			4 yrs.	13,500
Ohio	5	XN			23	6		X		POB*	25,000
Pennsylvania	3		X		10	6			X	4 yrs.	20,000
Texas	6	XN			21	6		X		4 yrs.	18,500
Virginia	14		X		7	4			X	4 yrs.	19,000
Wisconsin	15		D				XN			4 yrs.	17,000

[1] Source: Much of this information was obtained from the Council of Chief State School Officers.
A "Cabinet system" (Major policy decisions in all areas made by Governor and four department heads acting as a board.)
B Selected by Legislature
C Three autonomous 6-member commissions: 1. General Education 2. Teacher Training and Licensing 3. Textbook Adoption. CSSO is a member of each commission.
D No single state board responsible for elementary and secondary education.
† New constitution, when adopted, will drastically revise structure.
N Nonpartisan ballot
* Pleasure of Board

239

Certification Requirements in 16 Most Populous States

TABLE I

Requirements in Professional Education for Provisional Teaching Certificate

State	Professional Education Elementary*	Professional Education Secondary*	Practice Teaching
California^A	24 (12)	22 (9)	Elem. 8 (180 clock hours) Sec. 6 (120 clock hours)
Florida	20	20	6
Georgia	20	20	6
Illinois	16	16	5
Indiana	27	Jr. H. 24 Sr. H. 18	Elem. 8 Sec. 6
Massachusetts	18	12	2
Michigan	20	20	5
Missouri	20	20	5
New Jersey^B	30	18	150 clock hours
New York^C	24	18	Elem. 300 clock hours of supervised instructional experience Sec. 80 class periods of supervised instructional experience
North Carolina^D	24	18	6
Ohio	28	17	6
Pennsylvania	18	18	6
Texas	18	18	6
Virginia	18	15	Elem. 6 Sec. 4–6
Wisconsin	26	18	5

* Professional elementary and secondary totals include practice teaching except where noted otherwise.

^A These are the 1961 requirements. Certification regulations are being completely revised as the result of recent legislation. Proposals recently recommended to the state board appear in parentheses and exclude practice teaching.

^B Professional requirements do not include practice teaching.

^C New requirements become effective September 1, 1963, for secondary teachers and September 1, 1966, for elementary teachers. These professional requirements do not include practice teaching.

^D New requirements effective September 1, 1966 for all teachers.

TABLE II

General Education and Subject Matter Requirements for Provisional Certification

State	General Education	Specialization Requirements in Four Secondary Subjects			
		Eng.	Soc. Science	Math.	Foreign Language
California[A]	Elem. .. (45) Sec. 40 (45)	20	20	20	20
Florida	45	30	30	21	24
Georgia	40	30	33	20	27
Illinois	35	24	24	20	20
Indiana	50	40	40	40	40
Massachusetts	..	18	18	18	18
Michigan	40	30	30	30	30
Missouri	Elem. 46[B] Sec. 25	24	24	24	24
New Jersey	30	18	30	18	18
New York[C]	Elem. 75 Sec. 60	36	36	18	24
North Carolina[D]	48	36	42	30	30
Ohio	Elem. 60 Sec. 30	24	45	18	20
Pennsylvania	60	36	36	12[E]	24
Texas	50% of baccalaureate prog.	24[F]	48[G]	24[F]	24[F]
Virginia	48	24	30	18	24
Wisconsin	Pattern approved by state superintendent	34	54[H]	34	34

[A] Requirements as of 1961. These standards are being revised. New state board recommendations, pending approval, appear in parentheses.

[B] 10 of these 46 hours appear to be primarily professionalized-content courses.

[C] These are the new requirements effective 9/1/63 for secondary teachers, 9/1/66 for elementary teachers.

[D] New requirements effective 9/1/66 for all teachers.

[E] Dual certificate. Applicant must have a minimum of 12 semester hours in both physics and mathematics.

[F] This is part of a dual academic specialization certificate. 24 semester hours are required in each of two fields that do not have to be related. Thus 48 semester hours is the requirement with two subjects as majors (24 apiece).

[G] Related fields major with 48 semester hours in the social studies.

[H] Broad field major effective 1/1/64.

Appendix G
Further Information Concerning Certification Evasion

As a supplement to the statements in Chapter 3, the following information may be of interest. Some details of the situation in ten of the 16
states are given below:

Michigan has an incidental teaching provision that permits a certified
teacher with the permission of the Superintendent of Public Instruction
to teach a subject not covered by his certificate.

Texas can issue an emergency permit upon the request of an employing superintendent who certifies the existence of an emergency situation
within his school district. This permit is valid for one year only for those
who hold a bachelor's degree, or have 90 hours of preparation and two
years of teaching experience. In Texas, as in many other states, the
emergency certificate is renewable if certain courses are taken to make
up the deficiency.

Indiana has new certification regulations that permit a person to receive a limited certificate if the candidate holds a baccalaureate degree
from an accredited institution and presents a planned program of study
designed to meet the requirements for provisional certification. The program must be completed within five years from the date of issuance of
the original limited certificate. At least 7½ semester hours of credit have
to be taken annually. The candidate for a limited certificate on the
secondary level must have completed 15 semester hours of work in the
area of endorsement.

Ohio superintendents can secure emergency certificates for teachers
who do not meet certification requirements. The State Board of Education permits public and private (Ohio is the only state of the most populous 16 that certifies non-public school teachers on both the elementary
and the secondary level) school administrators to hire teachers on
emergency certificates upon "evidence of a scarcity of suitable teachers
otherwise certified."

Illinois provides that the Office of the Superintendent of Public Instruction may evaluate for temporary approval the application of a
teacher who does not meet the requirements for provisional certification.
All applications for temporary approval must be approved by the local
County Superintendent.

Wisconsin issues permits, limited to one year or less and to one specific job, to persons who do not satisfy the minimal certification requirements. The administrator must file a written request asserting that a

certifiable teacher is unavailable. The permit teacher must complete a minimum of 6 semester hours of approved credit each year. The state superintendent has the authority, at his discretion, to grant or refuse these permits.

Missouri issues short-term or two-year elementary and secondary certificates to persons who have the bachelor's degree but lack some of the requirements for standard certification. Elementary teachers, to acquire the two-year certificate, must have completed at least 5 semester hours in professional education and may not have more than 24 semester hours of deficiencies to make up. Two-year secondary certificates will not be issued to teachers who have more than 5 hours of deficiencies in their teaching fields or in professional education. A two-year certificate will be granted to an applicant who has met the requirements in the teaching field if the deficiency in professional education does not exceed 12 semester hours.

Virginia provides that the holder of the collegiate certificate may have the practice-teaching requirement waived upon completing satisfactorily two years of teaching and 9 semester hours of professional education. Even the requirement of 9 semester hours may be modified or waived at the discretion of the Superintendent of Public Instruction. Thus it is possible for a "liberal arts" graduate in Virginia who has the requisite preparation in a subject-matter area to enter secondary school teaching with no professional education courses. With two years of successful teaching experience eliminating the 6-hour practice-teaching requirement, a person would only have to complete 9 additional hours or three courses in professional education to earn Virginia's permanent certificate, the collegiate professional. The person teaching on the nonrenewable collegiate certificate has four years to complete the professional requirements, although the certificate can be extended for two one-year periods on the basis of extenuating circumstances. Special licenses can be issued to applicants who have earned not less than 60 semester hours of college credit if local school administrators submit satisfactory reasons, such as not being able to find a certified person for a teaching position. To renew a special license, the holder must complete annually 6 semester hours of college credits in approved courses.

Massachusetts may grant a waiver upon the request of a school committee, which certifies that it is unable to obtain the services of a teacher who has met the standard certification requirements. The practice teaching can be waived after a semester's teaching experience. As a result, a secondary school teacher may take only two or three courses in professional education to satisfy the certification requirements. This waiver system gives great flexibility to local school boards in Massachusetts to employ suitable liberal arts graduates. A teacher in Massachusetts may teach outside a certified field provided such teaching does not exceed 20 per cent of the full teaching program. (A similar provision in New York and Pennsylvania permits a teacher to teach one period a day out of his licensed field.) A secondary school teacher in Massachusetts may not devote more than 50 per cent of teaching time to subjects in which he has not majored. A teaching major requires 18 semester hours of preparation. A person may thus teach up to 50 per cent of his time in his minor area, which requires only 9 hours of preparation.

Pennsylvania regulations stipulate that the State Council (Board) of Education shall provide for the issuance of certificates by county or district superintendents to meet any emergency shortage of teachers. The emergency certificate may now be issued by the county or district superintendent for a period not to exceed three months, provided the applicant has completed at least four years of college preparation or 120 semester hours. Emergency certificates originate with the county or district superintendents and may be extended by them. A record of the issuance of the emergency certificate must be filed with the Department of Public Instruction.

The reader, in light of the numerous end runs I have described, may be wondering what sanctions the state can impose upon local school districts that do not adhere to the certification regulations. My staff and I made this query at the capitals we visited and found that in many states little, if any, *effective* action was being taken to enforce the certification requirements.

There is general agreement that the state, through its educational agency (state Education Department), has the authority to ask the attorney general to impose legal pressure upon local school boards and administrators. Such legal sanctions are rarely invoked in most states, as a letter from the state director of teacher certification will usually result in immediate compliance. State certification authorities told us that it was rarely necessary to invoke legal sanctions because the overwhelming number of school administrators report accurately the certification status of their teachers and make every effort to adhere to state regulations.

It must be noted, however, that the legal powers of most Education Departments have never really been tested. The threat of a letter from the chief state school officer or certification official to invoke sanctions has been sufficient to compel all but a handful of recalcitrant local school authorities to comply with state Education Department requests and rulings on certification matters.

In most states there have been few, if any, cases in which the state Education Department officials have invoked financial or any other specific sanctions against school districts that violated certification requirements. Pennsylvania is one state which at least makes an effort to impose financial sanctions against derelict districts. Section 2518 of the Pennsylvania school code provides: "In the event that after the first day of July, 1959, any school district or county board of school directors with respect to area technical schools, for a period of two successive years, employs in the same position teachers who hold only an emergency certificate for any grades or subjects which they teach, such school district or board shall forfeit the sum of $300 for each teacher so employed or for each position so filled." $300 does not seem a very high price to pay for employing a good teacher continuously who is deemed essential by the superintendent!

The information we obtained in Harrisburg indicated the extent to which forfeitures were invoked. In 1961–62 there were 542 cases, and penalties totaling $258,000 were assessed against 243 employing school districts. There seems to be a stiffer fine of $3,100 to $3,300 per teacher for a person employed without any certificate. School districts are by this sanction deprived of an entire unit of reimbursement from the state. Twenty-three districts were thus fined in 1961–62.

New York presents an interesting example of how difficult it is for state certification officials to enforce certification regulations stringently. As of September 1, 1958, emergency certificates were no longer issued in New York. Instead, superintendents are required to maintain a list of all professional persons uncertified for all or part of their assignment and for all uncertified substitutes who exceed thirty-five days of service in any school year. All employing school districts° are required to report to Albany each summer all uncertified classroom teachers who served during the previous school year.

Despite this procedure in registering uncertified teachers and the prestige of one of the leading and most powerful state Departments of Education, end runs continue to persist in New York.

The 1960–61 certification report indicated that 8,079 teachers in New York State, exclusive of Buffalo and New York City, were uncertified. A total of 1,880 of the 8,079—or 23% of the total—took less than the 6 semester hours of college work required of holders of less than the

---

° In New York, as in Pennsylvania and New Jersey, emergency permits must be signed by both the superintendent and the president of the local school board. Indiana, Ohio, Wisconsin and many other states require only the signature of the superintendent.

standard certificate who wish to continue teaching. 261 of the 1,880 were granted waivers at the request of their superintendents. The balance, or 1,619 (20%) of the 8,079 uncertified teachers, thus served *illegally* in the schools of New York State in 1960–61. The Bureau of Teacher Education and Certification of the influential New York State Education Department thus did not have the power to compel 1,619 teachers to fulfill the state certification requirements.

It must be noted that many states utilize their authority of accreditation or classification of schools to enforce certification standards and regulations. Ohio has reportedly revoked high school charters because schools have poorly prepared faculties. Missouri will restudy a school's classification if too many teachers are inadequately trained. The issuance in Illinois of an excessive number of temporary approvals (equivalent to emergency certificate or permit) to a school's faculty will threaten its accreditation.

Regional accrediting associations play a role in enforcing certification standards. The Commission on Secondary Schools of the North Central Association, with its authority to accredit schools in nineteen states, wields tremendous influence and has its own certification requirements. In more than one state we have been told that school administrators are more concerned with satisfying the North Central requirements than with meeting the certification regulations of their own state.

The reader must not underestimate the power residing in education departments and regional associations that actively exercise the authority to accredit schools. Students of a school that loses accreditation or is reclassified can lose their chance for admission to a desired college. With the pressure for college admission mounting nationally, the community pressure upon schools to maintain or improve their accreditation status is steadily increasing.

Source: *School District Organization, Journey That Must Not End,* published by American Association of School Administrators and Department of Rural Education of the National Education Association. 1962, Washington, D.C.

Trends in the Number of School Districts

Year	Number of School Districts
1932	127,649
1948	105,971
1953	67,075
1961	36,402

Percentage of Decrease in the Number of School Districts for Various Periods

Years	Percentage of Decrease
1932–48	16.98
1948–53	36.70
1953–61	45.73

Number of School Districts Less the Number of Nonoperating School Districts

Year	Number of School Districts	Number of Nonoperating School Districts	Net Number of Operating School Districts
1948	105,971	17,131	88,840
1953	67,075	11,891	55,184
1961	36,402	4,677	31,705

Number and Percentage of Decrease in One-Teacher Schools

Year	Number	Percentage of Decrease
1930	148,711	.....
1948	74,832	49.68
1961	15,018	79.93

247

TABLE I:
Number of School Districts and Trends, 1932–61, United States, by States

States	No. of School Districts[1]				Rank in No. of School Districts				Decrease in School Districts						Rank in Per Cent of Decrease		
									1932–48		1948–53		1953–61		1932–48	1948–53	1953–61
	1932[2]	1948	1953	1961	1932	1948	1953	1961	No.	%	No.	%	No.	%			
	2	3	4	5	6	7	8	9	10	11	12	13	14	15	16	17	18
Alabama	112	108	111	114	42	41	40	38	4	3.6	+3	+2.8	+3	+2.7	28	38	39
Alaska	17	23	28	30	49	49	48	47	+6	+35.3	+5	+21.7	+2	+7.1	41	40	43
Arizona	500	322	329	297	28	30	27	26	178	35.6	+7	+2.2	32	9.7	7	37	27
Arkansas	3,193	1,589	423	418	15	19	25	24	1,604	50.2	1,166	73.4	5	1.2	4	5	34
California	3,589	2,429	2,018	1,650	13	15	14	8	1,160	32.3	411	16.9	368	18.2	11	15	24
Colorado	2,041	1,884	1,147	341	21	17	19	25	157	7.7	737	39.1	806	70.3	22	9	3
Connecticut	161	174	172	176	39	36	35.5	32	+13	+8.1	2	1.1	+4	+2.3	40	33	38
Delaware	126	126	115	92	40	39	39	41	0	0.0	11	8.7	23	20.0	...	24	23
Dist. of Col.	1	1	1	1	50.5	50.5	50.5	50.5	0	...	0	...	...	...	...	...	...
Florida	67	67	67	67	44	43.5	43.5	42.5	0	...	0	...	...	...	...	...	...
Georgia	272	189	203	199	33	35	33	31	83	30.5	+14	+7.4	4	2.0	12	39	33
Hawaii	1	1	1	1	50.5	50.5	50.5	50.5	0	0.0	0	0.0	0	0.0	...	...	...
Idaho	1,418	1,011	216	118	24	24	32	37	407	28.7	795	78.6	98	45.4	13	3	13
Illinois	12,070	11,061	2,607	1,552	1	1	10	9	1,009	8.4	8,454	76.4	1,055	40.5	21	4	16
Indiana	1,292	1,196	1,144	888	25	23	20	17	96	7.4	52	4.3	256	22.4	23	28	22
Iowa	4,870	4,856	4,558	1,391	12	9	5	11	14	.3	298	6.1	3,167	69.5	35	27	4
Kansas	8,748	5,643	3,903	2,303	4	6	7	4	3,105	35.5	1,740	30.8	1,600	41.0	8	12	15
Kentucky	384	256	227	207	31	32	31	30	128	33.3	29	11.3	20	8.8	10	21	28
Louisiana	66	67	67	67	45	43.5	50.5	42.5	+1	+1.5	0	0.0	0	0.0	38	0	0
Maine	518	493	491	462	27	27	24	21	25	4.8	2	0.4	29	5.9	26	35	20
Maryland	24	24	24	24	48	48	49	48	0	0.0	0	0.0	0	0.0	0	0	0
Massachusetts	355	351	351	438	32	29	26	22	4	1.1	0	0.0	+87	+24.8	17	0	44
Michigan	6,965	5,434	4,736	1,981	9	7	4	5	1,531	22.0	698	12.8	2,755	58.2	34	18	8
Minnesota	7,773	7,606	5,298	2,420	6	2	3	3	167	2.1	2,308	30.3	2,878	54.3	17	13	10
Mississippi	5,560	4,194	1,417	150	10	11	16	35	1,366	24.6	2,777	66.2	1,267	89.4	14	6	2

State																
Missouri	8,764	8,422	4,331	1,735	3	1	6	7	342	3.9	4,091	48.6	2,596	59.9	27	8	7
Montana	2,439	6,800	1,201	1,025	17	4	18	15	+4,361	+178.8	5,599	82.3	176	14.7	42	2	25
Nebraska	7,344	6,991	6,276	3,348	8	3	1	1	353	4.8	715	10.2	2,928	46.7	25	23	12
Nevada	266	211	185	17	35	34	34	49	55	20.7	26	12.3	168	90.8	25	19.5	1
New Hampshire	244	239	235	230	36	33	30	28	5	2.0	4	1.7	5	2.1	32	31	32
New Jersey	552	561	557	588	26	26	22	19	+9	+1.6	4	0.7	+31	+5.6	37	34	41
New Mexico	98	104	100	99	43	42	42	40	+6	+6.1	4	3.8	1	1.0	39	29	35
New York	9,467	4,609	2,961	1,280	2	10	9	12	4,858	51.3	1,648	35.8	1,681	56.8	3	10	9
North Carolina	200	172	172	173	37	37	35.5	33	28	14.0	0	0.0	+1	+0.6	19	0	37
North Dakota	2,228	2,267	2,111	1,066	19	16	13	14	+39	+1.8	156	6.9	1,045	49.5	38	26	11
Ohio	2,043	1,583	1,365	840	20	20	17	18	460	22.5	218	13.8	525	38.5	16	17	17
Oklahoma	4,933	2,664	1,888	1,255	11	13	15	13	2,269	46.0	776	29.1	633	33.5	5	14	19
Oregon	2,234	1,363	893	510	18	21	21	20	871	39.0	470	34.5	383	42.9	6	11	14
Pennsylvania	2,587	2,540	2,502	956³	16	14	11	16	47	1.8	38	1.5	1,546	61.8	33	32	6
Rhode Island	39	39	39	41	47	47	47	45	0	0.0	0	0.0	+2	+5.1	0	0	40
South Carolina	1,792	1,737	103	109	22.5	18	41	39	55	3.1	1,634	94.1	+6	+5.8	30	1	42
South Dakota	3,433	3,409	3,385	2,964	14	12	8	12	24	0.7	24	0.7	421	12.4	24	25	26
Tennessee	194	150	150	154	38	38	37	34	44	22.7	0	0.0	+4	2.7	15	0	31
Texas	7,932	5,145	2,146	1,539	5	8	12	10	2,787	35.1	2,999	58.3	607	28.3	9	7	20
Utah	40	40	40	40	46	46	46	45	0	0.0	0	0.0	0	0.0	0	0	0
Vermont	268	268	263	262	34	31	29	27	0	0.0	5	1.9	1	0.4	0	30	36
Virginia	125	125	127	131	41	40	38	36	0	0.0	+2	+1.6	+4	3.1	0	36	30
Washington	1,792	628	551	419	22.5	25	23	23	1,164	65.0	77	12.3	132	24.0	2	19.5	21
West Virginia	450	55	55	55	29	45	45	44	395	87.8	0	0.0	0	0.0	1	0	0
Wisconsin	7,662	6,385	5,463	1,967	7	5	2	6	1,277	16.7	922	14.4	3,496	64.0	18	16	5
Wyoming	400	359	322	212	30	28	28	29	41	10.2	37	10.3	110	34.2	20	22	18
Grand Total	127,649	105,971	67,075	36,402	..	..	..	..	21,678	16.98	38,896	36.70	30,673	45.73	..	..	..

[1] In a few instances the number of school districts reported are different from the number cited. The differences are usually accounted for by the difference in definitions of school districts. In some states as in New Mexico and Georgia subdistricts have at times been reported as school districts. An effort has been made to include only districts that are quasi corporations with boards or chief school officers that have responsibility for, and either complete or partial autonomy in, the administration of all public schools within their respective borders.

[2] Deffenbaugh, Walter S., and Covert, Timon, *School Administrative Units*, Pamphlet No. 34, U.S. Office of Education, Washington, D.C., January 1933, p. 4–5.

[3] Operating units only embracing 2185 basic administrative units.

TABLE II:
Number of School Districts by Size, United States, by States

States	Number and Per Cent of School Districts Employing											
	9 Teachers or Fewer						40 Teachers or More					
	1947–48		1952–53		1960–61		1947–48		1952–53		1960–61	
	No.	%	No.	%	No.	%	No.	%	No.	%	No.	%
1	2	3	4	5	6	7	8	9	10	11	12	13
Alabama	0	0.0	0	0.0	0	0.0	84	77.78	84	75.68	109	95.61
Alaska	....	....	....	....	13	43.33	....	....	....	....	5	16.67
Arizona	155	48.14	144	43.77	113	38.05	22	6.83	39	11.85	56	18.86
Arkansas	1,242	78.16	45	10.64	50	11.96	63	3.96	95	22.46	100	23.92
California	1,591	65.50	1,197	59.32	780	47.27	230	9.47	334	16.55	434	26.30
Colorado	1,658	88.00	903	78.73	109	31.96	29	1.54	33	2.88	62	18.18
Connecticut	51	29.31	46	26.74	25	14.20	54	31.03	61	35.47	97	55.11
Delaware	91	72.22	73	63.48	47	51.09	11	8.73	19	16.52	23	25.00
District of Columbia	....	....	....	....	0	0.0	1	100.00	1	100.00	1	100.00
Florida	0	0.0	0	0.0	0	0.0	61	91.04	61	91.04	2	97.01
Georgia	0	0.0	0	0.0	1	.50	181	95.77	183	90.15	181	90.95
Hawaii	....	....	....	....	0	0.0	....	....	....	....	1	100.00
Idaho	614	60.73	97	44.91	27	22.88	18	1.78	33	15.28	45	38.14
Illinois	5,098	46.09	500[1]	19.18	552	35.57	754	6.91	1,050[1]	40.28	412	26.55
Indiana	435	36.37	351	30.68	248	27.93	86	7.19	120	10.49	174	19.59
Iowa	4,224	86.99	2,375	52.11	7	50	52	1.07	66	1.45	143	10.28
Kansas	4,323	76.61	3,431	87.91	1,519	65.96	40	0.71	50	1.28	81	3.52
Kentucky	16	6.25	5	2.20	6	2.90	139	54.30	142	62.56	163	78.74
Louisiana	0	0.0	0	0.0	0	0.0	67	100.00	67	100.00	67	100.00
Maine	384	77.89	325	66.19	286	61.90	28	5.68	34	6.92	63	13.64
Maryland	0	0.0	0	0.0	0	0.0	24	100.00	24	100.00	24	100.00
Massachusetts	106	30.20	85[1]	27.07	119[2]	27.17	115	32.76	125[1]	35.61	232[2]	52.97
Michigan	3,603	66.30	2,984	63.01	1,000	50.48	120	2.21	150	3.17	500	25.24

Minnesota	4,721	62.07	3,179	50.00	1,427	58.97	59	0.78	82	1.55	139	5.74
Mississippi	3,707	88.39	1,200[1]	84.69	0	3.0	21	0.50	301[1]	2.12	135	90.00
Missouri	6,114	72.60	2,873	56.34	810	46.69	42	0.50	90	2.08	143	8.24
Montana	1,039	15.28	838	69.78	700	68.29	15	0.22	24	2.00	25	2.44
Nebraska	4,970	71.09	4,300	58.51	2,570	76.76	14	0.20	25	0.40	38	1.14
Nevada	157	74.41	144	77.84	1	5.88	4	1.90	6	3.24	14	82.35
New Hampshire	162	67.78	157	66.81	126	54.73	15	5.44	14	5.96	25	10.87
New Jersey	171	30.48	117	21.01	52	8.84	145	25.85	175	31.42	356	60.54
New Mexico	68	65.38	15	15.00	4[3]	4.04	25	24.04	39	39.00	473[3]	47.47
New York	2,069	44.89	1,013	24.21	168	13.13	245	5.22	335	11.31	530	41.41
North Carolina	0	0.0	0	0.0	0	0.0	162	94.19	166	96.51	.....	.....
North Dakota	1,914	84.43	1,710	31.30	275	25.80	7	0.31	7	0.33	5	.47
Ohio	649	41.00	413	30.26	88	10.48	142	8.37	205	15.02	235	27.98
Oklahoma	1,024	72.22	1,743	92.32	864	68.84	41	1.54	50	3.18	79	6.29
Oregon	1,190	87.31	549	61.48	275	53.92	35	2.57	48	5.38	88	17.25
Pennsylvania	1,381	54.37	1,028	41.09	35	3.66	311	12.24	550	21.98	556	58.16
Rhode Island	5	12.82	5	12.82	2	4.88	21	53.85	21	53.85	26	63.41
South Carolina	1,226	70.58	0	0.0	0	0.0	60	3.45	103	100.00	103	94.50
South Dakota	3,296	96.69	3,238	95.66	1,811	61.10	11	0.32	12	0.35	26	.88
Tennessee	2	1.33	1	0.67	1	.65	117	78.00	120	80.00	125	81.17
Texas	2,886	56.09	1,133	52.80	525	34.11	275	5.34	213	9.93	373	24.24
Utah	1	2.50	1	2.50	0	0.0	27	67.50	27	67.50	30	75.00
Vermont	182	67.91	171	65.02	150	57.25	10	3.73	11	4.18	16	6.11
Virginia	0	0.0	0	0.0	0	0.0	119	95.20	120	94.49	131	100.00
Washington	358	57.01	284	51.54	.....	.....	88	14.01	88	15.97	.....	.....
West Virginia	0	0.0	0	0.0	0	3.0	55	100.00	55	100.00	53	96.36
Wisconsin	4,464	69.91	4,377	80.12	1,632	32.97	57	0.89	64	1.17	196	9.96
Wyoming	324	90.25	242	75.16	133	62.74	20	5.57	17	5.28	23	10.85
Grand Total	66,571	62.82	41,302	61.58	16,551	45.47	4,330	4.09	5,478	8.17	6,492	17.83

[1] Estimated.
[2] Data reported for 1958–59.
[3] Data reported for 1959–60.

TABLE III

Number of Public School Systems, by Enrollment-Size Group and Number of Pupils Enrolled: United States, 1961–62

Enrollment Size (number of pupils)	School Systems		Pupils Enrolled	
	Number	Per Cent	Number (in thousands)	Per Cent
1	2	3	4	5
U.S. total	37,025	100.0	37,800	100.0
25,000 or more	132	0.4	9,947	26.3
12,000 to 24,999	266	0.7	4,321	11.4
6,000 to 11,999	671	1.8	5,542	14.7
3,000 to 5,999	1,495	4.0	6,266	16.6
1,800 to 2,999	1,686	4.6	3,903	10.3
1,200 to 1,799	1,591	4.3	2,336	6.2
600 to 1,199	3,159	8.5	2,703	7.1
300 to 599	3,486	9.4	1,505	4.0
150 to 299	3,081	8.3	672	1.8
50 to 149	4,214	11.4	387	1.0
15 to 49	6,581	17.8	173	0.5
1 to 14	4,632	12.5	44	0.1
None[1]	6,031	16.3	. . . . .	. . . . .

[1] Systems not operating schools.

NOTE: Data are for 50 States and D.C.

SOURCE: U.S. Department of Commerce, Bureau of the Census, Release No. CB62-82, taken from *Digest of Educational Statistics*, United States Office of Education.

Within 7 Middle Western or plains states (North Dakota, South Dakota, Nebraska, Kansas, Minnesota, Iowa, Missouri) there are concentrated:

42% of the nation's school districts
81% of the nation's nonoperating districts
53% of the nation's one-teacher schools
48% of the nation's districts providing elementary education only.

These 7 states, however, enroll less than 9 per cent of all schoolchildren in the nation.

Size of School District

Year	9 or Fewer Teachers	Percentages of All Districts	40 or More Teachers	Percentages of All Districts
1948	66,571	62.82	4,330	4.09
1953	41,302	61.58	5,478	8.17
1961	16,551	45.47	6,492	17.83

Findings in Elementary Professional Education

A VAST MAJORITY of elementary teachers complete their preparation for employment in four years (8 semesters). Judging from 35 institutions selected from those I visited, the time devoted to general education ranges from 39 to 90 semester hours. The professional sequence of courses given by professors of education occupies from 11 to 29 semester hours. Special methods courses (selected from specified offerings in general education or from a list of "elective" courses set up for prospective elementary school teachers) occupy from 12 to 36 semester hours. Clearly, within an 8-semester program there is great variety in the allocation of time to subject-matter courses that may be regarded as general education, special content courses for teachers, or completely free subject-matter electives. There is also great variety in the allocation of time to the professional sequence (including both the foundations and the special methods courses), and to practice teaching.

There is some uniformity in that all institutions offered at least 3 semester hours in educational or child psychology, and all offered practice teaching. With very few exceptions, all institutions required some special methods courses in language arts including reading, arithmetic, social studies, and science, with either special content or special methods courses being added in physical education, music, and arts and crafts. Regardless, then, of differences in viewpoint regarding the extent to which some kind of general education prepares an elementary school teacher in the necessary subject fields, all institutions preparing elementary school teachers make some effort to provide special content and methodology directly related to the curriculum of the elementary school and what teachers are expected to do in it.

Earlier we have seen that teachers, elementary school teachers included, are prepared in every type of institution for higher learning in the United States. One can discuss differences and similarities among these institutions with only a limited degree of validity on a state-by-state basis; to be more accurate, one must examine programs on an institution-by-institution basis. Certainly, no broad generalizations can be made to describe similarities or differences among single-purpose teacher-preparing institutions, "liberal arts" colleges, or multipurpose colleges and universities.

A few single-purpose institutions educate only elementary school teachers. In these, the general education requirements and the teaching of these general education courses tend to be slanted toward the fact

254

that all the students enrolled are going into elementary school teaching; there are special content courses for prospective elementary school teachers (and, as I have stated, the distinction between these and general education requirements in this type of institution is difficult to determine); and there is considerable emphasis on observation, participation, and practice teaching. Again, one will find two such institutions quite far apart on one or another of these items. Nevertheless, the "tone" of this kind of institution is markedly different from the tone of the average "liberal arts" college. A student who chose to enter such a single-purpose institution because it was conveniently located and who did not really intend to teach would find it very difficult to escape from "the shadow of future teaching" as a dominant characteristic of daily campus life.

For those who are interested in more details, a summary of 35 different elementary programs is given below. These are found in institutions visited by either my staff or me. The programs include those from 11 state universities, 9 private universities, 11 state or municipal colleges and 4 private "liberal arts" colleges. There are 16 states represented: California, Washington, and Colorado in the West; New Jersey, New York, Pennsylvania, and Massachusetts in the Northeast; Illinois, Indiana, Iowa, Ohio, and Minnesota in the Middle West; and Texas, North Carolina, Florida, and Georgia in the South. Thirty-three of the programs summarized here are four-year preparation programs, and two of them are programs that take five years of preparation. The following figures will give some idea of the proportionate amount of time spent in various aspects of the program.

General Education: In the 33 four-year programs the requirements for general education range from 39 to 90 semester hours. It should be noted that this includes general psychology, geography, foreign language (not generally required), and any course not taken by prospective elementary teachers at their respective institutions.

Professional Core: This category includes all courses in educational foundations, introduction to education, educational psychology, child growth and development, guidance, tests and measurements, educational sociology, and history and philosophy of education. In the 35 institutions, the professional-core requirements range from 11 to 29 semester hours.

Special Content and Methods Courses: This category includes all courses in the content of the elementary school plus such courses as children's literature, speech for elementary teachers, health and physical education, nutrition, and all methods courses. In the 35 institutions, the support courses showed a range of from 12 to 36 semester hours.

Major or Concentration: Only 16 of the institutions require the prospective elementary teacher to take a major, a minor, or a concentration in some academic area other than education. This includes a wide variety of so-called content areas ranging from "Family and Community Living" to such traditional areas as foreign languages and the sciences. In the 16 institutions in this category, the requirements for a major or concentration were from 14 to 15 semester hours.

Free Electives: Twenty-three of the institutions represented in this summary allowed the student a number of free electives in his four-year course. These electives range from 2 to 32 semester hours. It is perhaps deceptive to call these "free electives." In reality, many students use most of their electives in taking courses to buttress their program of professional training. An example of this is one institution that reports 20 elective hours; however, faculty members there indicate that the majority of these hours are taken in courses that will help the elementary teacher in the content areas of the elementary school.

Total Requirements: The 33 four-year programs represented in this summary require a range from 120 to 136 semester hours for graduation.

In Table I are shown the ranges and average semester-hour requirements in professional education, including the special content courses. Unfortunately, such averages sometimes obscure the most startling differences that are of significance. For example, many programs have very heavy requirements in arts and crafts, music, and health and physical education, while other programs look on these areas as electives. These interesting contrasts disappear through the statistical summarizing. A more direct comparison of the requirements in arts and crafts, music, and health-physical education with the requirements in reading-language arts, arithmetic, social studies, and science provides some very interesting data. (Remember—these courses are courses that are taken only by prospective teachers!)

Out of 35 programs:

8	required more	*arts and crafts*	than	reading-language arts
13	"	"	" "	" "	" "	"	arithmetic
16	"	"	" "	" "	" "	"	social studies
15	"	"	" "	" "	" "	"	science
7	"	"	*music*			"	reading-language arts
14	"	"	"			"	arithmetic
14	"	"	"			"	social studies
13	"	"	"			"	science
14	"	"	*health-P.E.*			"	reading-language arts
17	"	"	"	"		"	arithmetic
21	"	"	"	"		"	social studies
19	"	"	"	"		"	science

Of course, not all programs had this uneven balance of course requirements. Some required as much or more work in reading-language arts,
arithmetic, social studies, and science. It should also be kept in mind
that most programs allow a few electives, and in many cases students
are urged to take these electives in support of methods courses in the
traditional subject areas.

TABLE I:

Range and Average Semester Hours Credit for All
Required Professional and Special Content Courses—
35 Elementary Programs

Name of Area or Course	Number of Inst. Where Required	Range of Sem. Hrs. Credit	Average Sem. Hrs. Credit
Intro. to Educ.	24	1 to 4	2.7
Psych.-Development-Measurement	35	3 to 17	3.7
Soc.-Hist.-Phil. Foundations	24	2 to 6	3.7
Curriculum or Educ. Problems	8	2 to 6	2.5
Prac. Teaching	35	5 to 14	8.9
General Methods	9	2 to 4	2.8
Reading	19	2 to 4	2.5
Language Arts	27	2 to 5	3.6
Arithmetic	34	1 to 5	2.4
Social Studies	32	1 to 3	2.3
Science	34	1 to 6	2.2
Health & P.E.	33	2 to 7	3.4
Child's Literature	23	1 to 3	2.3
Music	32	1 to 5	2.9
Arts & Crafts	30	1 to 6	3.3
Speech for Teachers	6	2 to $2\frac{2}{3}$	2.1
Handwriting	3	$\frac{2}{3}$ to 1	.8
Drama for Child	1	2	2.0
Audio-Visual Ed.	8	$\frac{2}{3}$ to 3	1.7
Food & Nutrition	2	2 to 3	2.5
Required Prof. Electives	4	3 to 4	3.2
Elem. Curriculum	3	1 to 4	2.8

Table II is an attempt to show the extremes in course requirements,
using 8 selected programs. This table also enables one to compare the
course requirements in art, music, and physical education with the traditional subject courses.

TABLE II:
8 Selected Four-Year Programs for Preparing Elementary Teachers Showing the Extremes

GEN. ED.	58	58	60	63	45	55	68	59
WHEN 1st COURSE	Jr.	Fr.	Fr.-Soph.	Soph.	Soph.	Soph.	Jr.	Fr.
PROFESSIONAL CORE								
Intro. to Ed.	...	2⅔	4⅔	3	3⅓	...	2⅔	2
Phil.-Soc. Found.	3	2	2⅔	...	...	3	4	...
Psych. Found.	5	5⅓	6	3	3⅓	6	4⅔	17
Prac. Tch.	15	8	8	8	6⅔	6	5⅓	10-stu. tch. 3-fld. exp.
Totals	23	18	21⅓	14	13⅓	15	16⅔	32
METHODS & SUPPORT COURSES TAKEN ONLY BY ELEM. TCHRS.								
Reading	2	...	...	2	1⅔	...	2	3
Lang. Arts.	...	4	2⅔	2	...	3	2	3
Arith.	2	2	2	2	1⅔	3	2⅔	2
Soc. Stu.	2	2	2⅔	2	1⅔	3	2	3
Science	2	2	2	2	1⅔	3	2	3
Health & P.E.	3	4⅔	4	2	3⅓	4	4⅔	4
Child's Lit.	...	2⅔	2	2	3⅓	3	(Students take their	2
Music	2	5⅓	6	2	3⅓	4	20 "free" electives	2
Arts & Crafts	2	4⅔	5⅓	2	3⅓	6	in support courses)	in gen. educ.
Speech	...	2⅔	...	2	...	...		2
Other	Drama-2	Writing-2	...	AV-2				
	AV-2	Elective-2	...	Curric-2	Elec-3⅓	Curric-3		3
Totals	19	33	26⅔	24	23⅓	32	15–25	27
Major	...	...	...	...	45	...	...	...
Minor	...	...	...	21	...	18	...	...
Electives	25	16	13	...	...	...	10–20	10
GRAND TOTAL HOURS	125	125	120	124	126⅔	120	120	128

Practice Teaching: Full-time practice teaching is required in 26 of the programs; the other 9 require only part-time practice teaching. This ranges from as little as 6 weeks in 1 institution to 16 weeks in 6 institutions. An average figure would be 12 weeks of full-time practice teaching, and this is found in 7 of the institutions. Of the 9 institutions having part-time practice teaching, 1 of them has as little as 10 weeks while 2 institutions require part-time practice teaching over 2 semesters or 1 entire year. Five of these institutions require 16 weeks of part-time practice teaching.

In 27 of the institutions there is a seminar accompanying practice teaching while in 8 there is no such seminar.

Students practice-teach at only 1 grade level in 25 institutions, while in the other 10 institutions they practice-teach at 2 grade levels.

Supervision of student teachers is handled by the methods and curriculum instructors in 21 institutions. Seven other institutions have special staffs of supervisors who do this as a full-time activity. In several institutions, especially in California, these supervisors are jointly employed by the school system and the college. In 7 other institutions all of the practice-teaching supervision is handled by doctoral students who are neither full-time faculty members nor instructors in the methods courses.

Cooperating teachers are paid for their work with practice teachers in 16 of the institutions, while 19 other institutions do not pay. However, in some institutions that do not pay, cooperating teachers are given tuition vouchers enabling them to take courses free of charge on the campus. Payments to cooperating teachers range from as little as $15 in one institution to as much as $80 in another institution. In 5 institutions cooperating teachers are paid $40 and in 7 they are paid $50 for each of their student teachers. For the most part this money comes from the regular college budget. However, in 2 institutions students are assessed a $50 fee, and this money is paid to the cooperating teachers. In the state of Washington, the principal is paid $10 for each student teacher in his school.

Only 12 of the institutions covered in this report have a campus or laboratory school, and 23 of them do not have such a school. A number of these schools are in actuality public schools that have been assigned by the local administration to cooperate with the college or university. In these cases the school is partially subsidized by the institution, although the ultimate administrative control is retained by the public school district. It should be noted that only a small fraction of the practice-teaching operation is carried out in these schools. They are basically used for the purpose of observation and demonstration teaching.

In 32 of the programs surveyed, prospective teachers have an opportunity to either visit schools or actually participate in classroom activities during their training program. This generally coincides with the point at which the students begin their professional work. For example, in 17 of the programs students begin their participation and observation during their freshman and sophomore years. In 15 others they get participation and observation in their junior, senior, or graduate year. There are 3 institutions where students get no observation or participation prior to their practice teaching. (It should be noted that these are all small "liberal arts" colleges located in relatively small communities.) One aspect of this observation and participation is the utilization of social and community agencies such as Boy Scouts, youth clubs, and child guidance clinics. Seven institutions utilize such agencies in connection with their teacher training programs.

Nine of the institutions included here have a so-called "September Experience": they begin their practice teaching on the first day of the public school year thus giving students some experience with the organization and initiation of a new class in an elementary schoolroom. Twenty-six of the institutions surveyed do not have such an experience.

PART II
"Support and Special Methods" Courses for Elementary Teachers

The following thumbnail descriptions are thought to be representative of the several courses taken by many prospective elementary teachers. There is a great deal of variation from one institution to another—and also among the several instructors within some institutions. However, the "typical" courses might be as follows:

Teaching of Reading

(1) A consideration of the *skills* required in learning to read; e.g., the recognition of words through their phonetic sounds, relating printed symbols to known objects or ideas, breaking words into syllables, determining words through the way they are used in phrases and sentences, etc.

(2) Consideration of the reading skills required in the upper grades, e.g., comprehending the direct and implied meaning of printed matter,

developing greater speed in reading, skimming printed material effectively, reading to locate details or the main idea, etc.

(3) Acquaintance with a variety of textbooks, workbooks, and related instructional devices such as teachers' manuals, flash cards, and visual aids.

(4) The consideration of reading problems and appropriate remedial techniques.

(5) Techniques of planning reading lessons, grouping children for instruction, conducting various kinds of reading lessons, evaluating children's reading skills, and assigning appropriate advanced or remedial work.

Language Arts in the Elementary School

(1) Usually includes all of the above (Teaching of Reading) in programs that do not require a separate reading course.

(2) Also includes a consideration of spelling, speaking, listening, and penmanship skills in the lower grades and the application of these skills in the upper grades.

(3) Acquaintance with the methods and instructional materials used in teaching these skills.

(4) May also include attention to grammar and creative writing as aspects of the language development of children.

(5) In many cases there is an attempt to relate the language program to the children's experiences in art, music, dramatics, and social studies—especially in the nursery school, kindergarten, and primary grades.

Arithmetic in the Elementary School

(1) Generally includes attention to the development of basic quantitative "understandings" as opposed to computation. This includes the decimal system, number systems with bases other than 10, sets, basic concepts of algebra, and arithmetic concepts such as algorism, ordinal, factorials, prime numbers, etc. Most instructors in such courses say students can do computations but that they do not understand the meaning of arithmetic ideas and processes to the degree required to help youngsters develop such understandings.

(2) The organization and management of the elementary arithmetic program.

(3) Acquaintance with instructional materials (texts, visual aids, drill material).

(4) The techniques used in introducing children to the concepts and processes of arithmetic.

Science in the Elementary School

(1) Considerable time is spent in identifying the facts and principles of astronomy, geology, physics, chemistry, and biology that are relevant for the elementary school child.

(2) Acquaintance with textbooks, visual aids, and related printed material relevant to elementary science.

(3) Opportunity to become familiar with and actually manipulate science apparatus.

(4) Consideration of the organization and management of the elementary science program from grade to grade.

(5) Attention to the techniques of introducing science to elementary school children.

Social Studies in the Elementary School

(1) Consideration of the purposes in teaching social studies.

(2) Studying varied approaches to the organization of the social studies curriculum, i.e., fused social studies vs. history and geography taught separately.

(3) Making lesson plans for teaching from day to day or over longer periods of time (the so-called "unit" plan).

(4) Locating and selecting desirable textbooks, reference books, and related instructional materials.

(5) Learning how to relate the facts and understandings of social studies to the children's communities and to other communities in the world (e.g., Eskimo, farm children, city dwellers).

(6) Developing skill in using the library, periodicals, maps, globes, charts, films, and other aids in teaching social studies.

(7) Learning how to help children develop habits of critical thinking such as distinguishing fact from opinion, recognizing bias, making generalizations, and defining details from generalizations.

(8) Making and using tests and other evaluation techniques in social studies.

Music in the Elementary School

(1) Renewing acquaintance with traditional children's songs from this and other countries.

(2) Considering the various kinds of musical experiences for elementary children, such as listening and appreciation, acquaintance with musical instruments and their unique features, and knowledge of various musical forms as folk songs, operettas, marches, lullabies, etc.

(3) Learning how to read notes (the meaning of musical terms and symbols) and how to teach these skills to children.

(4) Considering varied approaches to teaching music, i.e., note singing vs. rote singing.

(5) Acquaintance with singing books for children and the related materials and visual aids used in teaching music.

(6) Discussing the place of music in the overall school program and the main purposes for its inclusion.

Art in the Elementary School

(1) Consideration of the place of art in the total school curriculum and the appropriate artistic experiences for children of various ages.

(2) Acquaintance with and an opportunity to experiment with a variety of art media and materials that are appropriate for elementary school children.

(3) Discussion of basic art forms and the elements of color and design that might be introduced to children.

(4) Learning how to introduce art lessons and involve children in artistic experiences.

(5) Learning how art can be correlated to other subjects such as social studies and the language arts program.

Health and Physical Education in the Elementary School

(1) A consideration of personal, family, and community health problems and their solution.

(2) Identification of physical education activities appropriate for children of various ages, including rhythms, small-muscle activities, and large-muscle activities; individual and group sports and games.

(3) Discussion of the role of health and physical education in the total school program and how they may be correlated with other subject areas.

(4) Acquaintance with texts and curriculum guides in this area as well as techniques for introducing children to health and physical education experiences.

Children's Literature

(1) Renewing acquaintance with a wide range of books appropriate for children at various ages, which may have been read but forgotten by the future teachers.

(2) Introduction to a variety of anthologies of children's literature and

to publications that review and evaluate the current offerings of publishers in this field.

(3) Establishing techniques for the location and criteria for the selection of reading materials for children of various ages.

(4) Determining what purposes may be attained through various types of children's books and how the reading of appropriate literature enriches the child personally and contributes to the overall school program.

(5) Discussion of techniques for making books readily available to children and for stimulating their interest in reading a variety of literature appropriate to their age groups.

Findings in Secondary Professional Education

Twenty-seven institutions which my staff and I visited are considered here. They represent 13 states: 6 from the Northeast; 8 from the South; 7 from the Middle West, and 6 from the Far West. Nine are private institutions; 9 are state universities; 3 are state single-purpose institutions; 2 are multipurpose state colleges; 2 are private "liberal arts" colleges; 1 is a multipurpose city college; and 1 a private single-purpose institution. Because the major requirements vary so widely and are considered elsewhere, I am considering here only the professional requirements.

The First Professional Course

Disregarding psychology other than educational psychology, the student was likely to take his first professional course in the freshman year in 6 of the institutions, in the sophomore year in 14 of them, in the junior year in 5 of them, and in the senior year in 2.

There is considerable variation in the nature of the first professional course. This variation is only partly indicated in this paragraph, for courses with similar titles differ widely in content. Two institutions expected students to begin their professional study with simultaneous courses in educational psychology and social foundations of education; 9 institutions expected the first course to be educational psychology; 8 expected it to be introduction to education; 7 expected it to be social foundations of education; 1 expected it to be methods and materials in teaching the major subject. In the last-named institution the special methods course normally came in the fall semester of the senior year. It had been preceded by general psychology and was followed by a semester devoted entirely to professional work.

The Amount and Kind of Educational Psychology

The range in the amount of educational psychology required was from 3 to 9 semester hours.

It is difficult to tell what is in educational psychology courses from their titles or even course descriptions; however, some value may be derived by listing the courses required and the number of institutions requiring each.

Educational psychology	18
Human development	7
Measurement and evaluations	6
Adolescent psychology or development	3
Learning	3
Learning and measurements	2
Guidance	2
Human behavior	1
Educational psychology and measurement	1

It should be added that the introduction-to-education course often includes some aspects of psychology. Further, several institutions included measurement and/or guidance in the description of the general methods course or some other course in secondary education.

It might be noted that educational psychology is often the initial professional course and usually comes early in the program; however, in one institution it accompanied practice teaching, and in another institution educational measurement was required subsequent to practice teaching.

The Amount and Kind of Social Foundations

On the surface it would appear that the range in the amount of social foundations in education required was from 0 to 9 semester hours. Only one institution seemed to require more than 6 semester hours. Sixteen institutions required one course that seemed to be predominantly social foundations; 8 institutions required two; and 3 none.

The 3 that seemed to offer no such courses would undoubtedly protest that they do have a considerable amount of social-foundations content in their programs, and other institutions would probably insist that they offer more social foundations than is apparent. I have here ignored the introduction-to-education course that sometimes is oriented heavily in the direction of social foundations, sometimes has considerable psychology content, and often is a potpourri. Other courses also have some social content, but it is obvious that there is little agreement on what or how much social foundations of education should be required in a teacher-education curriculum. There is also little agreement on how what is included should be organized. I can't resist quoting the professor of education in one institution, which has a course in the introduction to education but no regular social foundations course. He said, "We try to permeate social foundations all through the curriculum." It might be noted that the only institution that did not require either an introduction to education or any social foundations course introduced a course in "Social Foundations in Education" the year following my visit.

From study of catalogs and courses of study, and from discussion with faculty members in the institutions, I conclude that all 27 institutions did, in fact, somehow require the equivalent of 3 semester hours or more in something that might be described as social foundations of education.

Two institutions required a course in history of education, one of 3 semester hours and one of 6. Two others required a course in the philosophy of education, one of 2 hours and one of 3. One required a 3-hour course in the philosophy of education and a 4-hour course in the history of education. Aside from the variations just listed, the confusion with regard to social foundations of education can be seen in the following list of titles of courses which I have considered to be all or predominantly social foundations: Education and Modern Society, Social and Philosophical Foundations, Psychological and Philosophical Foundations, American Public Education, School and Society, Problems in American Education, Principles of Secondary Education, Foundations of Education, The Modern Secondary School, Teaching in School and Community, American Education, Social Foundations of Education, The Secondary School, Fundamentals of Secondary Education, Fundamentals of Education, The Teacher and the School, The American Secondary School, and The School in American Society. Even in the titles, this list indicates that there is little evidence of agreement; only four institutions used one title; three used a second, and two used a third. The remainder of the institutions in our survey employed unique titles for their foundations courses.

It might be noted that social foundations is often the initial course and usually offered early in the program; however, in 4 institutions it was offered at or near the end of the program with an attempt being made to have it follow practice teaching.

Courses in Methodology

This section deals with courses that consist wholly or predominantly of methods and materials of instruction. In the main, these courses fall into two categories: those that treat of secondary school teaching in general (herein referred to as "general methods courses"), and those that treat the teaching of a specified field or subject (herein referred to as "special methods"). These appellations are arbitrary and hardly accurate, for such courses commonly treat of much more than methods, including such matters as objectives, organization, and materials of instruction as well as methods of teaching. Some institutions require courses in audio-visual education, and some require special seminars accompanying practice teaching.

The Total Content

Combining the required courses in general methods, special methods, seminars accompanying practice teaching, and courses in audio and visual education, the range in required methodology in the 27 institutions was from 3 semester hours to 11 semester hours, with 5 institutions at the lower extreme and 3 at the upper.

Special Methods

All 27 institutions required courses in special methods. Two institutions did not offer special methods in all the academic areas. Both these institutions required special methods of students majoring in the areas in which such courses were offered. One required general methods only of students in whose fields special methods courses were not available; the other, requiring general methods of all, required students for whom special methods courses were not available to elect substitute courses in education. Five institutions required special methods courses in both the student's major and minor.

The range in the number of semester hours required in special methods was from 2 to 8, but 20 of the institutions required 3 or 4 semester hours. The 2 institutions requiring 8 hours required special methods courses in both the major and minor teaching fields.

Twenty of the institutions expected special methods to be taken prior to practice teaching, although in exceptional instances the course might accompany it. Very rarely, in a few institutions and then only by specific exception, it might follow practice teaching. Five institutions offered special methods concurrently with practice teaching; 2 institutions extended special methods over more than one term so that some of it preceded practice teaching and some accompanied it.

General Methods

Seventeen institutions required general methods (one of these required general methods only if special methods was not available); 14 of the 17 institutions gave 3 hours' credit for general methods, the other 3 gave 2.

Practice-Teaching Seminar

Seven institutions required a seminar accompanying practice teaching. Credit for this seminar varied from 1 to 4 semester hours. It would seem that such a seminar is more akin to special methods than to general methods. (It should be noted that many but not all institutions required regular group meetings of student teachers and instructors but do not give separate credit.)

Audio-Visual Education

Four of the 6 California institutions required courses in audio-visual education. Three gave 2 semester hours of credit for the course; the other gave 1. It should be noted that California certification required a course in audio-visual education. Two of the institutions considered here had a special arrangement whereby the State Department of Education accepted their regular methods courses as including an adequate amount of audio-visual education.

Related Considerations

Even though they further confuse the picture, two other considerations are necessary to fill in the material of formal instruction in methodology.

Instruction in measurement and evaluation might be considered as instruction in methodology; however, because separate courses in measurement and evaluation are usually classified under the heading of educational psychology, I have included them under that heading.

Many courses that do not consist predominantly of methodology do deal in part with curricular purposes and organization. Eleven of the 27 institutions required general courses in secondary education that meet this description. Three of these 11 did not require general methods. The other 8 required both general and special methods, and 4 of them required general methods, special methods, and the practice teaching seminar.

Practice Teaching

The range was from 4 semester hours to 11. Sixteen institutions required 6, 3 required 8, 3 required 9, 1 required 10, and 1 required 11. Several institutions allowed a student to elect more than the minimum requirement.

The figures for the minimum requirement in clock hours are estimates except for 2 or 3 institutions. Most institutions specified full time for half a semester or a certain number of weeks or a full quarter on the one hand, or a certain number of hours a day for a quarter or a semester. The lengths of quarters, semesters, class periods, and school days vary. In arriving at these figures, I have assumed a school day to be 5 clock hours in length, full-time practice teaching for half a semester to go on for 8 weeks, full-time practice teaching for a quarter to go on for 10 weeks, part-time practice teaching for a semester to go on for 15 weeks, and part-time practice teaching for a quarter to go on for 10 weeks. These assumptions are conservative, so the figures that follow are really minimal.

The lowest minimum requirement was 110 clock hours, in one institution only; 4 institutions required 150, 2 institutions 180, 10 institutions 200, 1 institution 220, 1 institution 225, and 7 institutions 250. The mean requirement in these 26 institutions was approximately 200. (For the 27th institution, which gave 6 semester hours of credit for practice teaching, I have no way of estimating the number of clock hours required.)

The variation in requirements obviously is great. So is the relationship between semester hours and clock hours. One institution, which specified 110 clock hours, gave the same amount of credit as another that specified 220 clock hours. Two major universities 10 miles apart required 8 weeks of full-time practice teaching, but one gave 6 semester hours' credit and the other 9. Another major university with the same time requirement gave 8 semester hours' credit. On the other hand, the central tendency pretty clearly is to equate a semester hour of credit with approximately 30 clock hours of observation and practice teaching. (This is a common, though not universal, rule of thumb; several state Departments of Education follow such a procedure.)

Miscellaneous Requirements

Eight institutions required 2 or 3 semester-hour courses in introduction to education; 2 required 2- or 3-hour courses in observation and participation; 2 required 2-hour courses in health education; and 2 required the student to elect a 2- or 3-hour course in professional education.

INDEX

271

ABOUT THE AUTHOR

DR. JAMES BRYANT CONANT was born in Massachusetts in 1893 and educated at Harvard University, where he became assistant professor of chemistry; later, head of the chemistry department. From 1933 to 1953 he was president of the University. From 1947 through 1952 he was on the General Advisory Committee of the Atomic Energy Commission. In 1953, he became U.S. High Commissioner of Germany; later he was made ambassador to that country, a post he held until February of 1957.

Since returning to the United States, Dr. Conant has, under a grant from the Carnegie Corporation, devoted himself to studies of American public education. He is the author of over a dozen books, the two most recent being *The American High School Today* and *Slums and Suburbs.*